The Furniture of Sam Maloof

The Furniture of

SAM MALOOF

by Jeremy Adamson

with photographs by Jonathan Pollock

SMITHSONIAN AMERICAN ART MUSEUM

W. W. NORTON & COMPANY

The Furniture of Sam Maloof

by Jeremy Adamson
with photographs by Jonathan Pollock

Published on the occasion of the exhibition *The Furniture of Sam Maloof,* organized by the Smithsonian American Art Museum and shown at the museum's Renwick Gallery, September 14, 2001–January 20, 2002.

Chief, Office of Publications:
  Theresa J. Slowik
Designer: Karen Siatras
Editor: Timothy Wardell
Editorial Assistant: Sara Mauger

Typeset in Celeste, Univers, and Goudy and printed in Singapore on Nymolla paper by Tien Wah Press.

Library of Congress
Cataloging-in-Publication Data

Adamson, Jeremy Elwell, 1943-
  The furniture of Sam Maloof / Jeremy Adamson.
        p. cm.
Includes bibliographical references and index.
  ISBN 0-393-73080-8 —
  ISBN 0-393-73085-9 (pbk.)
  1. Maloof, Sam. 2. Furniture designers—California—Biography. I. Maloof, Sam. II. Title.
  NK2439.M28 A83 2001
  749.213—dc21

                                    2001003691

The Smithsonian American Art Museum is dedicated to the preservation, exhibition, and study of the visual arts in America. The museum, whose publications program also includes the scholarly journal *American Art,* has extensive research resources: the databases of the Inventories of American Painting and Sculpture, several image archives, and a variety of fellowships for scholars. The Renwick Gallery, one of the nation's premier craft museums, is part of SAAM. For more information or catalogue of publications, write: Office of Publications, MRC 970, Smithsonian American Art Museum, Washington, D.C. 20560-0970.

SAAM also maintains a web site at **AmericanArt.si.edu.** For further information, send email to **info@saam.si.edu.**

Smithsonian American Art Museum
Washington, D.C. 20560-0970

FRONTISPIECE: Sam Maloof in rocking chair, 2000. Photograph by Bob Carey.

FRONT COVER: Fiddleback maple chair (detail), 1984. Photograph by Jonathan Pollock.

BACK COVER: Sam Maloof in the studio, 1979. Photograph by Jonathan Pollock.

Contents

The Smithsonian American Art Museum is deeply grateful to those who have made possible *The Furniture of Sam Maloof.* These generous benefactors contributed to this book, the exhibition, and related programs.

Dr. and Mrs. Lane Ameen

Eileen and Carlton Appleby

Mr. and Mrs. Peter S. Bing

Anna and Harry Borun Foundation

Herbert and Jeanine Coyne

Mr. and Mrs. Nijad I. Fares

Mr. and Mrs. A. Huda Farouki

Dr. and Mrs. Joseph J. Jacobs

Albert and Rosemary Joseph

Mr. and Mrs. Peter Lunder

Lynx Investment Advisory, LLC

Sam and Alfreda Maloof Foundation

Nancy and Edwin S. Marks

John and Rebecca Moores

Ghassan M. Saab

Mr. and Mrs. James F. Sams

Peter and Ann Tanous

The Museum is grateful to Betty and James F. Sams, Peter and Ann Tanous, and Violet and Joseph J. Jacobs for their generous help in securing broad support for this exhibition, book, and programs.

Foreword

This book is published on the occasion of a retrospective exhibition of the work of one of America's best known and most admired craftspeople, Sam Maloof. Organized by Dr. Jeremy Adamson, senior curator of the Smithsonian American Art Museum's Renwick Gallery and the book's author, the show includes some sixty-five pieces of sculptural, hardwood furniture made between 1950 and 2001. Reaching back to the earliest products of his furniture-making career, the exhibition broadens our appreciation of Maloof's contribution to contemporary design in America, underscoring both his trail-blazing role in the blossoming studio furniture movement and the unusual, decades-long constancy of his vision as a designer-craftsman.

As Dr. Adamson's richly detailed text reveals, Maloof's fifty-year-long career as a Southern California furniture craftsman exactly parallels the growth and development of the nationwide crafts movement. Utilizing for the first time the rich resources of the Maloof workshop papers, Adamson develops an intimate portrait of Sam Maloof from his boyhood years in Chino, California, through his years of struggle as a designer-craftsman in the 1950s and 1960s, to his emergent leadership role in the American crafts movement in the 1970s and early 1980s, and finally to the success and worldwide renown he earned in the late 1980s and 1990s. Throughout, this engaging biography is intertwined with the material and ideological history of American studio crafts—from the earliest polemical debates about "art versus craft" to an analysis of landmark exhibitions—in order to provide a contextual study which will long remain a fruitful scholarly contribution to the field.

One of the many rewards of preparing this exhibition and book has been the delight of discovering so many other Maloof admirers. They are an extremely generous group, offering their cherished artworks for loan and their financial support to make the project as great as possible. I want to convey my personal gratitude to each of them.

Elizabeth Broun
Margaret and Terry Stent Director
Smithsonian American Art Museum

Introduction

Sam Maloof is America's most renowned contemporary furniture craftsman. No other twentieth-century woodworker has received such attention in the media, nor garnered as many awards. Topping this list, in 1985 Maloof was the recipient of a John D. and Catherine T. MacArthur Foundation fellowship— the coveted "genius" grant typically awarded to scientists, scholars, and authors. To date, he is the only American craftsman to have been so privileged. Following up on this celebrity, in January 1986 a feature writer from *People* magazine visited his Southern California workshop and enthusiastically declared the furniture designer-craftsman to be the "Hemingway of hardwood."

But fame was not a sudden occurence for Maloof; it had been gradually building for decades. Since 1949, when he precipitously switched careers from graphic arts to woodworking, a stream of notices about his designs had appeared in a variety of local and national newspapers and magazines. Public television programs on his furniture-making activities also helped create public recognition for his well-designed and expertly crafted furniture, as did, of course, the appearance of his work in exhibitions across the country.

Sam Maloof's fifty-year career as a woodworker is a study in the changing landscape of American design. During the 1950s, the self-taught woodworker was an acclaimed member of the Southern California modern movement, then in the forefront of American architectural and home furnishings design. Maloof's walnut pieces, with their simple, clean-lined compositions and softly sculpted details, were regularly commissioned by leading architects and decorators. They were perfect complements to the new "California-style" houses with their flat roofs and spare, open interior plans. Maloof's first major client was Henry Dreyfuss, the world famous industrial designer, who asked the fledgling woodworker to design as well as fabricate furniture for his new contemporary-style home and office in Pasadena. It was an extraordinary commission, during which Maloof developed the fluid, sculptural style that he would follow for the next five decades.

Early Maloof furniture appears to be similar to Scandinavian Modern, the international style that was beginning to find favor in the United States in the early 1950s. In quality of assembly and finish, however, they were superior to the factory-made models from Sweden or Denmark—a fact not lost on early clients. In design, Maloof's chairs were equal to the best of Scandinavian Modern, those by Hans Wegner or Finn Juhl.

At popular exhibits of modern home furnishings held in the Los Angeles area, as well as in the critically acclaimed *California Design* shows held annually at the Pasadena Art Museum, hundreds of thousands of area residents were able to admire Maloof's chairs, tables, and desks. This exposure prompted more direct orders than his operation—ably managed by his wife, Alfreda Ward Maloof—could effectively execute. Contending with back orders would be a constant feature of his working life. Sam Maloof is one of only a handful of furniture designer-craftsmen active after 1945 to make his livelihood through working full time with his hands. Most of today's eminent artist-woodworkers teach or rely on other means of support.

In the summer of 1957, Maloof attended the first national conference of the American Craftsmen's Council (ACC). It was a landmark event, not only for him, but in the history of the postwar crafts movement. Geographically scattered potters, weavers, enamelists, and woodworkers discovered they were members of a growing, nationwide community of craftspeople searching for a fulfilling way of life in an increasingly industrialized society. As the context for Maloof's work changed from "California Modern" to an American craft movement, he became an outspoken proponent of the ACC and its mission. He served for a quarter of a century as a trustee of the national organization, tirelessly promoting the moral values of working with one's hands and extolling the virtues of the "craftsman lifestyle." During the late 1960s and the 1970s, when working wood was enthusiastically endorsed by many in the counter-culture, he assisted would-be woodworkers to overcome the professional and technical hurdles he himself had confronted. Generosity to others in the field is a personal trademark.

Along with Wharton Esherick (1887–1970) and George Nakashima (1905–90), Maloof was widely recognized by 1970 as a leading member of the "first generation" of postwar studio furniture makers. Collectively, the furniture aesthetic

Cork-topped desk, 1953; maple, walnut, and cork; 28¾ x 23 x 54¼ inches; unsigned; Prototype dining chair, 1952; maple, walnut, and leather; 29¼ x 21 x 19⅞ inches; Sam and Alfreda Maloof Foundation.

Two-drawer desk, 1992; fiddleback maple and ebony; 29¼ x 26 x 49¾ inches; unsigned; private collection.

of these individuals was based on a modernist reverence for the beauty of solid hardwoods, a love of simple, sculptural forms, and above all, function. Even members of the so-called "second generation" of postmodern furniture artists who employed mixed materials in personally expressive work acknowledged Maloof to be a role model for his dedication to quality and commitment to a way of life. While Maloof's career paralleled the growth of the contemporary craft movement, his consistent body of work enjoyed an uneasy relationship to the movement as it evolved. His functionalist approach to design and his traditional ways of working were scorned by younger craftspeople who believed that the creation of utilitarian objects contributed to crafts' low esteem. Unlike Maloof, they were typically graduates of formal art programs and were idea-oriented. They admired avant garde painters and sculptors for their critical and financial success.

Under the leadership of Rose Slivka, editor of the ACC's monthly magazine, *Craft Horizons* (now *American Craft*), many sought to erase the border between crafts and fine art by rejecting traditions of function and multiple production. Instead, they focused on the creation of one-of-a-kind, deliberately useless "objects" destined for museum exhibitions or private collections. The ceramic sculpture of Peter Voulkos and the woven constructions of Lenore Tawney, for example, addressed aesthetic issues more closely allied to contemporary painting and sculpture than those of the potter's wheel or the handloom. In the new field of studio furniture, Wendell Castle's furniture-as-sculpture and Thomas Simpson's painted, fantasy pieces marginalized function.

By the late 1970s, although Maloof's simple, ergonomic designs were widely admired, they were out-of-step with mainstream craft-as-art, if not with the

expectations of his expanding client base or the values of the ACC leadership. In 1975 Sam Maloof was among the first class of inductees into the ACC's College of Fellows and in 1988 received its prestigious Gold Medal. In the 1980s, as crafts became increasingly "artified" and the market for unique forms boomed, Maloof's practical designs and traditional techniques found a more appreciative audience among amateur cabinetmakers. Instead of critical acceptance in *American Craft,* his work was now celebrated in the pages of *Fine Woodworking.* During the 1980s and 1990s, the number of woodworking demonstrations he conducted exceeded the number of museum exhibitions in which his work appeared. To the legions of cabinetmakers active in basement workshops across North America, he was a woodworking hero. His autobiography, *Sam Maloof: Woodworker* (1983), proved an inspirational best-seller, as did the instructional, hour-long videotape, *Sam Maloof: Woodworking Profile* (1989), produced by Taunton Press. The videotape provided a close-up introduction to Maloof's working methods as well as to the justly famous house he had designed and built, and decorated, room by room, over three decades.

Low-back dining chair, 1965; walnut and leather; 30 x 19 ¾ x 19 ½ inches; shop brand: "designed. Made/ MALOOF/ California"; Sam and Alfreda Maloof Foundation.

Low-back bar or counter stool, 1958; walnut and leather; unsigned; 30 x 22 ¼ x 19 inches; Arthur Raymond Family.

Rather than follow fads and fashions in the marketplace, or simply change for the sake of change, from the outset Maloof committed himself to a singular vision. New designs evolved from existing ones. As a result, there is a timeless quality to his work. To judge a Maloof chair, it is best to compare it to others in his evolving repertoire, not to twentieth-century design movements. Evolution, not revolution, is the hallmark of his stylistic development. After creating a satisfying prototype—for example, the low-back chair known as the "Evans" model—he would work towards perfecting the form over decades. The repeated design would be subjected to an increasingly sculptural treatment, creating greater tactile as well as visual beauty. Straight lines gradually became curved; simple curves slowly deepened. In his famous rocking chairs, single curves are transformed into compound ones, creating a more dynamic composition. A Maloof chair can be seen to artistic advantage from any point of view. Right-angle joints become rounded, parts flow into one another, resulting in greater fluidity. The organic character of Maloof's chairs is heightened by his use of signature-style "hard lines"—clean ridges that rise out of smooth forms to emphasize contours. Tactile accents highlight individual parts and help tie arms, legs, and seats into a single, sculptural unit. Maloof chairs silently cry out to be touched.

Notwithstanding these transformations, Maloof's chairs remain strictly functional. Although sculptural, they are not conceived as sculpture per se, or as artworks that appeal to the intellect. The balance between art and utility is strictly maintained. As beautiful as it appears, a Maloof rocking chair is remarkably comfortable. Art at the service of utility is the essence of Maloof's philosophy of design. It is a motto that has sustained a tradition of fine craftsmanship.

Drop-leaf cabinet, 1960s; walnut; 34 1/2 × 53 1/4 × 17 1/2 inches; shop brand: "designed. made/ MALOOF/ California"; Sam and Alfreda Maloof Foundation.

Acknowledgments

This book could not have been written without the direct and indirect assistance of Alfreda Ward Maloof, Sam's wife and business manager. During his fifty-year career as a furniture designer-craftsman, Freda not only kept the accounts and paid the bills but, without her husband's full knowledge, carefully assembled an unmatched archive of his activities both as a craftsman and a public figure. I knew Freda only during the last year of her life, but gained her confidence sufficiently to be permitted initial access to the voluminous office files and collections, hitherto out of bounds to outsiders. After her death, Sam generously allowed me full access and during successive trips to the Alta Loma site, I came more fully to appreciate the documentary riches that Freda carefully assembled. A treasure trove, the Maloof workshop papers are a testament to her firm belief—in the early years, often against all odds—in Sam's creative destiny. Like so many others who encountered her over the years, I treasure her memory.

Sam, too, deserves no less an acknowledgment for his remarkable openness in sharing his life experiences with an outsider. My debt to the man as well as to the craftsman is great. I am also indebted to his son, Slimen Maloof, who provided not only a variety of insights into his parents' lives but significantly into the history of the workshop and its activities. Indeed, he opened my eyes

to subtleties in Sam Maloof's evolving techniques and style to which I otherwise would have remained blind. Workshop employees Mike Johnson, Larry White, and David Wade likewise proved unfailingly helpful as they explained features of their work, introducing me into the world of the woodworker and the universe of Maloof furniture. Like others drawn into Sam's intense orbit, I share with them—and with Slimen—a special kinship.

I also wish to acknowledge a special kinship with Jonathan Pollock, the photographer with whom I worked to achieve the excellent results in color reproduced in this volume. Jonathan had already photographed Sam's work during the years 1977–83 and so was familiar with many of the problems presented by Maloof's subtle shaping of wood. For several months in mid-2000, under trying conditions he patiently photographed and re-photographed individual pieces until the final compositions and lighting finally matched his perfectionist's eye.

At the Smithsonian American Art Museum (SAAM) I wish to express my special gratitude to director Elizabeth Broun and to Renwick Gallery curator-in-charge, Kenneth R. Trapp. Both provided me the necessary autonomy to tackle the subject in my own way and to ensure I had the personal and institutional support needed to conclude it. Research librarian Patricia Lynagh willingly put up with my requests for interlibrary loans and my need for physical space. At W. W. Norton, we've appreciated the sage advice of Nancy Green and Jim Mairs. In the publications department, I am indebted to the commitment of chief Theresa Slowik and her staff in seeing the manuscript reach publication status. In particular, senior editor Timothy Wardell and designer Karen Siatras deserve special thanks for their fine professional skills in ensuring the final product was realized in such an exceptional fashion.

The Museum is grateful for support from a number of donors, whose generosity enhanced the exhibition and its programs. In addition to the groups and individuals mentioned earlier in this publication, we would like to thank Arab Bank PLC/Nofal Barbar, Mr. and Mrs. Rafic Bizri, Mr. and Mrs. Alfred E. Goldman, Mr. and Mrs. Joseph M. Haggar Jr., Mr. and Mrs. Theodore M. Hamady, Mr. and Mrs. Casey Kasem, Dr. and Mrs. Michael J. Langan, Kay Sekimachi and Bob Stocksdale.

This book is dedicated to the life and memory of
Alfreda Ward Maloof (1911–1998), wife, mother, business manager
and believer in all things just, worthy and beautiful.
Without her abiding belief in Sam's creative abilities,
and without her love, steady support and encouragement,
there would be no Maloof furniture to celebrate.
Her gentle spirit resonates throughout his work, his life, and this book.

Chapter One

BACKGROUND

Samuel Solomon Maloof was born on January 24, 1916, in the town of Chino, California, thirty-seven miles east of Los Angeles. It was a significant local event, long remembered in the small farming community surrounded by citrus groves, truck gardens, and dairy farms. After a succession of six daughters, his mother, the much-loved proprietor of a downtown women's shop, finally had her longed-for son. Several days later, family, friends, and neighbors celebrated Sam's arrival at a block party. The chief of police closed the intersection of Sixth and B Streets and the Maloofs, Lebanese immigrants, served Middle Eastern food, while a Mexican band from the nearby barrio played. People gathered, admired the baby, ate delicacies, and danced in the street.

Following an established family pattern, in 1905 the future woodworker's father, Slimen Nasif Nadir Maloof, and his young bride, Anisse, had emigrated to the United States from Lebanon, then part of Syria and thus a region of the expansive Ottoman Empire. Indeed, they had traveled overseas on Turkish Ottoman passports. From Ellis Island, the young couple went to Pawtucket, Rhode Island, to join other relatives. There they decided to journey west to Southern California where Nasif's sister, Holla, an earlier immigrant, owned and operated a store in Santa Barbara. Merchants by both tradition and inclination, but speaking little English, the new arrivals peddled goods acquired on credit from area Jewish wholesalers. From her horse-drawn carriage, Anisse also sold the delicate lace, crochet work, and embroidered linens she herself expertly made. For his part, Nasif peddled vegetables as well as dry goods along area roads before the couple settled down, just after the birth of their first child, Mary, in the booming town of Colton.

Given the number of Maloofs in Southern California—it was a common family name among immigrant Arabic speakers—the wholesalers asked Nasif to take another surname to keep their records and accounts straight. As was often the case with newcomers from the Middle East, he took his father's first name as his last—Slimen—which the Jewish traders accurately translated into Hebrew as Solomon. It became the family's official patronymic. Young Sam Maloof thus grew up as Sam Solomon. It was not until after his discharge

Maloof family photograph (detail), 1926. Ten-year-old Sam is seated next to his younger brother, Jack, and his sister Eva.

from the Army in late 1945 that he and his brother Jack legally changed their surname back to the original Maloof.

But Sam Solomon might not have been born in California at all. In 1912, at his grandfather's urging, his parents had returned to Lebanon. Although Slimen Maloof had emigrated to America in the late nineteenth century, he still owned considerable land in the northern mountain village of Douma. Homesick, he returned to Lebanon to work his terraced hillside orchards. As a tradition-minded patriarch, Slimen deeply desired to reunite his widely scattered kin and beseeched his children in America to return to their ancestral home. Nasif, with Anisse, and their three daughters, but not his sister Holla, dutifully sailed back to the Levant. With his American business profits, Nasif built his father a home on the edge of a cliff overlooking the valley below. Before finally resettling in Douma, however, he needed to return to California with his family to close his affairs. His father insisted that he leave two daughters behind as assurance Nasif and Anisse would return. It proved a fateful decision. With the sudden outbreak of World War I in 1914, the girls were marooned. Ottoman Turkish soldiers occupied the village and the inhabitants suffered greatly; Slimen and his wife starved to death, and the girls barely managed to survive. They were not repatriated until 1925 (through the efforts of the Red Cross). By that time, Nasif and Anisse had settled in Chino, opened a small dry goods store, and added six siblings to the family. They all lived in the rear of the one-story building. Up front, Anisse worked behind the counter selling a variety of goods, including printed cottons, dressmaker's supplies, and her own embroidery and crochet work, while Nasif peddled goods and produce in the outlying areas by carriage. Many of Chino's barrio inhabitants worked in a nearby sugar beet refinery, the town's largest enterprise, and shopped at Maloof's. Like his parents, young Sam learned to speak Spanish—as well as Arabic—before English. As a toddler, he was looked after daily by a Mexican housekeeper. Unlike their nine American-born children, Nasif and Anisse never fully mastered the English language.

A gregarious and energetic child, with a happy, infectious personality, young Sam, according to family lore, was soon running the household.[1] Learning was a top priority at home and, as a youngster, he was tutored by his older sisters at the kitchen table. Before he entered the first grade, he could read and write. He loved to draw—"as a little boy . . . I was always drawing," he later recollected, "I cannot recall when I *wasn't* drawing."[2] When he wasn't scooting along the Chino sidewalks on his tricycle, the curly headed, four- or five-year-old could be found seated outside his mother's store, pencil firmly in hand, with a sheet of paper spread out before him on an upturned citrus crate. He was also highly dextrous, and when Anisse missed a kitchen knife or a pair of shears, she invariably found him using them as tools with which to carve or fashion a wide variety of childhood toys—swords, guns, and wheeled vehicles. Many were unusually intricate for a child craftsman: the cylinder of a wooden pistol actually rotated, and the front axle of a truck was attached to handmade metal springs. Sam laboriously cut spirals from the top of a tin can and ruined the household's best scissors. Other children often brought broken toys to him to be fixed: he had an unusual ability to make them right again.

In 1920, the year Jack—Anisse's ninth child—was born, Nasif acquired a second dry goods store, this time in the fertile Imperial Valley, near Calipatria. It was a thriving business and he lived there alone for two years, returning to Chino to visit his family twice yearly. He was a remote and dignified man, and took pride in his status as a merchant. He wore a shirt and tie every day, even in old age. As a father, he remained a rather distant, though much respected, figure to his young son. His personality was wholly unlike that of his outgoing, open-hearted wife. Maloof adored his mother, and clearly inherited her sunny disposition. Nasif was a particularly handsome man and Anisse would fume that the women of Chino only visited her store with regularity when her mustachioed husband was behind the counter during his semi-annual visits.

In 1922, the Chino store was sold and the entire family moved to the Imperial Valley where Maloof entered school. He completed the third grade before the Calipatria business itself was sold and all the Solomons returned to Chino in 1924 to open yet another dry goods emporium (fig. 1). Four years

Fig. 1 The Solomon (Maloof) Family. In 1926 the family (plus four children of daughter Mary) was photographed on the steps of their doctor's home in Chino. Daughter Olga, in the center, died of tuberculosis two days later. Ten-year-old Sam is seated on the far left.

later, the peripatetic family (with the exception of daughter Olga who, after returning from Lebanon, had died of tuberculosis in 1926) moved yet again, this time to the neighboring town of Ontario, an agricultural colony named in 1881 by the founding Chaffey brothers after their native Canadian province. Here Maloof finished elementary school and completed two years at Chaffey High School before yet another move in 1932—back to Chino, this time for good.

The Depression had wiped out the Solomons' business in Ontario, but they were able to purchase a modest, two-bedroom bungalow on Sixth Street. It was a difficult period. Nasif's health deteriorated—although he lived to be 94 years old—and retail businesses were no longer profitable. In 1933 the family's problems were compounded when Maloof's oldest sister, Mary George, and her six children were forced to move in with her parents and siblings after her husband's death left her without means of support. At one point, there were seventeen Solomons and Georges living under one roof—"stacked up like cordwood"[3]—including all of Anisse's eight surviving children. Maloof was then a senior at Chino High School. But moving in with relatives was a familiar pattern during the Depression in Chino and elsewhere. None of the children knew they were poor; all their friends and neighbors were in the same boat. To ease the strain, two of the older sisters, college graduates, moved across the street into their doctor's house, and with Maloof's help, a needed addition was built onto the back of the bungalow. Brimming with affection, high spirits, and self reliance, many of the young had part-time jobs, and the family tended a small truck garden along with chickens, goats, and rabbits. These provided a steady flow of fresh vegetables, eggs, milk, and meat; the household, a virtual commune, provided for the basic needs of all.

During their summers in high school, Maloof and his brother were gainfully employed; Jack worked at a nearby Gilmore gas station and Maloof in a local grocery store, Blumenfield's. The latter job paid a dollar a day for seven days' work. Six of those hard-earned dollars, however, had to be taken in groceries. So on Saturday nights, his younger sisters hauled bags of canned and dried foodstuffs home to Sixth Street in a child's wagon. In grade school, Maloof had demonstrated a talent for precise lettering; teachers with illegible handwriting often had him inscribe their lessons on the blackboard. In high school, he developed his talent for calligraphy into an art. In the mid-1930s, this skill was put to good use in Chino. In the downtown area, the teenager hand lettered many of the store signs and window cards in a most professional manner. Indeed, for more than two decades, his free-standing "Welcome to Chino" sign stood proudly on Central Avenue. He earned the princely sum of $10 when he painted "Chino Mercantile Company" on the brick facade of a one-and-a-half story store. Just before he started, the owner had him sign a liability waiver in case he fell. Until then, he hadn't thought about that possibility, and, fearful of heights, ordered brother Jack to hold the ladder as firmly as he could.

As is often the case with immigrant families, the Solomons stressed education as the route to success in America, and in high school—both in Ontario and Chino—Maloof was enrolled in college-preparatory classes. His parents hoped he would become a doctor, lawyer, or other professional—certainly not a designer-woodworker (in Arabic, simply a "carpenter") who earned his living by his hands. He proved a good, if not outstanding student—he was on the dean's list his final year—but at high school his childhood interest in art deepened and matured. Among the 3,500 students at Chaffey High, his talent stood out for art teacher Charlotte Reid. As a freshman, he was allowed to take junior-year classes in life drawing and anatomy. Articulated skeletons, fellow students (fully clothed), and plaster casts provided classroom models. It proved an excellent introduction to fine draftsmanship and figure drawing, and helped lay a foundation for his future work in commercial art after graduation.

At Chaffey High, Maloof also took an elective course in the vocational program—woodworking. This class was not given much priority by school administrators. It was a "gut" course, and both the students and their teacher were deeply apathetic. Moreover, as there were no funds to purchase wood, the students spent most of their class time sweeping the workshop floor, keeping the idle equipment clean, and chatting. As a result of this inactivity (Maloof wanted to go out and scrounge his own materials, but succumbed to peer pressure), his annual report card displayed four "Fs"—not an auspicious start for someone who would develop into a furniture maker with a worldwide reputation for excellence in design and craftsmanship. Decades later, Maloof gave a slide talk about his furniture to the local Rotary Club, telling members about this ignominious beginning, and even naming the teacher, a Mr. Dean—who happened to be in the audience.

At smaller Chino High School, located just half a block from the Solomons' bungalow, Maloof came under the influence of an attractive young art teacher, Eleanor Corwin, who was not much older than himself. There were no well-equipped art studios at Chino High, as there had been at larger Chaffey, just two well-lighted rooms at the rear of the building. Corwin, too, recognized her student's innate talent and allowed him to work on his own projects with little supervision. Maloof continued life drawing, and honed his skills in calligraphy, caricature, and cartooning. By graduation, he could draw all the Disney characters to perfection (fig. 2), and to the delight of his school friends he even created his own comic strip, dreaming of selling it to a newspaper syndicate.

One of his artistic accomplishments at Chino was winning a school poster contest—his entry depicted a leaping baseball player catching a high fly ball. At the bottom was the stern, but handsomely lettered, admonishment: "Athletes Don't Smoke." Maloof firmly followed the advice. A committed non-smoker, he was an outstanding athlete, playing on Chino High's varsity football, basketball, and baseball teams. After graduation, he maintained his enthusiasm for competitive sports, playing in an intercity basketball league with the Chino Red Lions. By the 1939–40 season, this team had a remarkable 72-game winning streak (fig. 3). A local sports reporter called him the "bronze Syrian" and he even briefly considered a professional career in minor league baseball.

Aside from academic art courses under Eleanor Corwin, at Chino High Sam Solomon also enrolled in two practical elective courses in the school's vocational program: in his junior year he took mechanical drawing; and as a senior, architectural drafting and design. He passed both these courses with

Fig. 2 Airbrushed cartoon by Sam Solomon, 1934. Sam's earliest artistic endeavors were in the field of calligraphy and caricature. Reproduction by permission of Sam Maloof.

flying colors, and the technical instruction proved exceedingly helpful after graduation and during his Army years. The year-end project in the architectural class was to design a house. Plans, elevations, and even a model were prepared. Maloof's was a lavish design: his teacher declared it would cost $25,000—a Depression-era fortune—to construct. Again, the training and insights acquired came in handy when, in the mid-1950s he began to plan and build his own landmark residence and workshop in nearby Alta Loma.

During his senior year—at Miss Corwin's insistence—Sam Solomon entered a Southern California poster contest for high school students. Since there were projects of more pressing interest to complete, he was a reluctant competitor, but the contest called for a design that would suit reproduction by silkscreen, and since he was one of only a handful of students familiar with the process, he took up the challenge. The subject was theatrical: a production of *Oliver Twist* by the Pasadena Players to open on February 5, 1934, at the Padua Hills Theater. The popular playhouse was located among the olive groves in the foothills of the San Gabriel Mountains overlooking the nearby college town of Claremont. The "home of trees and Ph.D.s" and two important art departments— at Scripps and Pomona Colleges—picturesque Claremont was the home to a significant artists' colony.

The sponsor of the contest was a local businessman, Herman H. Garner, founder-owner of the successful, Claremont-based Vortox Manufacturing Company. In 1930 Garner had paid for the construction of the 300-seat concrete theater, along with its attached dining room, outdoor terrace for post-performance

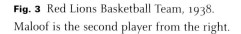

Fig. 3 Red Lions Basketball Team, 1938. Maloof is the second player from the right.

receptions, graceful pergola entryway, and separate gift shop. The handsome Mission-style buildings stood on a small mesa some 1,800 feet above the town and in the years ahead, Maloof would come to know it intimately. The hillside complex was to be the cultural hub of a private, 2,000-acre suburban development, "Padua Hills," planned by Garner and several Claremont partners. The picturesque home sites with views over the valley and adjacent arroyo were intended to attract artistically minded homeowners.[4] Many of Maloof's artist friends, including ceramicist Harrison McIntosh and sculptor Albert Stewart, and his future employer and mentor, painter Millard Sheets, would live in contemporary-style houses built along its winding, tree-lined streets.

Simply and expertly designed in black, Maloof's *Oliver Twist* poster won over other submissions from students around the region. Millard Sheets, then a young but established California watercolor artist and chairman of the art department at Scripps College, was the judge. The prize was a class trip—there were forty seniors in all—to see a performance. Afterward, at a reception on the terrace where desserts were served, Herman Garner casually asked Sam what he planned to do after graduation. The teenager replied that he hoped to get a job to earn enough money to attend college. Garner then asked the poster winner to contact him closer to graduation time about possible employment in Vortox's art department.

Ten days before graduation, Eleanor Corwin asked Maloof whether he had yet met with Garner. He replied that he had no phone or car available and had not bothered. Chagrined, Miss Corwin immediately phoned Vortox, made an appointment for her prize pupil, and drove him the fourteen miles from Chino to Claremont for his interview, waiting in the parking lot in front of the Spanish Mediterranean-style office building on South Indian Hill Boulevard. Herman Garner talked with him about his interests and his previous jobs, and then suddenly asked him whether he liked washing windows. Somewhat surprised, Maloof replied affirmatively and the Vortox president told him to report to the office on the Monday morning following Friday's graduation. He would work there as a graphic artist for five productive years, but to his disappointment, Maloof spent the first three months cleaning the factory windows, inside and out, scraping years of grime from the glass with a razor blade, inch by inch. But he completed the job without complaint, and in the fall of 1934 he joined the four-person art department (fig. 4). By January 1935, his biweekly paycheck was $30. Since he still lived in the family bungalow in Chino, almost half an hour's drive away, he needed a car and with the guarantee of full employment— a rare situation at the time—he splurged and bought a new, two-door Chevrolet sedan for the grand sum of $632.

The Claremont firm—still in operation at the original site—manufactured a proprietary oil-bath air filter for heavy duty internal combustion engines. They were installed primarily in tractors, military vehicles, and construction and drilling equipment. At Vortox, Maloof designed technical brochures illustrating the oil filters in cutaway drawings, as well as advertisements, stationery letterheads, and press releases (fig. 5). More significantly, he produced graphics for the Garners' outside interests—even their Christmas cards. Early on, he drafted

Fig. 4 Members of the Vortox Manufacturing Company Art Department, Claremont, California, about 1936. Reproduction by permission of Irene W. Garner.

the site plans for the entire Padua Hills development. He also designed and produced a variety of artwork for the Padua Hills Theater and Dining Room. His attractive, vignette illustrations and informal lettering style gave the artwork a casual, inviting look and helped to make the entertainment complex a successful attraction.

Beginning with the 1935–36 season, the much-loved Mexican Players became the resident troupe. Young men and women, mostly from the local area, acted and sang—often in Spanish—in plays based on Mexican tales and folklore, and performed costumed folk dances. (The performers actually did double-duty, serving beforehand as wait staff in the restaurant and afterward as musicians on the patio.) The Garners had a personal mission: to promote good will toward Mexico and the local Spanish-speaking communities. The plays, dances, and summertime fiestas were a means of validating and preserving the cultural heritage of old Spanish California, then rapidly disappearing in the region. Maloof attended many of the performances and, when needed, lent a hand painting sets, in the process meeting some of the local artists who in years to come would be among his closest friends.

Several artists' studios and crafts shops were located directly across from the theater complex—William Manker's ceramics studio, Stewart's Woodcraft Shop, and the Weaving Shop—while the main gift shop adjacent to the playhouse sold Mexican handicrafts. Regular exhibitions of work by professional painters, printmakers, and sculptors living in the Claremont area were also featured within the theater-restaurant complex. It was a stimulating artistic environment for Maloof, and it helped broaden his horizons. From 1935 to 1940, Maloof expertly hand-lettered the menus for the Padua Hills Dining Room,

Fig. 5 Brochure for the Vortox Manufacturing Company designed and hand-lettered by Sam Maloof, about 1936. Reproduction by permission of Irene W. Garner.

including the special annual Thanksgiving and Christmas dinners, as well as playbills and Padua Institute newsletters (figs. 6–8). At home, he was also besieged with requests to paint signs and posters for stores and groups in Chino. It seemed someone was always calling at the house on Sixth Street to get him to letter something for them.

After a year at Vortox, Garner allowed Sam Solomon two days off a week to attend classes at Chaffey Junior College in Ontario. Notwithstanding his high wages—so unusual during the Depression—his parents still wanted their eldest son to get a college degree. His brother Jack was enrolled in a degree-granting program and would later become a school principal. At Chaffey, the stench of a formaldehyde-cured cat carcass had driven him out of biology class and into the study of literature, a lifelong pleasure. But his heart was never really captured by higher education, and from 1937 to 1939, after quitting time at Vortox, he would drive once a week into Los Angeles where, enrolled in night classes at the Frank Wiggins Trade School (later the Los Angeles Trade-Technical College), he took commercial art courses, including advertising design and film animation (fig. 9). The teachers were professionals in their respective fields and, impressed by his skill, urged him—unsuccessfully—to join Wiggins' daytime teaching staff. Given the opportunities available to a skilled graphic artist in Los Angeles in the late 1930s—through his Wiggins connections, he was offered but turned down advertising art jobs at two area businesses—it is surprising he became a woodworker at all. In fact, he almost took one job in Hollywood's film industry that, if he had accepted the offer, would have ensured that his creations would have been seen globally.

In 1935 Maloof had answered a newspaper ad for the Walt Disney Company's animation school. He sent some of his accomplished Disney imitations, as well as samples of his own original cartoons, portrait caricatures, and elegant lettering. To his surprise, he was swiftly accepted into the training program and offered a stipend of $16 a week—with full-time employment in the Disney's studios to follow. He was ready to quit Vortox and move to Los Angeles, but there was an unmoveable force opposed to his leaving for the big city. "I was quite excited about it," he later reminisced, "but my mother wasn't. I'd never been away from home . . . and my mother . . . beat her chest and said 'All the bad women in Los Angeles,' and all that. So I didn't go work for Walt Disney, but I thought it would have been interesting to see what a bad woman was like."[5] Anisse's influence over her handsome, first-born son was strong, and she was dead set against his leaving home, then and when later opportunities arose. If he expressed such a desire, she would clutch her chest theatrically and cry, "Oh, my heart! My heart, if you go!" It would not be until the Army called him in 1941—a force more powerful than any mother's possessiveness—that Maloof was able finally to break the maternal bonds (fig. 10).

During lunch breaks at Vortox, the young graphic artist usually walked two blocks north to a restaurant that served a daily "merchant's lunch" for thirty-five cents. On the way, he would often stop in an alley and look through the open doors of a small but busy workshop on West First Street—a former automobile garage—intrigued by the array of up-to-date machine tools and

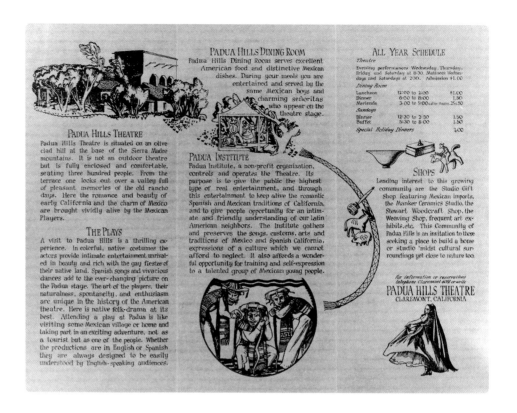

Fig. 6 Brochure by Sam Maloof for Padua Hills Theater and Dining Room, about 1937. The owners of Vortox, Mr. and Mrs. Herman Garner, founded the cultural center in the hills above Claremont to promote Mexican theatricals and music. Reproduction by permission of Irene W. Garner.

woodworking equipment inside and the interesting projects under construction. By this time, Maloof was somewhat familiar with woodworking. In the summer of 1934 he had enrolled in night classes held in Chino High's workshop where he learned the rudiments of carpentry and joinery. The main reason he went was to use the saw and other equipment to construct two needed plywood cabinets for the family's Sixth Street house. Along with a pine kitchen work table, still extant, these were the first pieces of Maloof furniture.[6]

In 1939 he was working on a complex project at Vortox—a large display about the company's filters destined for an oil field industry convention in Tulsa (fig. 11)—and the West First Street workshop possessed a bandsaw he sorely needed to cut out large wooden letters. He didn't really know the owner; only occasionally had they exchanged laconic greetings in passing. So one day, he approached a workman inside and inquired whether he might ask the boss if he could use the saw to cut the letters. The reply was not reassuring: "I would not ask him. Sometimes he goes weeks without talking to me." During this discouraging interchange, Maloof later recalled, "[the owner] walked in and he said, 'May I help you?' I got up my nerve and told him what I was doing. He said, 'Well, I have noticed your interest in the shop because you stand out in the alley looking in. Have you ever used a bandsaw?' 'Oh, yes!' I never had. [But] I went ahead and he liked what I did."[7] In fact, he liked it so much that he offered Maloof work after 5:00 PM and soon, a full time job—which he gladly took. It proved one of the most important professional decisions he ever made.

The owner was Harold E. Graham (1904–69), an innovative industrial designer who had studied at the Chouinard Art Institute in Los Angeles and the Schule Reimann in Berlin, a crafts and design school with an emphasis on industrial products. As an artist-craftsman, he was best known for his architectural murals in metal—typically in an art deco style. By 1934, he had won three first prizes in the exhibitions of local craftsmen staged annually in the fall at the Los Angeles County Fair in Pomona, as well as awards in the 1934 Allied Arts Festival. When Maloof encountered him, he was a part-time instructor in the Scripps College art department and a friend of Millard Sheets's. Indeed, he and Sheets were partners in a short-lived design firm that included Padua Hills ceramicist William Manker. Graham was justly famous for his remarkable seasonal window displays made for Bullock's downtown department store in Los Angeles during the years 1936–42. At Christmas and Easter, thousands flocked to Wilshire Boulevard to admire the complex, animated dioramas—pioneers of their kind in California.

At first, Hollywood decorator Tony Duquette created watercolor sketches for the thematic displays, which he handed over to Graham who figured out how to fabricate the myriad individual components and puzzle out the technical means that would make Santa's elves hammer out miniature Christmas toys, while reindeer and Saint Nick himself pranced about and—later in the new year—to make Easter bunnies jump out of the Mad Hatter's head gear while colorful eggs rolled around. They were delightful attractions—and more interesting and challenging to work on than industrial graphics for the Vortox Manufacturing Company. But while he was employed by Harold Graham from late 1939 until he was drafted by the Army on October, 1941, Maloof continued to produce work for the Garners' Padua Hills concerns. The visual style he had developed for the theater and dining room graphics was too ingrained in the public's consciousness for him to quit entirely.

At Graham's, Maloof for the first time began to work with wood in earnest, learning to handle a variety of power tools. Aside from the Bullock's displays, Maloof helped make the clean-lined, semi-industrial brass and wood furniture that his new boss had designed for his new house—a one story, art deco-style dwelling on South Indian Hill Boulevard that Graham had planned himself,

Fig. 7 Sam Maloof's playbill for the Mexican Players production of *Sandunga del Corazon,* Padua Hills Theater, 1938. Reproduction by permission of Irene W. Garner.

Fig. 8 Hand-lettered Thanksgiving Day menu by Sam Maloof for the Padua Hills Dining Room, 1940. Reproduction by permission of Irene W. Garner.

Fig. 9 Sam Maloof, advertising design, student project while attending Frank Wiggins Trade School, about 1938. Reproduction by permission of Sam Maloof.

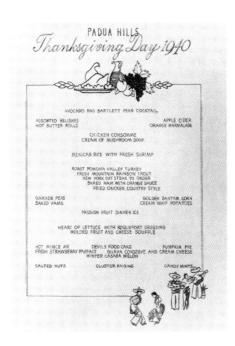

Fig. 10 Maloof with his parents, Nasif and Anisse, 1938.

and one which he was largely building himself. It proved an instructive and influential experience. The legs of the dining table and chairs were comprised of curved wooden ribs made for convertible tops of 1930s touring automobiles, which Graham had purchased in a job lot. The twenty-three-year-old also assisted in the construction of commercial cabinetry and special display units for cosmetics departments that Los Angeles area stores regularly ordered from the West First Street workshop. Most of Graham's projects began with simple, rough sketches; seldom did the designer complete detailed mechanical drawings or plans before commencing. The final design simply took shape during the fabrication process. As a designer-craftsman, Graham set an example that Maloof would follow. "Everything that he designed he was able to build," Maloof later recalled, "which was very rare among industrial designers. I think I learned as much from Harold as any person I ever worked for. This is when I became interested in working with furniture."[8]

It was an apprenticeship—of sorts. There was no formal training; Maloof simply picked up the needed expertise by watching, often surreptitiously. "I never had any instruction at all. In fact with [Graham], he'd not say, 'This is how you use a table saw. This is how you use this or that.' He'd just say,

'Sammy, do this, do that.' But I always looked out of the corner of my eyes . . . and watched what he was doing."[9] The sidelong glances were long and concentrated: Graham was a perfectionist, and there was no latitude for mistakes. But inexperienced Maloof did make the occasional error. One day, while working on a table top, he blurred the straight edge. To ameliorate the damage, Graham altered the design: with a router, Maloof rounded the flat, hardwood edge—a possible genesis of the famous California "Round-over Style" that Maloof perfected by 1960. He also learned fine joinery—from scratch. At the beginning, "if someone had said, 'make a dovetail,' I would not have known what they were talking about. Or a hip joint, or a finger joint, or a box joint."[10] But by the time he left Graham's for his Army service, he could make complex, triple-mitered joints with little difficulty.

Army Experience

Just before Maloof was drafted, Harold Graham's business had been turned into a small, but vital military workshop. Graham himself had been commissioned a captain in the United States Air Force and was not only producing displays for Bullock's, but also Link Trainers—operational, cockpit instrument panels used to instruct fighter pilots on the ground. He desperately wanted to keep Maloof on the payroll and, with the military's authority, offered his able assistant an Army sergeant's stripes if he would enlist and assist in making cockpit panels. But Maloof was sensitive to his status as a first-generation American from a small, farming community. Although he had rarely suffered discrimination, as a member of a racial minority still regarded as "foreign" in Chino, he felt it wouldn't be right to take a military posting that would keep him out of harm's way and allow him to live comfortably at home, while his

Fig. 11 Vortox product display for industry convention in Tulsa, 1939. Maloof designed and fabricated the elaborate display. He cut out the plywood letters using a borrowed bandsaw. Reproduction by permission of Irene W. Garner.

boyhood friends were sent overseas to fight. So, like the vast majority of his peers, he simply awaited his draft notice. It duly arrived, and he was inducted into the United States Army on October 11, 1941.

Private Sam Solomon was assigned to basic training at Camp Callen in San Diego. Eight weeks later, Pearl Harbor was bombed, war was declared on Japan, and all hell broke loose on base. Immediately, he and fifteen other raw recruits were shipped north to the Los Angeles suburb of Inglewood, where they joined a regular Army unit just transferred from Panama—the 65th Antiaircraft Artillery regiment. It was primarily composed of grizzled regulars; most had spent a quarter century in uniform, yet were still privates. Somewhat incongruously, veterans and anxious draftees were quartered at the Hollywood Park Turf Club, first in smelly horse stalls, then in tents on the infield. Early on, they nervously scanned the nighttime sky for Japanese planes, fingers on triggers. One evening, when the likelihood of attack had disappeared, and there was little else to do, Maloof sat on his bunk doodling cartoons of the unit's feline mascot—a Panamanian ocelot. In suitable, Disney-like fashion, he drew the creature doing all sorts of things, carrying artillery shells and firing the heavy guns.

A young messmate who worked in the battalion office saw the cartoons, and told Maloof the colonel was looking for a drawing of the unit's mascot, and asked whether he might show him the cartoons. Once again, fate intervened in Maloof's career. The next day, he was called out after morning muster by the old first sergeant and told to report to the battalion commander on the double. "Did you draw these things?" the colonel asked, "Yes, sir," Private Solomon replied nervously. "Can you do engineering drawings?" "Yes, sir." The colonel then handed over a badly drawn plan of an antiaircraft gun emplacement— "Redo this." Maloof redrew it professionally and immediately was detailed to battalion headquarters as a draftsman. A colonel from regimental headquarters then saw Private Solomon's first-rate artillery emplacement drawings and requested his transferral to the master gunner's department where there was an opening for a staff sergeant. In order to make the move, after only three months in the Army, in one week Maloof went from private to private first class, then corporal, and finally staff sergeant. It was one of the fastest promotions on record. After a couple of months at headquarters, he was promoted again, first to technical sergeant, and then master sergeant—the youngest in the Army, he was told—before being sent to the Aleutian Islands for further duty with the coastal antiaircraft artillery (fig. 12).

At his Quonset hut drafting table on Adak Island, he produced detailed engineering drawings for gun emplacements designed to defend against possible Japanese attacks on Allied bases. He also made surveys and produced maps from aerial photography, and learned to use a 35mm camera on the ground himself. When Hollywood actress Olivia DeHaviland made a morale-boosting visit to Kiska in 1943 (Maloof had been part of the invasion force), he acted as official regimental photographer. The colonel wished to escort her on a formal tour of the island, but she demurred, instead asking that the handsome young sergeant with the Kodak be the one to accompany her. Harking back to his days at Vortox, Sergeant Solomon also crafted large-scale displays—wall-size, painted maps of European and Asian theaters of war. These were used daily to update Allied military progress—or lack thereof.

From the island of Kiska, in 1943 he was reassigned to Divisional Headquarters of the Army's Alaska Department in Anchorage where he was appointed operations sergeant. While stationed in Anchorage, Maloof was sent to a coastal artillery surveying and drafting course at Fort Monroe, Virginia. The trip—his first to the East Coast—took him to Williamsburg, Washington, D.C., and New York City, where he visited museums and historic sites. His camera was always at hand to take snapshots to show to friends in Alaska and send back to family in Chino. Maloof liked Alaska. His Southern California roots notwithstanding, he enjoyed the cold weather and working outdoors in all weather. Accustomed to the communal atmosphere of his family's house, he also enjoyed the give and take of daily existence in cramped Quonset hut quarters. He also learned a cardinal rule: to survive the war and the weather, the diverse group had to think and act as one. Many of his fellow soldiers in the Aleutians and Alaska remained for decades his closest friends. As a master gunner, he relished the engineering part of his work, especially surveying and mapping. In fact, when the war ended—and he was marooned in Anchorage with little or nothing to do for a five-month period (except read all the novels of Thomas Wolfe)—he seriously considered the Army's request that he transfer to the Corps of Engineers and remain in the military.[11]

Nonetheless, he opted for a return to civilian life. The regimentation of Army life was numbing; the "hurry up and wait" pattern of existence was exasperating—as was the absence of creative outlets for an artistic mind. When he was finally mustered out, he swore he would be his own boss, to work when, where, and how he thought best for himself. But just as it was for innumerable wartime draftees, Maloof's experience in the military was in many respects a positive one. He certainly learned the practical value of his high school training in mechanical drawing and drafting. But more importantly, the military taught him discipline and responsibility—and emotional independence. "My Army experience . . . was probably the best thing that ever happened to me," he later reminisced, "I made a clean break with my mother. She was wonderful, but she was very protective and never wanted her children to leave home."[12]

Master Sergeant Solomon almost never made it home to Chino to see his mother again. Trying to stitch together a series of military flights to Los Angeles proved extremely difficult, especially in winter. In Seattle, he missed boarding one vital southbound connection. From the waiting room window, he watched it sit briefly on the runway during a passing snowstorm. Not long after it took off, it crashed on a mountainside. There were no survivors. But after a couple of days he caught another flight, and the final leg of his homeward journey, from Sacramento to Los Angeles, was in a car crammed with discharged soldiers driving at breakneck speed. Back safely in Southern California—and without a nickel in his uniform trousers—the returning veteran made his way home to Chino. But he did not stay long. Almost immediately, he moved to Los Angeles and into a one-bedroom unit in Westlake Bungalows—a pre-war rental development on South Grand View Boulevard opposite Chouinard Art Institute—and

Fig. 12 Master Sergeant Sam Solomon, Aleutian Islands, 1943.

looked for work. But with his brother Jack, he took time legally to change his name from Sam Solomon back to Sam Maloof.

Postwar Design Work

During his initial Army posting at Inglewood, he had taken his regimental cartoon to Angelus-Pacific, a commercial art firm in Los Angeles, to be made into a colored decal. Later unit designs he made for the Alaska Department had also been sent to Angelus-Pacific (fig. 13). The manager wrote to Maloof, asking that he look him up after the war ended. In December 1945, Maloof duly stopped by to ask about a job. Cartooning was a major enterprise at Angelus and he was instantly hired as a graphic artist, and began designing decals and logos for a variety of customers—the military, local schools and universities, oil companies, and area businesses.

He also did exquisite lettering for the firm, his high school skills honed at Wiggins now proving their worth. As his colleague and friend Harlan Chinn remembered, "Sam did all the lettering—fantastic letterman! He was unbelievable! He was a terrific designer."[13] At Angelus-Pacific, he also learned color separation for printing multi-color designs and also prepared silkscreens. A highly valued employee, in early 1946 his salary was raised from a dollar to $1.25 an hour and he was given a flexible work schedule. He had his own key to the firm's graphic art studio so he could work at his desk whenever he wished. He enjoyed the absence of regimentation, but his Army discipline paid off: he often worked sixty hours a week—late into the night and on weekends—on both company projects as well as his freelance work.

His rental unit at Westlake Bungalows was furnished with cheap, battered furniture—"traditional" American, in maple. To Maloof, it was repellently ugly, and in order to stand living in the apartment, he decided to design and make some key pieces himself. The manager was only too happy to use the old ones elsewhere. As a do-it-yourself craftsman, the most pressing problem Maloof faced was a supply of inexpensive wood (in the immediate post-war period, building materials for domestic use were costly and in short supply), but he solved it by buying a little plywood and scrounging discarded red oak boards used as packing materials in railroad freight cars, and dumped by the tracks. The next step was locating power tools. To gain access to needed equipment, he enrolled in adult night classes in woodworking at nearby Belmont High School and also on weekends back at Chino High, both of which had new saws and tools. The furniture he designed for Westlake Bungalows was his first serious essay in three-dimensional design, and the experience proved to be extremely significant in determining his future career as a woodworker. Pieces included a hi-fi cabinet and coffee table (made in Chino's wood shop), and a dining table.

Out of necessity, the designs had to be based on the varied dimensions of the stock he had assembled. Aesthetically, they were modern in style, reminiscent of the latest clean-cut, angular designs by modern designers on display in Los Angeles stores.[14] But if the materials were less than exquisite, the joinery and overall workmanship were excellent. A teacher friend at Chouinard, painter Loren Barton, was impressed by the up-to-date design and fine workmanship

M/SGT. SAM SOLOMON, 39165733
ALASKAN DEPARTMENT, HQ ADV. C.P.
U.S.ARMY, APO 980 % PM
SEATTLE, WASH.

ALASKA

U.S.ARMY

M·SGT. SAM SOLOMON
736 ½ SO. GRAND VIEW ST.
LOS ANGELES, (5) CALIF.

Fig. 13 The lid of Maloof's Army trunk, which he had shipped to a friend in Los Angeles. The regimental cartoon decals were based on drawings made by Sam.

and told him, in all seriousness, that she thought people would pay handsomely for such high quality, custom-made furniture—and that he might even make a living from it. It proved a defining moment. As he later put it: "this was the bug that planted itself."[15]

During the nine months he worked at Angelus-Pacific, like many veterans, Maloof began to consider seriously his career options. In 1946, he was thirty years old, but he had yet to find his true direction in life. He was innately skilled as a commercial artist, letterman, and typographic designer, but working in two dimensions was not wholly satisfying. When he had worked for Harold Graham, he had been introduced to the theory and practice of industrial design. It was an elite profession, and one that strongly attracted him. Indeed, in the machine age of the 1930s it was virtually an article of faith that design could solve many of society's problems; successful designers like Henry Dreyfuss and Raymond Loewy were national celebrities. To become more familiar with the field, Maloof had acquired a copy of Harold Van Doren's *Industrial Design: A Practical Guide* (1940) and read up on theory and practice.

Like other Angelenos interested in contemporary art and design, Maloof pored over copies of *California Arts and Architecture.* A monthly magazine published in Los Angeles, after 1940 it was edited by John Entenza, one of the West Coast's leading champions of modernism in architecture and the other arts, including music and theater.[16] By 1943, Entenza had completed its editorial transformation from a regional shelter magazine to a large-format journal of the avant garde, renamed *Arts & Architecture,* with an increasingly national audience (fig. 14). In 1946 Maloof met Richard Bird, the adventuresome chief designer and office manager for Raymond Loewy and Associates in Los Angeles, and another fan of Entenza's magazine. They became fast friends, and as a result of Bird's professional influence, and his own emerging interest in three-dimensional design, Maloof applied to and was accepted by the industrial design program at California Technical Institute. Unfortunately, in another twist of fate, the Caltech program was terminated before he could enroll.[17] But once again, providence appeared to redirect Maloof's life, this time in the form of Claremont artist and teacher Millard Sheets—Graham's friend and the judge of the 1934 *Oliver Twist* poster competition.

In 1943–44, while Maloof had been posted to the Aleutians, Sheets had been assigned to the India-Burma front as a war artist-correspondent for *Life* magazine, sketching scenery, and local and military life for illustration purposes. It had been a harrowing experience. India was then wracked by famine and the squalor and misery he encountered deeply moved him, imbuing his magazine images with a new-found expressiveness. Now back in Claremont, he planned to issue many of his watercolors—both Asian and American subjects—as colored prints, and was searching for an artist skilled in serigraphy to reproduce them. Before the war, many of Sheets's prize-winning pictures had been photomechanically replicated and sold by such organizations as American Federation of Arts, Associated American Artists, and Scribner's. The painter now wanted to raise the reproduction quality—and also maximize his profits—by controlling the process himself. When he learned that Maloof, whom he had known from his days at Graham's workshop, was doing screen printing at Angelus-Pacific, he drove into the city to talk about the project.

Sheets commissioned a colored print as a trial. With the assistance of Harlan Chinn, a friend at work more experienced in the multi-screen technique, Maloof produced a successful print from the watercolor Sheets had left. On that basis, the thirty-nine-year-old artist invited Maloof to return to Claremont and work in his studio. There were dozens of sketches to be squared for enlargement and printed. Moreover, Sheets also promised additional work as his full-time assistant on many of his other projects. Millard was California's most famous living artist, and Maloof promptly took up his offer of employment. After working for so long in the commercial art field, he was delighted to join the more rarefied universe of the fine arts—to say nothing of the stimulating environment of Claremont's artists' colony. Previously, his lack of university education had kept him on the margins of this more intellectual world. Moreover, he was happy to return to his bucolic roots in San Bernardino County. As a place to live, Los Angeles, a "jam-packed, war-boomed city,"[18] was not to his liking. After his return, Maloof would remain rooted in the Pomona Valley for the remainder of his active life.

Studio Assistant to Millard Sheets

Millard Owen Sheets (1907–89) proved to be the single most important influence on the development of Sam Maloof's aesthetic sensibility, artistic outlook, and cultural understanding. A visionary teacher, and a true polymath in the arts, he was a fine mentor to the younger man, opening intellectual and artistic vistas that gave Maloof a deeper appreciation of the role and meaning of art in

Fig. 14 Cover of *Arts & Architecture* magazine, July 1952. John Entenza's popular magazine, along with *House Beautiful* and *Interiors,* helped Maloof keep up-to-date with the latest postwar trends in modern architecture and furniture design.

human life. Listening to him (and his colleagues and friends) expound on the history and theory of art and design, examining his art collections and hearing his explanations of their importance (he was a leading collector of Oriental and pre-Columbian ceramics), and borrowing books from his extensive library in many ways proved a practical substitution for the university education that he had missed. "Millard really opened a whole new vista for me," Maloof later stated. "[He] introduced me into a whole new world of art, and I became acquainted with ceramics, weaving, and all of the different [craft] media."[19]

Born in nearby Pomona, Sheets, like Maloof, had been an inveterate sketcher since childhood. A successful artist in his teens, he enrolled in Chouinard Art Institute and graduated in 1929. Mural painting was a special study. In his senior year he held his first one-man show—a surprise sell-out—at the Newhouse Galleries in Los Angeles. (Only a decade later, the count had risen to an extraordinary forty one-man shows staged at museums and university galleries nationwide.) After graduation, he made a sketching trip to Europe, and returned in late 1930 to marry Mary Baskerville, sister of a fellow Chouinard student. Two years later, the twenty-five-year-old painter was asked to take over the art department at Scripps College and the couple moved to Claremont. The curriculum served not only the college's undergraduate women, but students at adjacent Pomona College. In 1934, the year Maloof joined Vortox, Sheets assumed the responsibilities of director of art at the Claremont Graduate School and began to assemble the finest art faculty in Southern California—painters, sculptors, printmakers, and studio craftspeople, many of whom Maloof came to know well. Essential to his doctrine as an art educator—developed from conversations with his philosopher friend Hartley Burr Alexander—was the notion that different art forms represented distinctive, non-verbal languages, each of which expressed and conveyed specific areas of human understanding and knowledge, otherwise not communicable through speech or writing.[20] He taught his students that art was an integral part of life, not something separate and apart, isolated on a pedestal. In the future, this idea was to become central to Sam Maloof's personal vision as a designer-craftsman.

A prolific and virtuoso watercolorist, by 1930 Sheets achieved such rich and novel effects with washes of pure pigment that his sun-drenched, somewhat abstracted views of the Santa Ynez and San Joaquin valleys looked almost like landscapes painted in oils. His painting style sparked so many imitators in the 1930s and 1940s that he was largely responsible for creating the California School of Watercolor Painting—the first West Coast art movement to achieve recognition in the East. But he was more than just a highly successful painter. A remarkably energetic and creative individual—and a handsome, athletic man with an infectious zest for life—the multi-talented artist-designer was a virtual "one-man renaissance."[21]

Although he was self-taught as an architect, during his career he designed almost one hundred banks, residences, stores, and institutional buildings, mostly in California and Texas. Given all his other activities, it is an astonishing number. (He is most famous for the many Home Savings and Loan buildings he designed in the Los Angeles area.) He also produced more than a hundred murals and glass mosaic decorations for a wide variety of settings—from bars, restaurants, and hotel lobbies to churches, sports clubs, and universities. (By the time Maloof started working on the window displays at Bullock's with Harold Graham in 1939, a large Sheets mural already graced the interior of the store.) But his work was even more diverse; it included interior design and decoration, magazine and calendar illustration, the design of the official seal of the County of Los Angeles, and in the mid-1950s, production designs for Columbia Pictures. Aside from his academic duties in Claremont, he even found time from 1953 to 1959 to direct the Los Angeles County Art Institute (now the Otis-Parsons Art Institute).

However, Sheets's greatest impact on the cultural landscape of Southern California proved to be as a director and organizer of art exhibitions at the Los Angeles County Fair. Through exhibitions, he was able to express his ideas about the indivisibility of art and life to a broader public. In 1931 he had succeeded his own artistic mentor, Theodore Modra, as director of the fine arts exhibitions at the Los Angeles County Fair, continuing the latter's emphasis on California arts and crafts. But after the war, Millard's shows became far more ambitious and serious in tone. Hugely popular, landmark events, they opened the eyes and minds of countless provincial Southern Californians to the wider universe of world art. Maloof was familiar with them all.

The first of the post-war series staged in the Fine Arts Building (itself a Sheets design) was an overview of Western art from the late rococo to 1950, *Masterpieces of Art from 1790 to 1950* (1950). In less than three weeks, it attracted 900,000 visitors. The next show was *One World of Art* (1951). An extraordinary, museum-quality display of masterworks from distinctive cultures worldwide, both ancient and modern, including America's recent enemies (in Sheets's view, in the post-war era, the universal spirit of art would abate hatred between peoples), this latter epic drew a million fairgoers. Subsequent exhibitions included *Six Thousand Years of Art in Clay* (1952), *Painting in the United States* (1953), and two highly popular interior design and home furnishings shows in which his vision of art as inseparable from daily life was most clearly evident—*The Arts of Daily Living* (1954) and his swan song, *The Arts of Western Living* (1955). In these two latter displays, Sam Maloof's modern furniture was integrated into contemporary-style architectural settings, and the displays helped launch his reputation as a maker of fine custom furniture. By 1954, Maloof furniture had already been included in two of the arts and crafts shows that took place concurrently with the fine arts exhibitions, but with less fanfare. These annual displays were organized by Sheets's colleague in the Scripps art department, ceramicist Richard Petterson, a friend of Maloof's and one of his early Claremont-area clients.

Maloof left his Westlake Bungalow unit in late 1946 and first returned to his family home in Chino, before moving into an apartment over a carport in the rear of a home at 353 Seventh Street in Claremont. Sheets admired some new pieces of angular, contemporary-style furniture that he made for this setting and at his request, Maloof designed and constructed several "clean cut" work tables in plywood for the studio.[22] But Sheets wanted Maloof closer at hand, available to work at all hours at a minute's notice, so he had him move into the spacious studio next to his house on Via Padova in suburban Padua hills. Maloof became an integral member of the family. Sheets and Maloof became close personal friends and companions, but as an employer, Sheets was often domineering and demanding. His personality could be overwhelming and the good natured, compliant Maloof soon found himself enmeshed in an intense, often emotionally exhausting relationship, one in which he played a subordinate, often submissive role. But the intellectual and artistic rewards of working with Sheets on a daily basis outweighed the frustrations he often felt.

Aside from silkscreening, Maloof's tasks were unusually varied. According to Sheets, "he did everything"[23]—even accompanying his boss and local artist Merrit (Mugs) Van Sant on a marathon, two-month painting tour of Mexico beginning in December 1946. During this odyssey they were befriended by the celebrated California jockey and art collector, Billy Pearson, then living in exile in Mexico. He would become a future Maloof client. Maloof's Spanish was of particular value to the travelers, as was his good-natured companionship. Back in Claremont during 1947 and 1948, Maloof collaborated on a number of Sheets's murals, typically enlarging Millard's small sketches into full-size cartoons and then applying the under painting. For the large-scale mosaics, he cut out all the copper templates. One interior decoration job took him into Los Angeles for late night work on Lawry's La Cienega Restaurant. He could begin work only after the 2:00 AM closing time, laboriously applying gold leaf on the long wall behind the bar until mid-morning. When it was finished, the owner thought the color too gaudy, so he had to return and tone down the bright gilding with a dark pigment wash.

Other disparate tasks included stretching canvases and making picture frames for Millard. In this regard, Maloof developed into a skillful frame maker and decorator, carving and toning the wood surrounds in a fashionably rough and primitive manner. He occasionally made picture frames for the Dalzell Hatfield Galleries, Sheets's Los Angeles dealer, and also designed the gallery's printed labels and exhibition brochures. For Sheets's county fair exhibits, Maloof's skills as a graphic artist came in handy. Working closely with Richard Petterson, he designed and hand lettered the original artwork for the catalogues, brochures, and posters. For one short period, Sheets even loaned him as a draftsman to his architect friend and former design partner, Harry Sims Bent, who had recently suffered a stroke. Bent had a reputation for being very difficult to work with, but he and Maloof became good friends. As the younger man drew up plans, the older one talked to him about architecture, regaling him with tales of clients and one of his early classmates—painter Georgia O'Keeffe. Working for Sheets was like being caught up in a whirlwind; Maloof often did not know where he would end up the following day, week, or month. It was certainly exciting, and a wonderful learning experience in the arts, but the question loomed: did working for Millard Sheets amount to a career for Sam Maloof? Or should the thirty-one-year-old jack-of-all-trades take a new, more personally satisfying direction, one that would take into account his rising interest in three-dimensional design?

Chapter Two

EMERGENCE

In June 1947, while waiting outside at Scripps College for one of Millard's morning classes to end, Sam Maloof encountered Alfreda Ward, then a graduate school applicant on leave from her job developing and administering arts and crafts programs for the Indian Service. It was love at first sight. Discharged from the WAVES in the summer of 1946, she was now living with her Swedish-born, invalid mother in a small house she had recently bought in Ontario, no money down and fifty dollars a month, as part of her G.I. benefits. She, too, was pondering her career options. Although she loved to teach, Freda had no strong desire to go back to the world of Federal bureaucracy. Moreover, she had her recently widowed mother to care for. A year later—and only one month after their first date—Freda and Maloof were married (fig. 15). She had known it would be the case the first time she had laid eyes on him—and so had Maloof. For more than fifty years, it proved a perfect union. Maloof hand lettered the wedding invitation and Millard Sheets served as best man.

After a short honeymoon spent driving along the coast from La Jolla to Carmel in his new maroon Studebaker, Maloof moved into his bride's home at 921 Plaza Serena. It was a modest, three-bedroom house with an attached garage whose door opened toward the street (fig. 16). Situated in a tract of similar working-class homes, it had been constructed in 1943 by the Kaiser Steel Company for workers at its factory in nearby Fontana, the first steel plant in California. A painter and weaver, thirty-six-year-old Freda was instantly accepted by Maloof's family and circle of friends. She had been born in LaVerne, and had grown up in the area, graduating from the University of California, Los Angeles, before becoming director of arts and crafts at the Santa Fe Indian School in the depths of the Depression.

Although Maloof now lived in Ontario and drove daily to work in Claremont, his work days continued in the same irregular pattern. At 4:30 PM, Sheets might decide he needed Maloof to stay in the studio and after a quick meal, they would work until midnight—or later. When he returned late one evening, with supper cold on the table, Freda quietly asked to whom he was married—herself, or Millard Sheets. The following day, and for the weeks and months that

Occasional chair (detail), 1950. Walnut, maple, and cord; private collection.

followed, Maloof left work promptly at 5:00 PM. His relationship with his possessive boss—who now thought that as a married man, his assistant was somewhat unreliable as a worker—began slowly to deteriorate, and in the early spring of 1949, Maloof finally got up the courage to tell Sheets he was going to quit. It was a difficult decision; it felt like asking for a divorce. Feeling hurt and abandoned, Millard did not talk to Maloof for two years. But their friendship was eventually restored and Sheets became a firm supporter of Maloof's woodworking career, commissioning work and helping to spread the word of his skill among potential clients.

Furnishing 921 Plaza Serena

When Maloof moved in with his new wife and mother-in-law in June 1948, the one-story house was sparsely furnished. At first, they survived with odd pieces and the wooden citrus crates that Freda had artfully covered and painted. The newlyweds were too poor to buy manufactured furniture, so in the fall of 1948 Maloof decided to design and build a suite of pieces that would be both practical and aesthetically pleasing. A contractor friend gave him several sheets of inch-thick, four-by-eight foot, fir plywood that had been used as forms for pouring cement. They were unusable when Sam got them, but Maloof took them to a local tombstone cutter and had the dried cement sandblasted off. During the process areas of soft wood were also removed, leaving a heavily textured surface. The cleaned sheets now looked just like high grade etched-grain plywood, a fancy builder's product then just coming onto the market. (At the time, new plywood with book-matched veneers cost two or three times as much as solid wood.)[1]

Fig. 15 Wedding reception, 1948. On June 19, 1948, a month after their first date, Sam married Alfreda Louise Ward.

The next problem was securing woodworking tools. Fortunately, Freda's father had left a variety of simple hand tools—a hammer, chisels, a jack plane, handsaw, carpenter's square, and a brace and bit—and from Harold Graham, Maloof borrowed an electric tilting table saw, "the type you work cock-eyed on."[2] (The table tilted, but the saw blade remained vertical.) It was his only power tool. Setting up a rudimentary workshop in the garage, he began to create contemporary-style furniture whose simplicity, utility, and economy of construction would soon gain him a nationwide reputation as a model home craftsman (fig. 17).

Analyzing the available space and limited needs of his household, Maloof had drawn up plans that included a long cabinet with doors on both sides. It served as a room divider, separating the living and dining areas in the small, open-plan house. The unit also had a built-in, metal-lined planter at one end above which louvers rose to the ceiling. An attached dining table and two simple benches abutted one side of the divider. A second, credenza-like cabinet stood against the wall, with over-sized round disks for door pulls. On the living room side, an additional cabinet sat on a long, low stand (a popular furniture format at the time), while several occasional chairs were grouped around a coffee table. The angular frames were made of salvaged red oak (originally used as railroad packing), their side rails and angled, short, back legs extending beyond the uprights. The backs and seats were made of tightly wound, wash line cord.[3] In design, the furniture was simple and unornamented, repeating the stark geometry of the pieces he had built for his Los Angeles and Claremont apartments, the unsightly plywood edges inset with strips of solid wood. Characteristic of Maloof's earliest work, squared legs canted out at an expressive angle. But the manner in which the dining table

Fig. 16 Freda and son Sammy in the yard of the Maloof home at 921 Plaza Serena, Ontario, 1950. The attached garage served as Sam's first furniture workshop.

Fig. 17 Maloof working in his garage workshop, 1950. He is seen attaching the back leg of a chair with dowels and glue. Courtesy *Better Homes and Gardens*.

and benches fit together with the two-sided, divider-cabinet was novel and space-saving (figs. 18–21).

The clean lines, functional nature, and consistent appearance of the pieces ensured that they did not overwhelm the small space, either physically or visually. In the living area, the decor included a length of printed fabric suspended from the ceiling, and in the dining zone split bamboo blinds were employed as "wall paper." A blond tonality predominated. The floor was covered with Skandia Flax, a sisal-like, woven carpeting, while the plywood furniture had been rubbed with an off-white finish, highlighting the sandblasted textures. Two of Maloof's contemporary-style, geometric wooden lamps (one round, the other rectangular) and a ceramic sculpture by his Claremont artist friend, Albert Stewart, graced the cabinet tops, while a large, primitive wooden mask was fixed to the louvered screen. It was an artful interior, composed and arranged with great taste, if little expense. It was famous among Sam and Freda's friends for its stylishness.

First Commission

Ceramicist William Manker from Padua Hills admired Maloof's early furniture. He also worked as an interior decorator, and when he was commissioned to decorate a new house in Pasadena, he turned to Maloof to produce a dining room set—a table, chairs, and a buffet with multiple interior drawers (fig. 22). When Maloof received this first private commission, he decided to leave Millard Sheets's employ. His son Sammy had been born prematurely in March 1949, and shortly after, at the age of thirty-four, Maloof decided to make his living as a self-employed furniture maker.

A graphic artist-turned-woodworker, Maloof first made an artful presentation drawing of the table and chairs (a host chair with arms for the ends of the table, and an armless model for guests), laboriously painting the background in black ink. The designs were pure geometry. There was no ornamentation, just straight lines and angled joins. But the proportions of the pieces were harmonious, and the spatial relationships between parts visually arresting. The table top floated above a supporting framework of slanted legs, while stretchers on chairs, placed just below the side and back rails of the seats, were a prominent part of the overall design.

In the end, the job proved an onerous learning experience:

When I asked for a down payment, [Manker] looked at me askance. 'You don't ask for a down payment,' he said. 'Only people working on a shoestring ask for a down payment.' Well of course that's exactly what I was working on, but I bought the wood myself—birch it was. I built a prototype for the chairs. I'd built chairs before, but not for sale, and I wanted to make sure these were going to be strong. So I made the prototype of birch, got up on the roof [of the garage] and dropped it on the driveway. It lit on the back leg and shot up like to knock me off the roof. The leg broke, but not any of the joints, so I went ahead and made the chairs. The buffet was all solid stock with triple-mitered corners. Very tricky joints. I made the drawers of solid wood, too, sixteen of them.[4]

Figs. 18–21 Furnishings designed and made by Maloof for his living-dining room in Ontario, California, 1949–1950. Made from sand-blasted plywood and scavenged materials, the furniture was simple and unornamented, but practical. Courtesy *Better Homes and Gardens.*

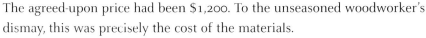

Fig. 22 First furniture commission, 1949. Maloof's first major order for custom-made furniture was a dining room set for a house in Pasadena.

Fig. 23 Arm chair, 1949. In late 1949 Maloof made lounge furniture for the Red Hill Country Club near Claremont.

The agreed-upon price had been $1,200. To the unseasoned woodworker's dismay, this was precisely the cost of the materials.

To compound this financial disaster, Manker had insisted on staining the ensemble a lifeless grey-brown without the client's prior approval. "Are you sure that's what they want?" Maloof had asked. "I'm the decorator," he had answered, "they'll take what I give them."[5] Maloof duly lacquered the stained surfaces, but when he and a cousin visiting from Rhode Island delivered the pieces, their reception was calamitous. The woman loved the designs, but hated the color and wanted it removed. At his own expense, Maloof transported the furniture back to his Ontario workshop and stripped and re-stained the pieces according to the client's wishes. The loss of time and anticipated revenues was extremely disheartening, and it almost ended his fledgling career as a furniture maker. To make ends meet—and they already lived very frugally—Maloof was forced to take numerous freelance graphic arts and frame-making jobs.[6]

"Handsome Furniture You Can Build"

Mary Sheets was another friend who had admired the Maloofs' interior decor. In the fall of 1949, when her brother, photographer Harry Baskerville, was commissioned by *Better Homes and Gardens* magazine to photograph an artfully furnished tract house for a projected article, she immediately directed him to 921 Plaza Serena. Delighted with what he encountered, Baskerville recommended the Maloof home to his editor who visited in February 1950, and ordered photographs taken of the interior. She also asked Maloof to prepare working drawings of his furniture simple enough for amateur craftsmen to follow. In March 1951, the magazine published a two-page illustrated feature on the Maloof home and its furnishings, offering the plans for twenty-five cents each. Years later, the unattributed designs could still be found for sale in amateur woodworking publications.

Entitled "Handsome Furniture You Can Build," the article situated Maloof's homemade furniture in its cultural context—the post-war American dream of owning a house and, for millions of homeowners, a frequent difficulty:

Many family budgets expire on the doorstep of a new home. They can't be revived to buy the basic chairs, tables, and cabinets every home needs. If you have watched high building costs shrink your bank account to near zero, you will be interested in the furniture pictured here. It was designed and built by Sam Maloof of Ontario, California. Sam is a professional designer and builder of fine furniture. But he has the interests of amateurs at heart—Sam is a young man with the responsibilities of a new business, a new family, a new home. He knows what it is like to have no furniture to move into a new home, for it happened to him. So Sam designed and built the furniture you see here, handsome, but simple enough so that it can be duplicated with hand tools by any unskilled handyman.[7]

Maloof was paid $175 for the plans—a sum he didn't expect—and the cash proved a godsend. The editors subsequently asked him to design some simple outdoor furniture for amateur craftsmen, but he never completed the project. Nor did his own entrepreneurial plan to sell his contemporary-style furniture in kit form materialize: for a one-man operation, the marketing hurdles seemed too high. As a result, he decided to restrict his work to private clients. Fortunately, over the next fifty years, he never lacked customers.

Maloof's early clients were local homeowners and organizations who learned about his design and furniture-making skills through word of mouth and telephoned to order work. In late 1949, a year he earned only $555 (less than his annual mortgage payments), he made lounge furniture for the Redhill Country Club near Claremont as well as furniture for other clients (figs. 23–26). The following year he constructed six pieces for Mrs. V. C. Maul of nearby West Covina—virtually his entire output in furniture that year—for which he received $1,160 (again, the amount barely covered expenses). Intended for the Mauls' new ranch-style house—and designed in close consultation with the homeowner—the furniture included a complex, walnut and birch radio/hi-fi cabinet with built-in speakers, drawers, and vertical slots for long-playing records (it also supported a television set on a swivel). The other pieces were a cork-topped, drop-leaf dining table (when not in use, it was placed against a wall), a low side table with two open shelves, and a bench-like coffee table with a black, slatted top.

Functional and straight-edged in design, the furniture was reproduced in color in an article in the *Los Angeles Times* Sunday Home magazine, on the Mauls' stylish residence (fig. 27)—a publication that

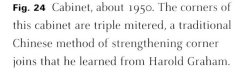

Fig. 24 Cabinet, about 1950. The corners of this cabinet are triple mitered, a traditional Chinese method of strengthening corner joins that he learned from Harold Graham.

Fig. 25 Coffee table, 1949.

for the next two decades would regularly promote Maloof's handcrafted furniture. Mrs. Maul's son was the architect, while her daughter handled the interior decoration, combining a series of then-fashionable hues—coral, sage green, cocoa brown—with natural materials—brick and redwood—and emphatic textures. The suburban house was a model of Southern California informality—the floor plan was open and inviting, and sliding glass doors led from the indoor dining area to an adjacent outdoor dining patio.[8]

Maloof's simple, clean-lined wood furniture eminently suited Southern California's new style of interior decoration. In the early 1950s, progressive Southland homeowners rejected period accessories and historical associations, favoring instead coordinated assemblies of contemporary furniture, fabrics, and decorative accessories. A model living room created by Scripps College ceramicist Richard Petterson for the school's ninth annual clay show and featured in the *Los Angeles Times* in early 1952, highlighted this new, creative approach. The display was filled with Maloof's latest custom pieces, new hand-printed textiles, and recent pottery by Petterson, Harrison McIntosh, Rupert Deese, Gertrude and Otto Natzler, and Raymond Koechlin.

Maloof's contributions included an advanced version of his original "string" chair, a cabinet on a low table stand, and a circular, cork-topped coffee table with multiple legs (figs. 28–30). The accompanying text stated the obvious: "For many years decoration was considered nonfunctional and unnecessary. Stark, antiseptic, machinemade 'art' was the style. But the pendulum has finally swung back. . . . Sterotyped, sterile factory products . . . fail to satisfy a need for individual expression by the artist or home decorator."[9] By the time the article was published, Maloof had a new private client, the most famous of all his many customers. The commission proved a turning point, for during its completion, the mature Maloof style began to emerge.

Henry Dreyfuss Commission

In the summer of 1951 Maloof had answered the telephone and heard a voice say: "My name is Henry Dreyfuss. You don't know who I am, but I know who you are. I've seen your furniture and I like it very much. I'm building a new house, and I would like to have you make furniture for me. [Can] we get together?"[10] Maloof was speechless. One of the era's most talented and successful industrial designers, with a design staff of thirty and offices in New York and Pasadena to serve his major corporate clients, Dreyfuss had been an idol of Maloof's since his days in Harold Graham's workshop. At the appointed meetingtime, Maloof drove into Pasadena and lunched with Dreyfuss's architect and staff in his office. Afterward, the eminent designer met alone with the little-known craftsman to look over the house plans (drawn up by architect Henry Eggers after Dreyfuss's own designs) and discuss the family's furniture requirements. It proved to be a big order—in all, twenty-five pieces. During the course of the discussion, Maloof stopped to clarify one important matter: "You want to design it, and you want me to make it?" "Oh, absolutely not" was the reply. "You're the designer and the maker; that's the reason I called

Fig. 26 Sofa, 1949.

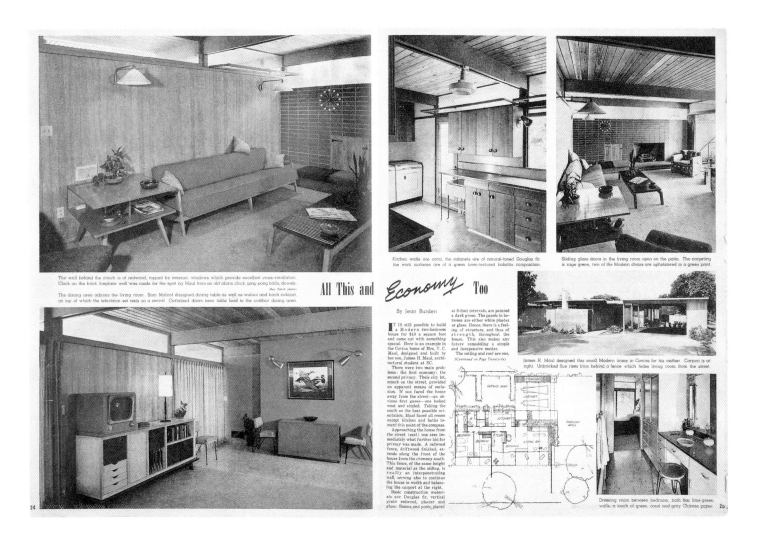

Fig. 27 V. C. Maul residence, Covina, California, 1950. The open plan house, with its contemporary furnishings by Maloof, was featured in the *Los Angeles Times* Sunday Home magazine. Courtesy *Los Angeles Times*.

you. I want you to design it, and I want you to make it."[11] It was an extraordinary vote of confidence as well as a challenge at the outset of his furniture-making career.

Which of Maloof's early pieces prompted Dreyfuss to call remains unknown, but Maloof's unadorned, geometric style was clearly coincident with the designer's own ideals. An art and design critic declared Dreyfuss to be "the foe of fancy ornaments and the exponent of clean lines."[12] Nonetheless, why the famous product designer with a bi-coastal practice would commission a fledgling furniture craftsman with a garage workshop in working-class Ontario, California, is a question difficult to answer. Probably, because he was a very private man in a very public profession, he wished to shield his domestic life from prying eyes, and Maloof's professional anonymity would help ensure it. (Although magazine editors often begged him to do so, Henry Dreyfuss never allowed the interior of the magnificent Columbia Street residence to be photographed.) Moreover, to get exactly what he wanted, it would be easier to work with a virtual unknown than with a noted professional who had a firmly developed style.

As an industrial designer, Henry Dreyfuss was far less interested in style than in ergonomics, and by the time he met Maloof, he already had calculated ideal dimensions for everyday furniture—the height of chair arms, the depth

Fig. 28 Occasional "string" chair, 1950. Walnut, maple, and cord (refinished); 29 ½ x 24 x 33 inches; unsigned; private collection. This contemporary-style chair was among the first of his pieces to incorporate turned legs. The open frame was tightly wrapped with washline cord to create a comfortable seat and back.

Fig. 29 Cabinet and stand, 1951. The 1xth Annual Ceramics Exhibition at Scripps College in Claremont included a model living room demonstrating how contemporary ceramics, furniture, and textiles could be artistically coordinated. Exhibited in the Scripps show was a moveable cabinet on a low table stand, a furniture format then popular with contemporary designers.

Fig. 30 Interior design display, 1951. In addition to the cabinet, Maloof contributed a "string" chair and a circular, cork-topped coffee table.

of seats, the angle of backs, and the distance from floor to table top. Indeed, for several years, Dreyfuss had been developing "Joe" and "Josephine," his "typical" human prototypes. Based on anatomical measurements of a wide variety of body types and sizes, as well as on scientific studies of the range of physical motion while standing or sitting, these models represented the "average" American man and woman for whom he designed all manner of products, from airline seating to power tools. Although his theories were not published until 1955, in reality "Joe" and "Josephine" were as much Maloof's clients as the actual Dreyfuss family.

Henry and his wife, Doris Marks, wanted a large refectory dining table that, with the extensions pulled out, could seat twelve people. As Maloof recalled: "He said, 'I think you should make that out of plywood, because I understand solid woods twist and warp and all.' Well, I could not tell him [otherwise]. . . . So I did it in plywood [covered with walnut veneer]. I wanted a solid edge on the plywood, so I made a "V" groove. I thought that was the way you did it. . . . But doing that "V" groove on large sheets of plywood [with the tilting saw], I was standing on my head practically."[13] The Dreyfusses also wanted a coffee table, something sturdy enough to rest their feet on and whose surface was stain-resistant. Maloof suggested a four-by-four-foot table topped with waxed Danish cork.

To test it, they asked Maloof to make up a corner sample. The top was three inches thick and a round walnut leg projected through the surface in which a large spline was inserted. As Maloof recalled, "They kicked it around and they spilled stuff on it and all, and they said, 'Fine, go ahead and do it.'"[14] A week after it was delivered, Dreyfuss called and said, "'Sam, the cork table you made—our son . . . spilled a bottle of India ink on it.' And I said, 'Oh, no,' to myself. 'But you were right. It came right off.'"[15] Unfortunately, while making the coffee table, Maloof had his first workshop accident: he caught the skin of

his knee cap in an electric sander, which ripped it off. Due to inadequate medical attention, he developed severe toxic poisoning and was incapacitated for weeks.

Dreyfuss also wanted four office chairs made out of teak. For this order, Maloof reworked the design of the host dining chairs he made in 1949 for William Manker's Pasadena client. But he altered the sturdy, angular form in several significant ways. For one thing, he eliminated the rear stretcher and raised the side one, making the chair look lighter; more importantly, to provide greater comfort, he shaped the hard inner edge of the arm into a smooth, rounded surface. But, at Dreyfuss's insistence, the back remained cushionless. Indeed, Dreyfuss wanted an uncomfortable chair. So Maloof raised the original cross rail so that it no longer supported the lumbar region but cut across the shoulder blades (fig. 31). There was a method behind Dreyfuss's unreasonable demand. During business meetings, he wanted his staff and clients to remain mentally alert and uncomfortable chair backs ensured short, productive meetings. But around the family dining table, it was a different matter. Comfort counted, and in addressing that particular issue, Maloof made a breakthrough in his own design philosophy. By introducing curves, shaped joins, and turned arms and legs, his geometric style relaxed into a softer, and more organic mode. Indeed, the prototype dining chair he developed for Henry Dreyfuss in mid-1952 was the beginning of his distinctive sculptural style.

Dreyfuss actually wanted two different sets of dining chairs. One was to be a reproduction in solid walnut of a radically simplified plywood chair that he already owned, but the design of the other set was left up to Maloof. Chairs are the most challenging of furniture pieces to design. Like a work of sculpture, a chair is viewed from different angles and a well designed one needs to remain aesthetically coherent from all sides. But dining chairs impose special demands. Since they are most commonly seen drawn up to an empty table, the back view is the most important. To solve this particular problem, Maloof designed a chair that was radically different from any he had previously fabricated. A simple, low-back model with arms and an upholstered leather seat, it used woods of contrasting color—light-toned maple and dark walnut (fig. 32).

Although geometric in outline—front and back posts were vertical and turned arms were attached at right angles—the seat

Fig. 31 Office chair for Henry Dreyfuss, 1952. In 1952 Henry Dreyfuss, one of the leading industrial designers of the age, asked Maloof to both design and fabricate furniture for his new home and office in Pasadena.

Fig. 32 Prototype dining chair for Henry Dreyfuss, 1952. Ultimately the design was rejected by the client, mostly on the basis of its heavily lacquered finish.

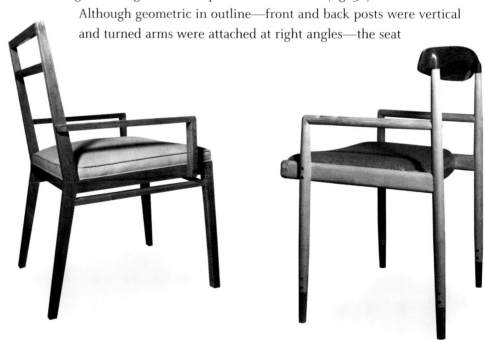

was set forward, away from the backposts, its apron extending beyond the front legs. Since it was now visibly isolated, the rear seat rail gained in importance as a design element, and Maloof shaped it into a gentle, visually appealing curve. To add interest, the light-colored legs ended in dark, tapered "feet" made of pegged walnut inserts (fig. 33). This decorative detail was similar to one employed on a chair with a floating seat designed by the celebrated Danish architect-designer, Finn Juhl, and manufactured by the Baker Furniture Company. Part of Baker's "Modern" furniture line, in the early 1950s Juhl's chair was prominently featured in advertisements in *Arts & Architecture*.[16]

But the most significant feature of Maloof's prototype was its subtly sculptured back rest. Carved out of a walnut blank, the flattened plane was gently curved and, as attached to the back posts, canted backward to provide maximum lumbar support. To achieve the right angle to the tilt, Maloof created a new type of hand-carved, organic joint that allowed the posts to fuse with the back in a purely sculptural fashion (fig. 34). The leg was fitted into the back rest like an arm anchored in a shoulder socket. He was justifiably proud of this joint (developed instinctively as he was carving the back rest), for it allowed him to adjust the support to suit individual needs. No manufacturer could have duplicated the fluid transition from round leg to flattened back rest, and in the years to come, such sculpted joints would become a hallmark of his work. But to Maloof's great disappointment, Dreyfuss rejected the prototype, mostly on the grounds of its finish. He criticized the ten layers of lacquer finish as "too plastic-looking." So Maloof made another prototype of the same design, but this time all in walnut with a glowing, hand-rubbed finish and a broader, more rectangular back rest (fig. 35). It was his first true "Maloof" design. But by the time it was finished, Dreyfuss decided instead he wanted the woodworker to replicate a manufactured chair he had just acquired. The updated design was later developed for Alta Loma client, John Chilton, who ordered four examples and a dining table in 1953.

During a business trip to New York, Henry Dreyfuss had purchased a simple wooden chair with flowing lines and a rubbed oil finish from Georg Jensen, the Fifth Avenue Scandinavian home furnishings store (fig. 36). Designed in 1949 by the Danish designer-cabinetmaker, Hans Wegner, it was from a limited production line produced at the small Copenhagen factory of Johannes Hansen. Only three examples were made each day, for in the modern Scandinavian tradition, the thirty-man workshop combined fine hand craftsmanship with machine fabrication. Characteristically, Wegner rejected the severity and spareness of machine aesthetic modernism with its reliance on steel frameworks, substituting soft, curving forms in natural hardwoods. Warm and sensuous, the individual parts of his chairs flowed together to create simple, sculptural compositions. Less geometric in outline than Maloof's prototype design, the principal feature of Wegner's chair was a highly sculptured back rest that curved forward in a half circle to incorporate strongly molded arms. The separate sections were seamlessly connected with sawtooth joints.

Not only was it beautiful to look at, it was comfortable to sit in. When it was introduced into the United States by Georg Jensen in 1950, Wegner's design

Fig. 33 Prototype dining chair, 1952. Maple and walnut, leather upholstery; 29 1/4 × 21 × 19 7/8 inches; signed with gold-on-white decal, "MALOOF"; Sam and Alfreda Maloof Foundation. For the first time Maloof employed turned and subtly shaped components. The walnut "socks" on the legs were a decorative feature highlighting Maloof's joinery skills.

proved an immediate hit. It was instantly nicknamed "The Chair." Its sculptural aesthetic represented a new, humanized version of modernism. After 1945, the geometric character of Bauhaus-inspired furniture had been greatly relaxed. To demonstrate this obvious change in style, in the spring of 1952 the Museum of Modern Art presented an exhibition, *New Design Trends.* The display paired similar household objects designed in the 1920s and '30s with contemporary examples. To reveal clearly the recent shift toward organicism in furniture design, a flowing easy chair in teak by Finn Juhl was contrasted with an angular, tubular steel-and-leather "Wassily" model from 1925 by Marcel Breuer.[17]

Dreyfuss thought his new Wegner model would make a fine dining chair when combined with Maloof's refectory table and so he shipped it to Pasadena. (He knew he could acquire additional examples from Frank Brothers' furniture store in Long Beach, then the West Coast's leading outlet for new Scandinavian and other contemporary designs.) But the arms of "The Chair" proved too high to fit underneath Maloof's table. Moreover, the seat was too deep for dining comfort. So he asked the woodworker to alter the height and depth and make four new copies. Reproducing Wegner's design proved a valuable learning experience. Maloof readily absorbed the Dane's more emphatic sculptural aesthetic, seeing possibilities for greater plastic developments in his own work. Indeed, as an exercise in the new Scandinavian inspired idiom, he designed and fabricated a Wegner-like prototype, but without extended arms and incorporating a curved seat (fig. 37). A unique piece, it proved to be the only example in his oeuvre of the direct influence of Scandinavian design. By the time the distinctive Nordic style captured the home furnishings market in the United States in the mid- to late-1950s, he had firmly established his own sculptural style, even more classic and restrained than that of the commercially driven Danes and Swedes who annually introduced new, more complicated designs.

Maloof charged Dreyfuss $1,880 for the twenty-five pieces of furniture he made for his new home (other pieces included cabinets, desk tops, and bedroom furniture). It was not a big return for what amounted to his total annual production for 1952, and Henry Dreyfuss, who had become very close to Maloof and Freda during the process, was anxious that the craftsman not set his prices too low. But he was more concerned about another issue. As Maloof later recalled, "Freda and I went there for dinner one night and he said, 'Sam, I've been terribly worried about you.' And I said, 'How's that, Henry?' 'You're working alone. . . . The only income you have is from your hands. And I've often thought, if you get sick, how would your family get along?' And I said, 'Well, they wouldn't.'"[18] Dreyfuss's suggestion for Maloof's financial security was a natural one: "You should design for production. I'll write a letter." At that point in his emergent career, Maloof was not wholly opposed to the idea. In the early 1950s, furniture designers were public celebrities; custom cabinetmakers were virtual unknowns.

In February 1953, Henry Dreyfuss duly wrote to his friend Hollis Baker, president of the Baker Furniture Company of Holland, Michigan, recommending Maloof as a designer. But after reviewing photographs of Maloof's work, Baker demurred. With numerous pieces by Finn Juhl in production, he felt he

Fig. 34 Sculpted backrest on prototype dining chair, 1952. This hand-carved joint was Maloof's first organic treatment of joinery and helped launch his distinctive sculptural style.

Fig. 35 Dining chair made for Mr. and Mrs. John Chilton, 1953. Based on the Dreyfuss prototype, Maloof further developed the chair's ergonomic back rest.

Fig. 36 Chair designed in 1949 by Danish cabinetmaker, Hans Wegner. In modifying this classic design for Henry Dreyfuss, Sam absorbed some of the Danish cabinetmaker's advanced sculptural style. The Metropolitan Museum of Art, Purchase, Edward C. Moore, Jr. Gift, 1961. (61.7.45).

Fig. 37 Scandinavian-style prototype low-back chair made by Sam Maloof, 1952.

had more than enough modern designs to satisfy the current market. At the same time, Dreyfuss also wrote on Maloof's behalf to a number of successful American designers of contemporary-style furniture—Paul McCobb, T. H. Robsjohn-Gibbings, William Pahlmann, Charles Eames, and George Nelson—seeking their advice on fees and charges. The text read in part:

I have a young friend, Sam Maloof, who is doing some excellent furniture designing and distinguishing himself by actually building the pieces in a fine, craftsman-like manner. He works alone in his own shop in Ontario, California. . . . Sam is anxious to design and build samples that can be turned over to manufacturers for mass production. Several manufacturers have already approached him and I would like to see him off to a good start. . . . Today, he came to me to ask advice about charging for such an effort. I am frankly not familiar with furniture charging methods. . . . Would you be helpful to him and give him some indication as to how much he might charge. . . . Your suggestions would be appreciated by both Mr. Maloof and me.[19]

Dreyfuss had stretched the point about manufacturers' interest, but he was factual about Maloof's "distinguishing" himself by not only designing, but fabricating his pieces. In the contemporary furniture industry, a one-man operation was an extreme anomaly. Indeed, Maloof knew no other individual furniture craftsmen and he felt isolated in Ontario.

Although he regretted the financial restrictions the scale of his business imposed on him, he balanced it against the inner satisfaction—indeed the joy—he got from making furniture by hand for individual clients who, like the Dreyfusses, became close friends. When they were unable to attend performances of the Los Angeles Philharmonic Orchestra in their box at Chandler Hall, Henry and Doris regularly would give Maloof and Freda their tickets, and the two couples even went on excursions to the Los Angeles County Fair, enjoying Ferris wheel rides together. A designer working for industry could never develop such personal relationships with consumers. As a result, Maloof wrote to the recipients of Henry Dreyfuss's letter, thanking them for the advice they had given (there appeared to be no accepted industry standard as to designer's fees and royalties) and furthermore stating that he had no interest in designing for machine production. Several months later, over dinner at the Dreyfuss home, Henry asked Maloof what his response to the designers had been. As Maloof recalled, "I told him I wrote to them, but I was not interested [in designing for industry], and he said, 'I thought that's what you'd do.'"[20]

As his orders grew, the tract house garage proved an inadequate work space and during the fall of 1952, Maloof repeatedly expressed a desire to move out into the country. One day, Freda, quietly exasperated, exclaimed, "You know, I'm tired of hearing you talk about it. Why don't you do something about it?"[21] Turning to the real estate section of the local newspaper, he found a small parcel of land with a house on it advertised for sale in rural Alta Loma, a village about ten miles to the northeast. He immediately called and made an appointment to see the property. Surrounded by miles of citrus ranches, the one-acre site off Highland Avenue had been part of a larger, five-acre grove of lemon and orange trees. At the end of a short dusty driveway stood a white, clapboard-sided grove manager's cottage. In Maloof's words, "a little dingbat of a house,"[22] it was nonetheless picturesquely situated directly beneath the spreading limbs of a huge avocado tree.

More than a century old, the tree was a magnificent specimen. Although the Maloofs didn't know it then, it was the largest of its kind in Southern California. But the house it sheltered was mean. Built in the 1920s, it was little more than a one-bedroom shack for the man who once maintained the rows of citrus trees. Nearby was a dilapidated chicken house. A garage door led into a musty, eighteen-by-twenty-foot space with a broken cement floor covered by a low pitched roof. Attached to the rear was an outdoor poultry run that had long since collapsed; weeds poked through the rusty fencing. But to the north, the view toward the street revealed the majestic backdrop of the San Gabriel Mountains. Cucamonga Peak lay directly ahead. The beauty and quietude of the place was deeply satisfying and Maloof determined then and there to root himself next to the enormous avocado (figs. 38–40).

The owner wanted $9,500 for the property, with a down payment of $4,000. For the Maloofs, it seemed an impossible sum. Their only assets included some small savings, the value of their life insurance policies, and their equity in the tract house. But the seller refused to swap their equity in 921 Plaza Serena. He wanted all cash. There were no family resources available to them—

Fig. 38 Sammy Maloof playing outside the grove cottage in Alta Loma, about 1955. The workshop that had been converted from a chicken coop can be seen in the background.

Fig. 39 Vista looking north from the Maloofs' property, 1979. Before construction of tract housing opposite Maloof's driveway on Highland Avenue, his family had an unobstructed view of the nearby San Gabriel Mountains. Reproduction by permission of Jonathan Pollock.

Fig. 40 Maloof in about 1965 under the immense avocado tree that had initially attracted him to the Alta Loma property.

Maloof's parents in Chino couldn't give them anything, nor could Freda's wheelchair-bound mother. A bank loan was also out of the question—Maloof's business was simply too risky. The dream of owning the modest property faded. Three months went by, and one day the owner telephoned. There had been no other offers, and the seller would now accept in trade the $3,000 equity. Finally, after cashing in their insurance policies and borrowing $200 from a friend, they made the down payment. On Easter Sunday, 1953, Sam, Freda, four-year-old son Sammy, and Freda's mother (called Mor-Mor by her family) moved their few belongings, including the sandblasted plywood furniture and the Wegner-style prototype chair, into the new residence. For Maloof, it was a true homecoming. He knew that he had found his physical and spiritual center and for the next half-century, the genius of the place influenced him deeply. The widening stream of work that flowed out of his grove workshop earned him honors and acclaim of a sort that he could never have obtained as a designer for industry.

Chapter Three

GROWTH

The mid- to late-1950s were years of growth for Sam Maloof—as well as for Southern California. Indeed, the fast-growing, prosperous Southland was a furniture designer's paradise. During this short, but concentrated period, Maloof's philosophy of design and craftsmanship matured, his repertoire of forms expanded and, as he incrementally acquired more tools and equipment, his woodworking skills and speed of production increased. Due to enthusiastic press coverage, his furniture also began to be widely known throughout the Los Angeles area and even east of the Rockies. His clean-lined, gently sculptured pieces were regularly featured in the *Los Angeles Times* Sunday Home magazine (a publication that, throughout the 1950s and 1960s, strongly supported his work), but it also appeared in such nationwide periodicals as *House Beautiful, Arts & Architecture,* and *Craft Horizons.* As a result, his reputation as a designer committed to the modern ideals of simplicity, function, and economy of means and materials spread rapidly and widely.

In the 1950s Maloof's furniture was regularly included in numerous exhibitions of contemporary-style household objects organized in the Los Angeles area. Extremely popular, they helped to develop and promote a "California look" in modern home furnishings. Indeed, Maloof's clean-lined pieces came to epitomize this emergent West Coast style and admirably suited the new "contemporary" homes then being built in record numbers throughout Southern California. In fact, working alone in his Alta Loma shop with a minimum of tools, by the mid-1950s Sam Maloof was the Golden State's outstanding "modern" furniture designer-craftsman. But at the same time, unwittingly, he was in the vanguard of the postwar studio furniture movement then emerging across the United States.

In the dynamic Southern California marketplace, Maloof's rivals were not custom cabinetmakers like himself, but celebrated designers who worked for leading manufacturers of modern-style wood furniture. They included the Scandinavians Hans Wegner, Finn Juhl, and Folke Ohlsson, among others, and their American counterparts Jens Risom (Risom Designs), Terence Harold Robsjohn-Gibbings (Widdicomb Furniture Company), Edward Wormley

Counter stool (detail), 1958. Walnut and leather; Arthur Raymond Family.

(Dunbar "Modern"), Paul McCobb (Directional Contemporary Furniture), Greta Magnusson Grossman (Glenn of California), and George Nelson (for Herman Miller). All of their lines were available in select Los Angeles area stores. But factory-made, their pieces clearly lacked the fine craftsmanship, attention to detail, skilled joinery, and warm patina of Maloof's handcrafted furniture— subtle qualities sought by discriminating clients in search of more personalized, hand-made furnishings.

Kneedler-Fauchere

After the workshop was relocated to Alta Loma, Freda's business records reveal accelerating production. In 1953 Maloof made thirty-seven pieces that earned $3,634 (almost twice what he had received from the Dreyfuss commission the previous year). In 1954 fifty-four pieces brought $7,876, while the following year eighty-four pieces sold for $11,733. In 1956 a total of 151 pieces (many of them sets of chairs) were delivered to clients for $26,959. But it was not all smooth sailing. After a serious accident sidelined him for several months (he suffered second and third degree burns over his face, arms, and upper body that almost ended his career), in 1957 completed orders only amounted to sixty-four, reducing revenues to $16,696. (In fact, Maloof would not surpass his 1956 earnings record until 1965, when ninety-six pieces sold for $34,782.) For almost two decades the business actually did little more than break even. Since he worked alone to ensure the highest quality workmanship, Maloof's production was limited and, to survive, he often worked long hours—from sixteen to eighteen a day, six days a week. It was a grueling schedule, but he had the physical stamina and inner drive to maintain it (figs. 41–44). Moreover, he did not want his wife to have to work outside the home to make ends meet. In large part, the increase in production after 1953 can be explained by an exclusive arrangement Maloof established that year with a leading interior design gallery in Los Angeles. As a result of this commercial connection, his work was seen and admired by the Southland's leading architects and decorators, and orders began to mount.

On April 16, 1953, Maloof had been contacted by Richard Whitney, the manager of an outlet about to open in the Robertson Center of Beverly Hills, which housed upscale decorator showrooms. Located opposite the handsome Herman Miller Furniture Company showroom designed by Charles Eames, the new store was to be the Los Angeles branch of a San Francisco firm, Kneedler-Fauchere, owned by designer Harry Lawenda and his wife, Dorothy. Among the finest shops of its kind, Kneedler-Fauchere sold only to the trade. The new showroom, its walls covered with Japanese grass-cloth wallpaper, stocked an array of upscale modern furnishings and yardgoods: Thaibok handwoven silks, textiles by Dan Cooper and Jack Lenor Larsen, Swedish printed cottons, Danish furniture, contemporary wooden lamps, and the pottery of Maloof's friend, Harrison McIntosh.

Whitney had learned about Maloof's furniture from the dean of admissions at Pomona College, and wrote offering to represent his work in Los Angeles on an exclusive basis. Maloof was cautious about entering into any contractual arrangements, but after meeting with Whitney, he agreed to supply some floor

Figs. 41–44 Sam Maloof working in his first workshop in Alta Loma, about 1955. Before erecting a more suitable structure in 1956–57, Maloof set up shop in a dilapidated chicken house on his rural property.

samples for the opening—a low-back dining chair (the second prototype made for Henry Dreyfuss but rejected for the Wegner reproductions) and two simple walnut benches whose seats were resilient nets of laced cord. Both were rectangular, but one had handles and was slightly curved (figs. 45 and 46). The latter was to become one of his most popular designs in the 1950s and 1960s. A ring binder on display contained photographs of other available designs. It proved a highly successful arrangement. After two years, he couldn't keep up with the burgeoning orders, and although the business relationship had its ups and downs, it lasted until 1960. "Once they introduced me to the architect or the interior designer," he later recalled, "I was on my own. Whatever the commission was, or whatever the price was, I'd give them one-third of the cost and the interior designer would take a third, then I got the remainder."[2]

In October 1953, Elizabeth Gordon, the influential, style-setting editor of *House Beautiful* magazine—and a friend of Millard Sheets's—visited the Los Angeles County Fair, saw Maloof's curved laced bench on display in the California arts and crafts exhibit, and ordered a similar one through Kneedler-Fauchere. Its retail price was $60, but since it was purchased through an intermediary, Barbara Treiman Interiors, with the various commissions and discounts allowed in the transaction, it cost Gordon $55.72, of which Maloof netted less than five dollars after paying air freight to New York.[3]

Nonetheless, the sale paid enormous dividends. Smitten with the simple but elegant design and fine craftsmanship, Gordon featured it in an article in the February 1954 issue of the magazine that was devoted to "The Pace-Setting Kitchen." In this modern workstation, the editor decreed there should be "beauty in everything you touch." To Maloof's surprise and delight, his laced bench was among the handful of "touchables" reproduced in color.

The text declared: "A handmade wood bench with a seat of laced string is entirely appropriate and practical in the kitchen. Yet its soft, flowing lines are very beautiful. . . . The kitchen bench is a poem of practical loveliness, designed and made by Sam Maloof. Here beauty works, and work itself has a wondrous beauty." The copy stated that the maker did custom work "on a line that is typically his own" and that Kneedler-Fauchere was the exclusive distributor of his "creations."[4] The power of publicity was soon demonstrated. Within days, Whitney received letters asking about the price and availability of the design.

Maloof's work was soon featured again in *House Beautiful*; this time in a May 1954 article on Millard Sheets's personal choice in home decorations. Entitled "Taste Portrait of One Man Who Played the Game," it illustrated one of Maloof's new occasional, or easy chairs commissioned by Sheets, now fully reconciled with his former assistant. The text noted that the famous head of the Scripps College art department "shops in all countries, all centuries. . . . [But] the furniture Mr. Sheets admires most is the work of new, young, custom cabinetmaker, Sam Maloof, whose work is beginning to attract connoisseurs."[5]

"Designer, Craftsman of Furniture"

Among the "connoisseurs" was Claremont art journalist Sherley Ashton. After visiting the workshop, examining pieces on hand, and interviewing Maloof, she

Fig. 45 Laced bench, 1953. Walnut and cord.

Fig. 46 Curved laced bench, 1960s. Walnut and leather; 16 1/2 x 29 5/8 x 16 5/8 inches; signed with shop brand "designed. made/ MALOOF/California." Sam and Alfreda Maloof Foundation.

wrote an in-depth article, "Maloof: Designer, Craftsman of Furniture," for the May/June 1954 issue of *Craft Horizons* (now *American Craft*). The journal of the American Craftsmen's Council (ACC), the bi-monthly magazine was the Bible of the nascent studio crafts movement in the United States, and the well-illustrated feature introduced Maloof's creations to a nationwide network of craft artists and patrons. It proved an important entree into a world that eventually would become the principal context and support for his work.

Ashton's article provides the first clear statement of Maloof's philosophy as a designer-craftsman—an individual who not only designed a piece but completed it from start to finish. From Sam's point of view, designing didn't stop with the completion of a working drawing; it was part of the fabrication process itself. Measured drawings were guidelines, not dictates. "Design doesn't just exist on paper," he was quoted as saying, "it pervades every step in the creation of a piece of furniture. For me, the individuality of a table or a chair begins when I select the length of wood from which I am going to shape it. And it continues to develop as I take out the bow, saw the raw piece, shape and turn the parts, and finally assemble the whole. Sometimes a chair leg will look a little heavy, or a table top a little thick. When they do, I change them."[6] In his search for perfection in both aesthetics and ergonomics, as he worked he subtly altered shapes, proportions, and transitions between parts. It was not only his prerogative as a designer-craftsman, but a necessity. As he later stated: "I do not feel that it is possible to make working drawings with all the intricate and fine details that go into a chair or stool, particularly. Many times I do not know how a certain area is to be done until I start working with a chisel, rasp, or whatever tool is needed for that particular job."[7]

One of Maloof's principal objectives was "warmth." In his view, the weakness of much contemporary American manufactured furniture was its "coldness"—the direct result of the separation of designer and craftsman in industry. Scandinavia offered a better manufacturing model. There, he pointed out, furniture designers and production cabinetmakers worked in tandem, not isolation, each appreciating and acknowledging the other's contributions. But his own role as an independent designer-craftsman represented the ideal: in one autonomous individual, the two identities were successfully combined, and quality was controlled from start to finish.

According to Ashton, Maloof thrived on the freedom and demands of his one-man operation. (It was exactly the type of self-directed, non-regimented life he dreamed of while in the Army.) "In the course of a day," the writer stated, "he may be salesman, designer, craftsman, supply buyer, and truck driver, but he is sublimely free to design and build, without interference from such commercial factors as cost accountants, advertising executives, sales managers, or shop superintendents whose foibles tend to destroy the subtleties of craftsmanship for the sake of profits." When asked whether he would ever want to design for factory production, he responded simply: "The smell of wood in my shop is more pleasing than a desk in an office."[8]

Maloof declared he wanted the light, fluid lines of his hardwood furniture also to convey "strength." While his designs retained the appearance of strength, his seating forms were designed with comfort and ease of use in mind (fig. 47). Instead of applying a set of ideal dimensions like those developed by Henry Dreyfuss, Maloof used his own body as a template, adjusting the height of arm and back rests and the proportions of seats to fit himself. Remarkably, it proved universally applicable; a Maloof chair fits virtually everyone.

In his otherwise unadorned furniture, visible joinery played an important aesthetic role. "If a piece is well put together," Maloof declared, "the joints will be pleasing to the eye and should not be hidden."[9] Corners of cabinets were triple-mitered—an old, but little used Chinese custom that protected veneered corners—and while other cabinetmakers might avoid them on account of their difficulty, he regularly made dovetail and tongue-and-groove joints with hand tools. Differences in color and graining patterns emphasized their presence. As a decorative as well as functional device, he inserted a wood spline of contrasting color into the top of pegged walnut legs where they projected through surfaces of tables and benches (fig. 48). In the 1950s, it was one of his signature joinery details.

The type of wood selected for individual orders was typically based on the dominant color of the room in which the piece was to be placed. Although in the mid-1950s he worked in teak, oak, ash, and birch, he told Ashton he preferred walnut for its warmth and "workability." But no matter what wood was used in a piece of furniture, the manner of its finish was a fetish: "I put as much time on finishing my pieces as I do on the combined steps of designing and putting them together."[10] After hours, sometimes days, of obsessive sanding to obtain perfect smoothness (his brother Jack, a school teacher, helped out on Saturdays), a transparent wood filler was rubbed into the open grain before a primary oil finish was liberally applied. Next, the first of two mixtures of turpentine and boiled linseed oil were firmly rubbed into the wood with cheesecloth. Finally, a coating of pure linseed oil was applied. After two days' drying time, the saturated surfaces were firmly rubbed down with pumice or rottenstone, and finally with an oil-soaked leather pad. The warm and mellow patina obtained by such a lengthy, labor-intensive process could never be matched by industrial methods. It was one of the charms that set Maloof's work apart from manufactured pieces.

In the early summer of 1954—a key year in terms of press notice—a reporter for the local Upland-Ontario *Daily Report* also visited the Alta Loma workshop and wrote admiringly: "Sam Maloof is destined, perhaps, to be one of the country's foremost designers of furniture. The young artist—and who says furniture designing is not an art?—has gained such recognition that [in *House Beautiful*] . . . you'll find a two-page spread showing some of his furniture— graceful, modern pieces that lend additional charm to the home of Claremont artist, Millard Sheets." It was when he was working as Sheets's assistant, the writer continued, that Maloof was "inspired to work in the third dimension," and all things considered, "furniture seemed the best medium for three-dimensional design." People who were "fortunate enough" to own a Maloof chair, the story continued, were as proud to display it "as they would a Van Gogh or a Cézanne painting." The craftsman had no intention of expanding his workshop:

"I want to keep it a one-man business. . . . Every piece is custom made. I want to keep it that way. People who want distinctive contemporary furniture are willing to pay the price." The only helpers he "enlisted," the reporter noted, were "his charming wife and five-year-old son."[11] The article was illustrated by a photograph of Maloof, Freda, and young Sammy sitting on the grass next to their cottage (fig. 49). Arrayed in front of them were ten pieces of Maloof furniture, early geometric designs of the 1949–52 period, as well as the newly introduced sculptural models. It is a telling record of his early progress.

In August 1954, Maloof's latest work was on display in the fifth annual *California Living* show, a major home furnishings trade fair held in Los Angeles's huge Pan-Pacific Auditorium. The Sunday *Los Angeles Times* Home section reported on the exhibit, featuring a new Maloof arm chair on its cover (fig. 50). Seen at an angle from the rear—thus showing the framework otherwise obscured by the loose back cushion—the photograph more fully revealed the chair's relatively complex, sculptural composition. Inside the magazine, there was an admiring article by design writer Virginia Stewart, "The Work of Sam Maloof—Strength, Beauty, Utility."

Familiar with the local scene, Stewart wrote: "As the number of maturely conceived Contemporary homes increases in Southern California, the demand for beautiful, enduring furniture continues apace. Just as these new homeowners are searching for good lighting, floor coverings, draperies, decorative accessories and paintings, they have also decided that their homes call for fewer and better pieces of furniture. Quality has become a prime requirement. To illustrate what quality means, especially in custom made furniture, the methods and beliefs of one of Southern California's upcoming designer-craftsmen, Sam Maloof of Alta Loma, are shown and detailed here."[12] The remainder of the text repeated ideas already expressed in *Craft Horizons*, but six of the accompanying illustrations showed rooms full of "quality" Maloof furniture commissioned by local clients (figs. 51 and 52), as well as a half-dozen details of his decorative joinery and a small model of a desk.

Before starting work on a new order, Maloof first visited the client's home, studying its layout and decoration, and drawing up a ground plan. Back in the workshop, he made simple mock-ups in folded paper—with windows, doors, and fireplaces marked—to evaluate the character of the architectural space. Not only did he want to satisfy the customer's needs, but also meet his own aesthetic standards. Always concerned with the overall artistic effect of interiors, he wanted to visualize how his pieces would relate to one another within the physical setting. Because his strong, simple designs needed adequate space to breathe, he firmly opposed "crowding up a room"—especially as new houses diminished in size as building costs skyrocketed in the late 1950s.

As part of his design process, in the 1950s Maloof also made scale models of new pieces. (It was a practice followed by Hans Wegner.) The correctness of proportions could be judged more easily in three dimensions than from plans. Shown to clients, these miniature prototypes supplemented scale drawings— and afterward, proved wonderful toys for his son. Next, he made a full-size prototype in redwood or pine for the customer's final review. He charged for

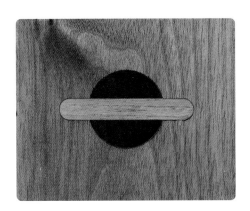

Fig. 47 Occasional arm chair with turned spindles, 1954. Walnut and leather; 37 ¾ × 30 ¼ × 28 ¼ inches; unmarked; private collection. This comfortable chair was one of a pair ordered in 1954 by Los Angeles painter, Emil Kosa.

Fig. 48 Joinery detail on a coffee table, 1960s. Walnut and maple.

Following pages:

Fig. 49 Maloof, Freda, and Sammy outside the workshop in 1953 with ten examples of Maloof furniture made since 1949.

Fig. 50 Cover, *Los Angeles Times* Home magazine, Aug. 8, 1954. Sam made this upholstered occasional chair for his former employer, Claremont painter Millard Sheets. Courtesy *Los Angeles Times.*

Fig. 51 Article on Maloof furniture, *Los Angeles Times,* August 1954. Photographs show rooms in the John Chilton home furnished with Maloof's pieces. Courtesy *Los Angeles Times.*

Los Angeles Times
MAGAZINE SECTION
AUGUST 8, 1954

HOME

California Living Show

Burton Frasher Jr.

See Page 13, 14

The Work of Sam Maloof —

Strength, Beauty, Utility

By Virginia Stewart
Illustrated on Cover

AS THE number of naturally conceived Contemporary homes and apartments increases in Southern California the demand for beautiful, enduring furniture increases space. Just as these new homeowners are searching for good lighting, floor coverings, draperies, decorative accessories and paintings, they have also decided that their homes call for fewer and better pieces of furniture. Quality has become a prime requirement.

To illustrate what quality means, specifically in custom-made furniture, the methods and beliefs of one of Southern California's upcoming designer-craftsmen, Sam Maloof of Alta Loma, are shown and described here.

"Design," as he practices and speaks of it, "exists not just on paper; it pervades every step in the creation of a piece of furniture."

He designs and makes by hand furniture to fill his clients' specific needs, furniture that will stand the test of time and has warmth. "Good Contemporary furniture goes well with any good antique. My chief concern is that every piece of furniture I make shall have usefulness, beauty, craftsmanship, the same qualities fine antiques have," says Maloof.

He wants the light, fluid lines of his furniture to convey also a feeling of strength. He believes that, ideally, a table should be in one solid slab and with—

(Continued on Page Fourteen)

Three-piece storage unit and chair were designed for Mr. and Mrs. John F. Chilton by Sam Maloof. Interior of this walnut cabinet is lacquered blue; the doors are sliding ones, corners are triple mitered

View of the Chilton living room at right shows a chair, occasional table of wood and cord, a coffee table and an end table cabinet designed, handmade by Maloof

Burton Frasher Jr.

Fig. 52 Living room, Carleton Appleby home, Alta Loma, 1954. The Applebys were among Maloof's early local clients.

the time spent making these three-dimensional models, but gave away the detailed drawings. The multiple-step process eventually proved too time-consuming and costly and by the late 1950s, he generally started fabricating the final piece in hardwood as soon as the order had been confirmed. Later, with the exception of measured drawings for case goods, he typically dispensed with drafting-board plans altogether.

Los Angeles County Exhibitions

In the postwar era, an interior design philosophy that coordinated contemporary furniture and crafts with modern architecture was heavily promoted in Southern California. In 1954 it was the theme of Millard Sheets's vast home furnishings exhibition, *The Arts of Daily Living,* staged at the Los Angeles County Fair. Demonstrating his cherished notion of the indivisibility of art and life, the show prominently featured Maloof's furniture. Maloof had first shown at the County Fair in the 1952 exhibition of California arts and crafts organized by Richard Petterson. The following year he was awarded second prize in furniture for a new cork-topped desk and an honorable mention for one of his curved laced benches (fig. 53). (The Pomona *Progress-Bulletin* had called his pieces "the main items" in the exhibit.)[13] But in Sheets's sprawling 1954 blockbuster—which filled the Fine Arts Building—Maloof had a whole suite of coordinated pieces on display, plus other, isolated examples. To local reporters, it was only natural. As the *Progress-Bulletin* put it, "of course, Sam Maloof's incomparable furniture is used with appropriate and lavish abundance."[14]

The Arts of Daily Living drew an immense crowd. During the sixteen-day-long fair itself, an astonishing 1,110,927 visitors passed through the turnstiles of the Pomona fairgrounds—almost one million of them touring through the show. In the opinion of the *Los Angeles Times,* it was "the best exhibit of its kind in the Fair's history."[15] The sprawling display included twenty-two architect-designed model rooms—so called "realistic depictions of idealistic living"[16]—which had been furnished and decorated according to Sheets's integrative precepts. Its success was not only a testament to the organizer's creative vision, but also to the public's overwhelming interest—at the time, almost an obsession—in contemporary-style household objects and decorative accessories.

In the new one-story, post and beam houses proliferating throughout the Los Angeles region, Colonial-style designs (until 1950, typical products of the American home furniture industry) were wholly out of place. Period-style furnishings might be suitable in older homes east of the Mississippi River, but in postwar Southern California, Old World design traditions had been firmly rejected. For inspiration and guidance in how to equip their newly built, ranch homes with appropriately designed products, Southland consumers increasingly turned to style-setting exhibitions such as *The Arts of Daily Living.* In this respect, Sheets's show—and Maloof's furniture—fulfilled Angelenos' needs and desires. As one writer put it: "most of the hundreds of thousands of visitors will find solutions to their own house problems . . . and ideas for adding vitality and interest through the use of arts and crafts."[17]

The exhibition was co-sponsored by *House Beautiful* and was lavishly featured in the October 1954 issue. The complex display was dedicated to Frank Lloyd Wright—the modern master of integrating interior design with architecture—and the layout was designed by the magazine's architectural editor, John de Koven, a former Wright disciple. (Wright himself visited the show before it opened to the public, walked slowly and imperiously through it, and departed by limousine without saying a word.) Carefully decorated with contemporary furniture, fine arts, and studio crafts, as well as the latest in fabrics, wallpapers, and floor coverings, each artistically coordinated environment had its own "stamp of personality." There was, for example, a Scandinavian-American dining alcove that included a Swedish tapestry, Finnish rya rug, and a circular table and four three-legged dining chairs by Hans Wegner. (Four months later, Wegner's chair designs would be featured in *Craft Horizons,* among the first illustrated articles to popularize his work in the United States.)[18]

Nearby was a larger dining room that featured a dramatic Oriental screen, a handcrafted wood table and four spindle-back chairs by George Nakashima—all arrayed on hogskin-covered parquet flooring. It was the first time that Maloof

Fig. 53 Maloof furniture in the 1953 Los Angeles County Fair arts and crafts exhibit.

had seen the work of this celebrated Japanese American architect and fellow furniture craftsman, whose work and self-designed home had been illustrated in 1950 in *Arts & Architecture.*[19] In the years to come, Nakashima, a devotee of graining patterns in slabs of hardwood, would become a friend and strong supporter, ultimately admitting, "Sam Maloof is one of the only craftsmen whose work I admire."[20] Not far from this eating area was an elegant, combined bedroom-dressing room suite. Over the king-sized bed hung a painting by Millard Sheets whose frame had been carved by Maloof, but the rooms also contained a pair of his now-famous walnut benches, as well as a glass-topped counter whose frame was constructed like a laced, three-seat bench.

A novel setting attracted a great deal of attention. It was a new type of domestic space—A Special Room for Television (fig. 54). Painted blue, it had a low-pitched wood ceiling with the visible beams and rafters typical of a contemporary-style California house. Designed by George Wright, a partner in the large Los Angeles architectural firm, Welton Becket and Associates, the model room was entirely outfitted, according to *House Beautiful,* with furniture "handmade by an up-and-coming young man in cabinetry, Sam Maloof." Indeed, the home entertainment center had been specifically designed "to give his pieces a functional setting, as well as to show how a small space can be fully developed."[21] The display contained an upholstered walnut occasional chair, a matching wide, spindle-back sofa with cushions, and two cork-topped tables— one an end model, the other a long, low coffee table on which the television sat. For inspiration, fairgoers could purchase a color postcard of the room.

In November, Angelenos were exposed to yet another modern home furnishings show—the first of the celebrated series of *California Design* exhibits staged between 1954 and 1971 at the Pasadena Art Museum (now the Norton Simon Museum). Important displays of contemporary California crafts and industrial design, Maloof's work was featured in all eleven shows. In his words, "[they] had a great influence not only in California, but throughout the United States."[22] Design specialist Virginia Stewart was the general consultant to the first show which, like all those staged annually through 1957, included objects from throughout the state. (From 1958 through 1961, the shows were restricted to Los Angeles County producers. Beginning in 1962, after which they were staged triennially, the exhibits were once again opened to all Californians.) In the 1954 exhibit brochure, the Pasadena museum director rightfully claimed that "'California' and 'Hollywood' . . . have long been used as catch words in describing or advertising new designs, especially in the apparel and home furnishing fields. . . . California is indeed a vital center of the best creative design and production for contemporary living." It was an appropriate show for a museum setting, he argued, since today's well-designed wares were "tomorrow's antiques."[23]

The objective of the exhibition was to educate Southland consumers about "good design" thus elevating popular taste and stimulating demand for creatively conceived objects that were manufactured locally. Each household item was clearly marked as to maker, price, and retail source and represented a wide range of designer-producer relationships: from the individual craftsman fabricating a

Fig. 54 A Special Room for Television at the 1954 Los Angeles County Fair. Maloof designed and made the furniture for this new type of domestic setting.

limited quantity in his own studio, like Maloof, to the industrial designer working for mass production, like Charles Eames. Aside from furniture, the display included samples of floor and wall coverings, printed fabrics, lamps and accessories, ceramics, tablewares, small household appliances, and even toys. Maloof contributed three pieces: a laced bench (now priced at $75), a low-back dining chair ($125), and an occasional arm chair ($325).

California Design was Los Angeles's answer to the *Good Design* exhibitions co-sponsored between 1950 and 1955 by the Museum of Modern Art (MoMA) in New York and the industry-supported Chicago Furniture Mart. These annual East Coast and Midwest displays included European as well as American products, both handcrafted and mass produced, and fabricated from a variety of materials, both natural and industrial. Inaugurated by MoMA curator Edgar J. Kaufmann, Jr., they were intended to educate manufacturers, retail buyers, and consumers by identifying (and promoting) well-designed products. Juried objects were given the organizers' distinctive seal of approval—a round, orange-and-black tag emblazoned with the logo "Good Design." (Items chosen for *California Design* were likewise identified with paper labels which were then used in subsequent sales promotions.) Design-conscious Southern Californians were well aware of the MoMA exhibits; they were regularly featured in *Arts & Architecture* and *Interiors* magazines, and discussed in *Craft Horizons*.[24] But there was an excitement to the annual West Coast displays that was missing in the more anonymous, New York–Chicago design shows. In Los Angeles, the exhibitors all knew each other and their products were off-shoots of the invigorating cross-fertilization between crafts and industry that in the 1950s was characteristic of Southland designers. According to one long-time participant, "Everybody talked to each other, and that created excellence and ingenuity."[25]

In 1955 Millard Sheets followed up his previous year's triumph with another blockbuster. His twenty-fifth and final show at the county fair (the following year he was accused of communist leanings and resigned), it was titled *The Arts of Western Living.* Like its immediate predecessor, it, too, contained a series of artfully decorated model rooms, but this time it focused on characteristic, Southern California settings. Rooms of different types were designed for city, suburban, beach, and desert homes. Again, Maloof's furniture was prominently featured. In the exhibit brochure, "Western living" was defined as "provocative and casual, a direct result of the personality of the region." The modern architecture of the Southland was distinctive, the text continued, for local architects had "adapted and realized a style of building and use of space different from any other part of our country."[26]

To drive the obvious point home, a full-scale California-style show house was constructed behind the Fine Arts Building (fig. 55). It had an informal, open interior plan and glass walls that integrated the adjacent patio and pool into the overall architectural scheme, underscoring the indoor-outdoor lifestyle fostered by the region's climate. The one-story, ranch-style residence lacked any historical reference and was a building type then proliferating throughout Los Angeles's expanding suburbs. During the 1950s, the city's population literally doubled in size; its growth rate "defied comprehension."[27] The number of new homes needed to house all the newcomers (then flooding into the state at the rate of 1,200 a day) fueled an unprecedented construction boom—and along with it, an enormous demand for suitably styled home furnishings. But the explosion in house building was a nationwide phenomenon. Between 1946 and 1958, some ten million new dwellings were built across the United States—an estimated nine million of them directly influenced by "the California style."[28] In the words of one well-known developer, a California-style house was not simply a "liveable dwelling," but "a way of life."[29] For many discriminating Angelenos, Sam Maloof's furniture was to be a crucial component of that lifestyle.

In his 1946 book, *Southern California Country—An Island on the Land,* Carey McWilliams had set the stage not only for postwar Los Angeles architecture, Sheets's vision of the synesthetic California interior, but also for Sam Maloof's modern designs. "A nearly perfect physical environment, Southern California is a great laboratory of experimentation," he wrote. "Here, under ideal testing conditions, one can discover what will work, in houses, clothes, furniture, etc. It is a great tribal burying ground for antique customs and incongruous styles. The fancy eclectic importations soon cancel out here and something new is then substituted . . . the importation-and-discarding process has been continuous."[30]

The notion of Southern California as a natural laboratory for new design experiments was at the heart of the highly respected Case Study House (CSH) program initiated by John Entenza and, beginning in 1945, sponsored by his magazine, *Arts & Architecture* (fig. 56).[31] These prototype dwellings were designed with Los Angeles-area professionals in mind. Like Maloof's principal clientele, they were "progressives" with moderate incomes and contemporary

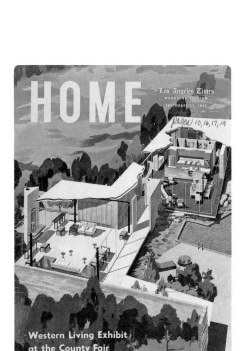

Fig. 55 Model home at the Los Angeles County Fair, 1955, constructed behind the Fine Arts Building. Courtesy *Los Angeles Times.*

tastes for whom the prewar ideal of a white picket fence and period architecture was anathema. Among the architects who first took up the challenge of designing Case Study Houses on a five-acre plot in Pacific Palisades were Charles Eames, Eero Saarinen, Richard Neutra, and William Wurster. After 1950, they were followed by a younger generation who designed houses for other sites, among them Raphael Soriano, Pierre Koenig, and A. Quincy Jones and Frederick E. Emmons. By 1963, twenty-six CSH projects had been planned and published, though not all had been built.

Keenly interested in developments in contemporary architecture and design, Sam Maloof was familiar with the program. The plans and photographs were regularly published in *Arts & Architecture* and before they were sold, the model homes were open to the public. During this viewing period, each house was carefully furnished by local decorators. In several instances, Kneedler-Fauchere used designs by Maloof. Like Scandinavian Modern pieces, Maloof's walnut tables, chairs, and stools were perfect complements to these high-style modern houses. They were not only simple, clean cut, and visually strong, but, more importantly, their softened edges and mellow finishes added a note of warmth and grace often missing in the austere, glass-walled structures.

Millard Sheets lamented the current isolation between architects and craftsmen. *The Arts in Western Living* was intended to demonstrate his belief that, in order to stimulate "creative living," architects, artists, and craftspeople must collaborate on schemes of interior design and decoration. (At the time, the majority of architects rarely concerned themselves with the type of furnishings that went into residences they designed. In part, the CSH program was intended to sensitize them to that issue.) So, almost a year before the show opened, Sheets convened a meeting of leading California artists and designers, organized them into collaboratives, and assigned them model rooms. Once a team's lead architect had determined the basic layout for one of the twenty-four interiors, each group met to plan the furnishings and decorations. Once a consensus had been reached on the overall scheme (color, light, and texture were central concerns), woodworkers, ceramicists, muralists, enamelists, painters, sculptors, and weavers worked independently on their contributions. The day when everything was brought together was magical. To the delight of the participants, empty spaces turned into dramatic, colorful settings.

Fig. 56 Pierre Koenig, Stahl House, Case Study House #22, 1960, Hollywood. *Arts & Architecture,* June 1960. Reproduction by permission of Julius Shulman.

In *Craft Horizons,* Claremont painter Paul Darrow, assistant director of the county fair's Fine Arts Department, noted the unusual, participatory character of the project. "It was a wonderful experience for all concerned," he wrote. "The interchange of ideas from one craft to another had a revitalizing effect on the different arts involved. A vitality and freshness was reflected in the work of the many participants united in a common project. The personal relationship between the many arts and the interchange of ideas and problems resulted in a new respect and understanding toward the allied arts."[32]

Maloof was a member of several teams. For the suburban living-dining room, he contributed a circular dining table and two low-back chairs. They were coordinated with a mix of pre-Columbian and contemporary Japanese pottery, a vivid hand-woven floor rug by Lea Miller, wood veneer wall papers, and a set of bright mosaic wall panels by Kayla Selzer. He also constructed a rectangular table and four upholstered, square-back chairs for Millard Sheets's stunning beach house—notable for its rough, interior stone walls and colorful decorations—as well as the furniture in Tony Delap Jr.'s compact dressing-sewing room: a new low-back counter stool with arms and a familiar laced bench. He also contributed a multi-purpose, counter-height table and bar stools with foot rests for informal eating, menu writing, and household account keeping.

A West Coast Style

In the coordination of contemporary crafts, furniture, and architecture, and the emphasis on natural light and bright color accents, the model rooms were paradigms of the new West Coast decorating style. In early 1956, Conrad Brown, New York editor of *Craft Horizons*, explored the Golden State's craft scene in preparation for the magazine's special issue on California. He reported what visitors to *The Arts of Western Living* must have noted and admired: "The most significant news from a state where modern interiors are the norm is that California craftsmen are leading the way in a movement to de-clinicalize the modern house and warm it up. Everywhere we went we found examples of pottery, mosaics, tapestries, rugs, enamel or ceramic plaques, or turned wood used as the focal point of a beautiful room, tying together all its decorative elements with what seemed like the brightest colors we had ever seen in the crafts outside of Italy. The magnificent climate and a consequent closeness to nature probably have a lot to do with it. Bright colors seem brighter and warm colors warmer in that brilliant saturation of sunlight that Californians work and play in and have so much right to boast about."[33]

In 1955–56 Maloof was invited to contribute work to two more important shows of household objects: *Contemporary California Designers,* the seventh annual Home Show staged in 1955 at the Oakland Museum, and *California Designed,* a large exhibition co-organized the following year by the Long Beach Municipal Art Center and the M. H. deYoung Memorial Museum in San Francisco. The latter was a comprehensive display, comprising 325 products by 128 designers and craftspeople. (In 1957 a smaller version was circulated nationally by the American Federation of Arts.) A number of Maloof's friends and supporters were on the Long Beach selection committee—editor John Entenza, decorator Harry Lawenda, furniture designer Greta Magnusson Grossman, and Richard Petterson. According to *Arts & Architecture,* the objects were chosen on the basis of "freshness and originality, as contrasted to overworked reproduction of modern design." In furniture, "function and utility were important considerations; finishes were soft and warm rather than slick and mechanical."[34]

Publicized heavily in both the popular and trade press, *California Designed* helped familiarize Maloof's name and work—as well as modern furniture and accessories by other designers—for a broad West Coast audience. Long Beach's weekly *Southland Magazine* decreed: "The fact that California is a leading exponent of casual living has been known nationally for years. Not so well known is the role its designers have played in contributing furniture, fabrics, and accessories compatible—even necessary—for the casual mode of life."[35]

For its part, *Living Young Homemakers* (a short-lived shelter magazine aimed at young married couples) asserted that the products on display fit the Southland's "expansive pattern of living," and declared: "Americans, who have a propensity for labeling everything have grown to give the tag *California Designed* an admiring respect. The Golden State's reputation as a source of good contemporary design is perhaps more noteworthy in the home field than in any other." California design was not parochial: "Like other alert currents of American life, [it] is internationally minded. Inspiration comes from the Far East, with influences of Scandinavia and Italy also apparent, translated, of course, into an American idiom."[36]

The Long Beach jurors chose four pieces by Maloof: his first double settee (fig. 57)—a form based on his basic, low-back dining chair (it retailed for $375); an occasional chair ($350); a low, table-bench ($135); and a walnut bar stool with foot rest ($115; fig. 58). Other furniture designers in the show included Charles Eames, George Nelson, Kipp Stewart, and Stewart MacDougall, and designer-woodworkers Paul Tuttle and John Kapel. During the run of the exhibit in Southern California, Maloof gave two illustrated lectures at Long Beach City College on the subject *Art in Modern Furniture.* In the four years since his plywood pieces had been featured in *Better Homes and Gardens,* he had progressed considerably.

Indeed, by the mid-1950s, Maloof was widely viewed as a key member of the trend-setting Los Angeles-area furniture design community. In July 1956, when the *Los Angeles Times* reviewed the semi-annual trade display of modern furniture at the Los Angeles Furniture Mart, the cover of its Home magazine, emblazoned with the banner "California Furniture," boasted how "fresh, original design has focused the nation's attention on our new products." Inside, under the headline, "Leadership Came West," the writer declared that in only twenty years the local industry had "built a world-wide reputation." While in 1935 there had been some 50 furniture factories doing $15 million in wholesale business, now there were more than 400 manufacturers with $250 million in annual sales. Statistically, in terms of output, Los Angeles stood third in the nation, the reporter noting: "The emphasis today, of course, is on Contemporary design."

Indeed, "modern" was synonymous with California. As Richard Petterson noted in *Craft Horizons:* "The modern idiom in the arts is almost universally understood on the West Coast. It is so prevalent in public architecture and in fine houses that people—the younger generation especially—take it for granted, understand it without half trying."[37] One of those who admired the "modern idiom" was Maloof's recent client, Helen Diddy. A color photograph of the dining table and six new, low-back chairs he designed for her new home in Arcadia was illustrated in the *Los Angeles Times* article on California furniture (fig. 59). The caption noted: "Designer Sam Maloof has established a reputation for custom-made furniture that is sturdy enough for hard use, yet has a feeling for lightness."[38]

Furniture by Craftsmen

In February 1957, Maloof's reputation was put to the test in the East when five of his pieces were featured in *Furniture by Craftsmen,* the fourth exhibition to be held at the recently opened Museum of Contemporary Crafts (MCC, now the American Craft Museum) in Manhattan. On display across the street from the Museum of Modern Art, it was the first substantial museum survey of the nascent studio furniture movement and for seven weeks, seventy-eight works by thirty-five woodworkers were on view. Maloof's contributions included the cork-topped desk and low back dining chair made in 1952 and shown at the Los Angeles County Fair, one of his celebrated laced benches (designed 1953), his new walnut settee (1954), and a double-back occasional chair upholstered in white leather (1956). It was the first time his work had been displayed within the context of one-of-a-kind, studio furniture by leaders in the field nationwide, rather than in a mix of Southern California industrial design and craft objects. In regard to artistic modern cabinetry, communication between the East and West coasts was virtually non-existent, but Richard Petterson and Elizabeth Moses (co-curator of *California Designed*) had served as West Coast project consultants and had strongly recommended his inclusion. The *New York Herald Tribune* reproduced a photo of one of Maloof's occasional chairs, praising its "handcarved arm rest and carefully fitted joints."[39]

The intent of the exhibition was to focus attention on studio furniture, a field long in eclipse. "That the work of the contemporary furniture craftsman has been one of the last of the crafts to claim the solo spotlight is not to its discredit," the catalogue stated. "Even the seasoned collector of contemporary handcrafted objects . . . as well as painting and sculpture has been reticent in accepting a fine sculptured chair or table, or a choice cabinet as a . . . work of art."[40] The unusual display was briefly covered in the *New York Times*, the reporter noting one of the differences between a craftsman's creation and mass-produced objects: "when a piece of furniture is treated as a work of art, one finds decorative inserts added . . . cork appears on a desk top by Sam Maloof."[41] However, while the ground-breaking exhibit included a variety of veneered, inlaid, mixed media, and metal pieces, it actually highlighted the use of solid, unadorned wood, then perceived by critics as a more sophisticated use of the medium.

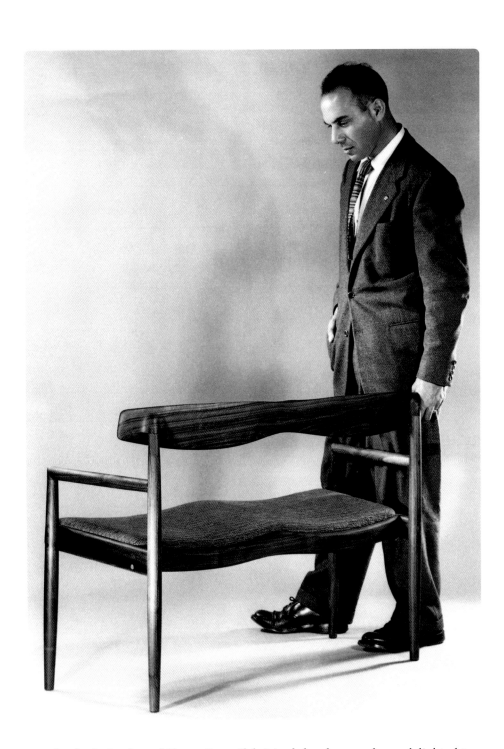

Fig. 57 Maloof with his first settee, designed 1954. Its appearance in the Museum of Contemporary Craft's ground-breaking 1957 exhibition of studio furniture marked the first time Maloof's work was shown in New York City.

Elizabeth Gordon of *House Beautiful* visited the show and was delighted to see an example of the curved bench she had purchased four years earlier. Indeed, she was so thrilled by Maloof's contributions that she called him up in Alta Loma and told him his pieces were among the most exciting she had encountered during twenty-five years as a magazine editor. She also inquired if Sam was Egyptian, or had studied Egyptian art. The answer was "no." "But why such a question?" he asked. "Your things have a very Egyptian feeling to them," she replied. It wasn't until he visited Cairo in 1959 and saw the ancient dynastic furniture at the Egyptian Museum that Maloof understood Gordon's query. A little wooden bench from King Tut's tomb was almost the same as his own design.[42]

Fig. 58 Low-back bar or counter stool, about 1955. Walnut and leather; 30 x 22 ¼ x 19 inches; unmarked; Sam and Alfreda Maloof Foundation. This popular design was introduced in 1955.

Greta Daniels, associate curator of design at MoMA, reviewed *Furniture by Craftsmen* at length for *Craft Horizons*. For Daniels, the show represented an unprecedented opportunity to investigate the place of furniture craftsmen in a highly industrialized society, one which by now might have rendered them obsolete. She determined that consumers who did turn to custom-made rather than manufactured furniture did so for particular reasons. They sought originality in design: the craftsman's "personal statement," use of solid hardwoods instead of less expensive veneers, careful attention to detail and finish, and the maker's freedom and ability to design for a specific setting. Since all the exhibitors readily used power tools, she noted the show was not a sentimental showcase for the "hand made." Nonetheless, mcc director Tibbs had selected numerous pieces that highlighted handwork—"the sculptured effect in solid wood and the joinery techniques which only the hand craftsman can achieve."

In terms of design, Daniels found the show rather dull. An "experimental spirit" was lacking, and while "speak[ing] the visual language of our time," the assembled pieces nevertheless reflected conventional approaches. She found some of them too fussy in their decoration (several tables had elaborate mosaic tile inlays) and others too complicated in design. She preferred "a quiet refinement of contour and proportion, fine detailing, finishes, and, particularly, a very personal choice of material, a living element which renders no two pieces alike." Work which satisfied her aesthetically included a simple, rectangular walnut chest with dramatic book-matched graining on the drawer fronts by Tage Frid (a Danish-trained woodworker teaching at the acc-sponsored School for American Craftsmen in Rochester, New York), and a "silky" yellow birch cabinet set on a dark walnut base by George Nakashima. The sole decoration on this latter case piece was an elegant and understated line of four walnut plugs running across the center of the top echoing the placement of hand-cut dovetails on the ends.

Daniels also praised Jean Russum's solid wood drop-leaf table whose oddly shaped oval top was intrinsically decorative, and John Kapel's laced, walnut and cherry bench (not unlike Maloof's model) for its Japanese temple-like design.[43] She also commended the strong, sculptural qualities of a three-sided telephone table and stool in solid cherry made by graphic artist-turned-woodworker, Wharton Esherick, then the reigning "dean of American craftsmen." With its thick rounded edges, the table was far more expressively shaped and massive in form than Maloof's more delicate, linear designs. The critic likewise admired the work of New Hampshire furniture maker, Walker Weed, a former Dartmouth College English major. His all-wood tables were simple, sturdy productions evoking New England traditions, yet, like Shaker furniture, were disarmingly light in feeling. Maloof's entries were not mentioned, but they must have been among those unidentified "other pieces" cited for their solid, "handmade" look, "spelling comfort and homeliness, and best defined as a continuation of traditional elements—without being an imitation of the past."[44]

An official of the Raymore Furniture Company of New York, then America's largest importer of Danish fine furniture, was highly impressed by Maloof's contributions to *Furniture by Craftsmen* and wrote to ask whether he could

acquire the reproduction rights for the settee, desk, and low-back chair. He wanted to simplify the designs for machine manufacture and have them mass produced in Denmark for sale across the United States. Maloof initially expressed interest in the venture—and even negotiated a royalty—but the financially lucrative deal (it would have netted him a fortune) was never consummated. The manufacturer wanted a "flexible" interpretation of the originals, but the craftsman insisted on only minimal design alterations.[45]

The landmark show also caught the attention of a writer for *American Forests,* the American timber industry's trade journal, and he traveled to a number of the exhibitors' studios, interviewing them for an article on the nascent craftsman furniture movement. It was an unusual subject for readers more familiar with logging camps and saw mills than artist-cabinetmakers' shops. For the author, the people he met were oddballs, "bucking" the industrial age by devoting their lives to fine woodworking. "In an age of mass production," he wrote, "we still have them—those master craftsmen with wood whose creations have brought joy to discriminating homeowners. They're a wonderful crew of individualists, and they're hidden away in the most unlikely corners all over the United States . . . up dark, rusty flights of stairs in an ancient loft building in New York City's Greenwich Village . . . on a rise in Pennsylvania's rolling farm land set in a grove of blossoming magnolias . . . in barns, garages, basements, cinder block shacks . . . in California, Wisconsin, New Hampshire, Ohio, Boston, New Jersey." As a group, he noted, they preferred to make original pieces, not copies or adaptations of existing patterns; it allowed them to change, modify, and experiment as they worked. They didn't advertise their wares, or sell through stores and galleries. Instead, business was generated by word of mouth, or by clients encountering a piece in a friend's home.

George Nakashima was named "the unquestioned leader among hand furniture craftsmen in America today." The forest products writer was attracted by his personal reverence for the inherent beauties of hardwoods. "The hours spent by the true craftsman in bringing out the grain, which has long been imprisoned in the trunk," the Japanese American woodworker was quoted as saying, "is an act of creation in itself." For his part, Maloof was not quoted, but seen in a photograph working in his citrus grove workshop.[46] The article was another proof that Maloof was part of a nationwide group of like-minded individualists, creative people who preferred the workmanship of personal risk to that of industrial certainty.[47] Within months, the Alta Loma craftsman would meet Esherick, Weed, and other leading Eastern furniture craftsmen at the ACC's first nationwide crafts conference held at Asilomar, California.

Asilomar

The first Conference of American Craftsmen was held June 12–14, 1957, at the Asilomar conference center overlooking the Monterey coast in Pacific Grove, California. (The rustic wooden buildings of the state-owned facility had been designed by Arts and Crafts-era architect Julia Morgan.) The ground-breaking meeting was not only pivotal in Maloof's career, but also a turning point in the postwar crafts movement. Never before had so many crafts adherents gathered together in one place. Among the 450 attendees, practicing craftspeople (avocational as well as professional) predominated, but they were joined by designers, museum curators, and educators from thirty states and Canada. Given the location, there were numerous Southern Californians. Maloof and Freda drove north to the Monterey Peninsula, as did Millard Sheets, Richard Petterson, Harrison McIntosh, and other friends from the Claremont artists' group. The theme that brought the geographically dispersed conferees together was one that vitally concerned them: Craftsmen Today. As they all knew from direct experience, in an era of escalating materialism, mass production, and planned obsolescence, craftsmen were isolated on the periphery of the American economy. Members of a subculture outside the mainstream of the larger technological and consumerist society, they suffered "the cold winds of economic and esthetic neglect."[48]

ACC president and conference organizer, Aileen Osborne Webb, intended to help correct that situation. She hoped the unprecedented get-together would give the conferees the opportunity and confidence "to insist on a place in society, and to be strong enough to define that place on their own terms."[49] As she put it in a keynote address:

Briefly, the aim of our conference is to afford participants from all over the United States the chance to meet, communicate, and cooperate in solving problems; to formulate, through discussion and interchange of ideas, a basic understanding of the place of the craftsman in our contemporary society—the philosophical and sociological role of the crafts, the need of a creative and experimental approach to design, and the craftsman's practical problems of production, marketing, and industrial affiliation.[50]

Each day was devoted to a particular theme. In the morning, a panel of speakers at a general forum treated the topic broadly, while in the afternoon, craftsmen broke out into media-based groups and continued the discussion as it related specifically to them. The first day addressed the socio-economic outlook. Keynote speaker Karl With, chairman of the UCLA art department, declared: "the overwhelming change from the basically . . . hand made world to a machine made world . . . leads us to the question—where are we, who are we, where do we go from here, where is our place in society?" Like Millard Sheets, he believed the economic future lay in successfully linking craftsmen with industrial designers, architects, and product engineers in "new teams" that would integrate "all the arts and architecture."[51]

The members of the afternoon wood panel (woodworkers were the smallest group of attendees) included Wharton Esherick as moderator, Tage Frid, Walker Weed, Arthur Espenet Carpenter, Bob Stocksdale, John Kapel, and Sam Maloof. Lawrence Peabody, a production furniture designer from Boston, served as chairman. The weather was warm and sunny, so they decided to meet outdoors. Charles Eames joined the group, sitting on the grass next to Sam. Pioneering wood turner and design teacher James Prestini opened the discussion, asking "What *is* the place of the wood craftsman in an industrial society?" Maloof promptly countered: "Why do you make bowls? For your own satisfaction, or for money?"[52] Prestini responded tartly that he would "rather make bowls for 10,000 people than 10." It was an awkward juncture. For a moment, everyone was silent. Then Maloof broke the silence and asserted that, to control the quality and character of the end product, it was imperative to restrict production to small batches. Otherwise, the woodworker lost his identity as a craftsman.

Peabody then declared that a craftsman should not repeat designs simply for the sake of making them by hand, but rather deliver them to industry to duplicate. Maloof firmly voiced his disagreement. As to the question whether a designer first had to be an expert craftsman in his field, Peabody firmly supported the view that a top designer had no need to be able to work in the medium for which he designed. Sam heatedly stated the opposite: "I believe that one *must* be a craftsman to be a good designer," and backed up his position with a vivid description of his own working methods, noting how, to achieve better aesthetic and functional designs, during the fabrication process he often modified his initial plans. Peabody then counter-argued that mass production was far more democratic and that designer-craftsmen "should design for industry so that more than a chosen few who can afford to buy individual, one-of-a-kind pieces can benefit." Commercial designing, he insisted, was more personally rewarding than creating pieces for single customers, since "many more homes are beautiful, have sounder values, because of [the industrial designer's] skill."

Riled by Peabody's comments, Maloof again took center stage, firmly asserting that, from an emotional standpoint, his personal contact with individual clients was for him far more intrinsically valuable than designing for an anonymous public—they became his friends. Moreover, since the demand for his work exceeded his ability to supply it, clearly many people were looking for the "quality article" which only the designer-craftsman could produce. As a result, he argued, many more furniture craftsmen would appear, allowing a greater number of consumers the opportunity to acquire distinctive, custom work. After the discussion was over, seventy-year-old Wharton Esherick approached Maloof, congratulated him on supporting the craftsman's position so firmly, and gave him some advice: "Young man," he said, "stick to your convictions and don't stray from the way you work and believe; remember what I've told you."[53] Maloof never forgot. Indeed, through what he termed "years of valleys and hills," the injunction helped sustain him. At the evening barbeque dinner, Prestini, too, came up to Maloof and confessed, "If I could work the way you do, I would."[54]

The theme of the conference's second day was design—in essence, the critical relationship of craftsmen to industry. In his keynote address, industrial designer Jay Doblin asserted that "good design" could not be accomplished if the designer set out to design for the "average" man. The direct result was "predigested" mediocrity. Instead, good design "must have behind it the drive of a competent person with strong convictions—one who designs for himself." But he criticized current practices among designer-craftsmen: "You are aiming too much for the gallery rather than the public. Stop designing for shows—this is as bad as designing for mass sales, possibly worse." Millard Sheets was a member of the morning panel and, along with fellow panelists weaver Anni Albers and potter Marguerite Wildenhain, supported the notion that the designer-craftsman should ally himself with modern production methods and view industrial machinery simply as artists' tools.

For his part, panelist Charles Eames underscored his conviction that the present-day world was deeply in need of the set of values attached to the word "craftsmanship." Without them, he stated, society would fail. But he also cautioned: "Areas of the crafts seem to suffer more from overdoses of originality and design than from a lack of it. You are conscious that somebody was conscious of being original, [and] therefore didn't really know what they were about."[55] Panel chairman Daniel Defenbacher, president of the California College of Arts and Crafts, likewise addressed the subject of overtly self-expressive work: "the so-called 'art' crafts are a rich source of [personal] satisfaction," he said, "however, these arts will be effete if they somehow do not show, at least in spirit, an awareness of industrial disciplines." Defenbacher did not want to deny fine artists the use of craft media and techniques, but he defined these crossover artists as "a new breed of sculptor," not craftsmen.[56] In his opinion, it was advantageous to maintain the distinction between art and craft, and to affirm crafts' functional identity.

On the second afternoon the wood panel again met outdoors, and the discussion on the practical application of design theories turned into a bull session. A central theme was the past—its value as a resource for modern design. Lawrence Peabody said he was glad to have been born in New England and to live in a late eighteenth-century house built by a local mill foreman. A truly American design, he said, could develop out of such vernacular traditions. Indeed, Art Institute of Chicago staffer Meyric Rogers insisted that the more a contemporary woodworker knew about the strengths and weaknesses of historical furniture, the better a modern designer he would become. New Hampshire woodworker Walker Weed agreed with this viewpoint, and noted that in his work he tried to "restate the good of the past." Tage Frid then shifted the discussion somewhat, expressing his feeling that too much attention was paid to appearance and too little to function. First and foremost, a chair had to be a comfortable place to sit. Maloof voiced his agreement wholeheartedly: it was central to his philosophy.

Prestini then asked: "Are we running the designer-craftsman out of business when we design for the machine?" The answer was no: given his flexibility and the slow pace of industrial change, the designer-craftsman would always be the leader. Sam pointed out that his creative flexibility was unlimited: simply by changing the angle of his tool as he worked, he could modify a design, while to achieve the same subtle alteration, a factory would have to be extensively retooled. At the end of the afternoon's discussion, a general consensus was reached: the proper role of the designer-craftsman in an industrialized society was probably best described as "an advanced researcher"—or prototype-maker—in the field of industrial design. The question then arose, if that was the case, why shouldn't industry support them financially, as it did in Scandinavia?

But the real outcome of the afternoon's discussion was not the conclusions reached, but the deepening sense of community among all the participants. As Maloof later recalled: "The woodworkers who were there formed friendships that endure to this day [1983]. There I first met Walker Weed, Wharton Esherick, Arthur Espenet Carpenter, John Kapel, and Tage Frid. Bob Stocksdale I had met previously, but this meeting cemented our friendship." There was a shared bond: "What we all had in common was that we were doing what we wanted to do," he later wrote, "None of us wanted to be tied up, or bound. I believe all of us were seeking spiritual well-being in what we were doing."[57]

The third day's program dealt more pragmatically with the subject of "professional practices"—business ethics, production problems, and distribution methods. It was a topic of real interest to Freda, and she was keen to learn how other furniture craftsmen operated. Based on his decades of experience, Wharton Esherick stated flatly that there was no simple answer to the problem of distributing and marketing an individual's work. Walker Weed reported that, like Maloof, he worked alone, selling the majority of his work directly to the customers who ordered the pieces. He operated out of an old, rehabilitated barn, but unlike Maloof, when necessary, he utilized the more advanced facilities of a nearby commercial cabinet shop, where the workers also planed and glued up his case goods. Weed noted that his shop records revealed that he worked 42.8 hours a week (far less than Maloof) and that in the past year he had made some 150 pieces (far simpler than Maloof's designs, they also lacked the latter's labor-intensive finishing)—half custom work, half repeated designs. He did not advertise; most of his new business came from personal recommendations, publicity from exhibitions, and articles in the press. Since he lived in rural New Hampshire and his customer base stretched south to Richmond, Virginia, and west to Chicago, unlike Maloof, Weed conducted most of his business by mail. He shipped his finished work by truck or rail express. Standardized pieces had fixed prices, he explained, based on an hourly wage predicated on his cost of living.

For his part, Maloof never developed such a rationally calculated pricing system, and it long remained a bone of contention between himself and Freda. One participant asked pointedly whether the "slave labor" of a craftsman's wife should be figured into the price. No response was recorded in the transcripts of the session, but it was nonetheless an important issue for Maloof. Without Freda answering the phone, handling the correspondence, meeting clients who visited their home, and daily administering the business end of the workshop, Maloof would have had to price his pieces much higher. He would have been forced either to hire an office manager, or take time out from his shop to do all the office work himself and thus reduce his production.

For the Maloofs, the real reward of this practical session—indeed for the entire conference—was not what they learned about others' business operations, but the gratifying knowledge that they were not isolated. Although small and financially insecure, their enterprise was actually part of a swelling national movement—with the ACC at its center. As textile designer and weaver Jack Lenor Larsen, another new friend of theirs from Asilomar—and one with whom in 1972 they would travel adventurously through Afghanistan—declared in a final, windup panel: "The top people came [to the conference] and have related themselves to the American Craftsmen's Council. Fifty years from now, we will date the beginning of a national movement to Asilomar."[58]

Commissions

In the mid- to late-1950s, Maloof's arrangement with Kneedler-Fauchere generated numerous commissions. His clients now included Hollywood celebrities, a downtown hotel, major corporations, and other important area business groups. In 1954, for example, Santa Monica decorator Peter Shore ordered six pieces for his Beverly Hills client, movie actor Gene Kelly. (All of the furniture was later destroyed in a house fire.) The next year, Maloof received a commission from Welton Becket and Associates to design and make furniture for the new Presidential Suite at the Beverly Hilton hotel. It was an important order, and he duly drew up and presented detailed plans. But the hotel's management decided that his unadorned, all-wood pieces would be too understated. Prominent guests paying premium prices, they argued, wanted something more showy, so they insisted that marble and brass be added to the walnut tables, chests, and bedstead. For economic reasons, Maloof agreed, but subcontracted the job to a commercial cabinetmaking shop; he simply couldn't face ornamenting his work himself.[59]

His most important corporate client of the period was the Scandinavian Airline System (SAS). In 1955 SAS hired Pasadena interior designer Guy Brink to furnish its new business and ticket offices in the United States, along with its first-class departure lounges at airports in Los Angeles, San Francisco, New York, and Washington, D.C. Brink secured Maloof's services through Kneedler-Fauchere and, over two years, the woodworker designed ticket counters, lamp and coffee tables, writing desks, sofas, and occasional chairs for the airline. He was a suitable choice; there was a clear affinity between his own spare style and Scandinavian Modern.

Fig. 60 Executive office furniture, about 1957. Maloof made custom office furnishings beginning in the mid-1950s.

Fig. 61 Tapered-back arm chairs commissioned for the office of Henry J. Kaiser Sr., 1959. They were used by senior managers in the headquarters of the Kaiser Steel Company in Oakland.

Years later, Maloof client Melville Kolliner recalled sitting in the SAS Viking Lounge at Idlewild Airport (now John F. Kennedy International Airport). Awaiting the departure of a flight to Copenhagen, he fell into conversation with a staff member from the Danish consulate. Spying what he assumed to be a Danish writing desk in the V.I.P. lounge, the diplomat proudly identified its designer and described his country's celebrated heritage in modern furniture. After listening for a few minutes, Kolliner, who knew the designer's true identity, invited him to pull out the desk drawer and look at the maker's name inside. To his surprise and confusion, the Dane spied a gold-and-white decal that clearly stated: "Designed/Made by/MALOOF/Alta Loma/California."[60]

In the 1950s large department stores also ordered pieces from Maloof through Kneedler-Fauchere—Saks Fifth Avenue in Palm Springs, Livingston's in San Francisco, Rankin's in Santa Ana, Matthew's in Beverly Hills, Goldwater's in Phoenix, and even Gimbel Brothers in Philadelphia and Milwaukee. Counter stools and lounge seating were popular items for these retail clients, but they also ordered furniture for executive dining rooms. Maloof later recalled an incident with one of his department store customers that demonstrated his remarkable ability to produce work quickly under pressure. In 1955 a soon-to-open Japanese emporium in Los Angeles ordered a set of eight chairs to be completed in time for the store's grand opening. After they were duly delivered a week in advance, he received a tearful telephone call from the decorator in charge. A dreadful mistake had been made; counter stools were wanted instead. Could he make them in time? Working night and day, Maloof completed the order, delivering them an hour before the deadline.

Lawyers' offices, on the other hand, wanted Maloof to supply all-wood conference tables and chairs, and businessmen, like H. F. Ahmanson, founder of Home Savings and Loan Company, ordered executive desks and high-back chairs, often swivel models (fig. 60). In the late 1950s, professionals had a wide choice of handsome modern office furniture. Indeed, the executive desk was one of the most studied of all forms. But a number of successful individualists found Maloof's solid, hand-crafted walnut desks more suitable symbols of personal and corporate integrity and stability than the sleek, wood and metal designs retailed by such leading manufacturers as Herman Miller.

In January 1959, Welton Becket and Associates commissioned Maloof to make a set of office furniture for Henry J. Kaiser Sr.'s executive suite in the new Kaiser Center in Oakland, then the largest office tower west of Chicago. After speaking with Mr. Kaiser, the woodworker fabricated a massive walnut desk designed in a broad curve: the boss sat on the inside, his senior managers arrayed in chairs along the outer edge. For her husband's offices, Mrs. Kaiser had selected a color scheme based on pinks, mauves, and purples, and to harmonize with these hues, Maloof upholstered eight tall, double-back conference chairs with bright pink leather. Before delivery, he photographed the colorful group outside the workshop (fig. 61). In 1961, another corporate client, Lawry's Foods of Los Angeles, ordered twenty-six pieces of Maloof furniture through Kneedler-Fauchere for two conference rooms in its downtown headquarters, including a long meeting table and ten matching chairs. Unlike Henry Kaiser, the president selected more sedate, black leather upholstery.

However, eighty-five percent of Maloof's individual orders came to him directly from homeowners, mostly Southern Californians. Among them were Dr. and Mrs. Jesse Bueno who, in 1956–57, commissioned seventeen pieces for their new Pasadena home (and also asked Sam to assist in choosing suitable wall-papers, fabrics, and accessories). In 1958 aircraft designer-manufacturer Arthur Raymond ordered nineteen pieces for his new, contemporary-style residence in Beverly Hills, including a large custom dining table with twelve matching chairs. For the living room, Maloof made two comfortable chairs and a large cork-topped coffee table (figs. 62–64). Strong color was a period characteristic. Originally, one of Raymond's arm chairs was upholstered in vivid "citron" leather, the other in a bright yellow fabric.[61]

New Workshop and House

By the date of the Raymond commission, the Maloofs had tripled the size of their Alta Loma property. Now three acres, it contained not only many more citrus trees, but a new workshop-house complex—the nucleus of what was eventually to become enshrined on the National Register of Historic Places. It began simply enough. In early 1956, Maloof and a friend who owned a cement mixer poured a twenty-by-forty-foot slab behind the old chicken house for the floor of a new shop. He couldn't afford to frame and roof it immediately, so during daylight, he worked outdoors on the slab, storing his work in progress in the chicken house at night.

This went on for several months until one day an 85-year-old friend, a retired contractor, called him up and said, "Sam, you can't just work outside like that, you've got to have a shop. Buy some lumber and I'll come over and put it up for you, no charge." Although he had no ready cash, he called up the lumber yard and explained the situation. As he later recalled, "they said, 'fine, we'll give you the lumber, you pay us whenever you're able.'"[62] Materials were delivered and Sam, the elderly contractor, and two preacher friends put up the studs and a tin roof. Walls would come later. With a more spacious place in which to work, he could now increase his production. In July 1956, Richard Whitney wrote to Harry Lawenda: "Sam . . . has greatly expanded his manufacturing facilities in Alta Loma, and now feels he can cope with the addition of [Kneedler-Fauchere's] San Francisco market."[63] During the next year-and-a-half, he gradually sheathed the workshop with redwood siding and demolished the old chicken house.

Maloof poured a second cement slab of the same size at right angles to the first, beside a carport erected earlier at the east end of the new workshop. This was to be the foundation for the new home he had long hoped to build. The old cottage was too cramped and outmoded. Sammy had moved from his parents' bedroom to a cot in the living room, and with the addition of two-year-old daughter Marilou, adopted in 1954, the family needed more spacious, efficient, and attractive living quarters. Constructed during 1957, the new residence featured a master bedroom with a glass wall facing the front which was created by enclosing the existing carport. Behind this room was a dining-living area

Following pages:

Fig. 62 Upholstered occasional chair with flared back and sculptured arms, 1958. Walnut and wool fabric (reupholstered); 35⅝ × 29¼ × 30¾ inches; signed with shop brand "designed.made/ MALOOF/ California"; Arthur Raymond Family.

Fig. 63 Upholstered, double-back, low-arm side chair, 1958. Walnut and wool fabric (reupholstered); 38 × 21¾ × 25⅛ inches; signed with shop brand "designed.made/ MALOOF/California"; Arthur Raymond Family. The arm, set too low for an arm rest, served instead as a handle with which to pull the chair forward. The tightly fitted upholstered panels could be popped out by hand for cleaning.

Fig. 64 Cork-topped coffee table, 1958. Walnut, plywood, and cork; 17 ½ × 33 ½ × 54 inches; unsigned; Arthur Raymond Family. In the period 1952–65, Maloof used waxed Danish cork inserts on a variety of table and desk tops.

Fig. 65 Exterior view of Maloof home and workshop, about 1960. In 1956, Maloof began construction of an attached workshop and home that was to be famous among artists, craftsmen, and design professionals for its personal style.

Fig. 66 View of Maloof guest house/ showroom, about 1960. After Maloof severed connections with the design studio, Kneedler-Fauchere, the well-proportioned structure served as his showroom, as well as guest house.

with a fireplace, an adjacent small kitchen, and just beyond, separate bedrooms for the children and their grandmother. For Maloof, it was an easy step from the workshop to the house, and for the next four decades, as the residence itself expanded incrementally, room by room, he moved effortlessly between his two virtually seamless worlds—shop and home (fig. 65).

Inside and out, details were simple and rustic. Instead of the sleek Case Study Houses in glass and steel he admired, the small residence was more like the idiosyncratic, highly personalized homes of fellow woodworkers Nakashima and Esherick, both of which Maloof had seen illustrated in magazines. A one-story structure, it had a flat roof with a beamed wood ceiling and was sheathed, inside and out, with redwood planks. Throughout, it was filled with Maloof's furniture—and a growing collection of Southwest Indian and contemporary crafts—and featured fanciful, hand-carved door latches. Outside, Sam and his brother Jack constructed low, coarse walls of fieldstone and concrete, defining the parking area and entryway to the shop. A corner of the roof of the master bedroom was supported by a column fashioned out of a twisting tree trunk.

The old cottage was dismantled in 1958 and in its place, under the spreading avocado tree, a thirty-six-by-thirty-six-foot redwood-sided guest house-cum-furniture showroom was constructed. It had a flat roof supported by wood posts that covered a six-foot-wide deck that ran around the building (fig. 66). In the masonry basement of the old cottage, for Freda's use he set up a photography darkroom. In the vicinity of the new buildings the Maloofs planted orange, olive, walnut, avocado, Japanese maple, and eucalyptus trees which, over the years, grew into a veritable arboretum. Behind the little house, Freda tended a garden that kept the family supplied with fresh vegetables and with Sammy and Marilou's help looked after chickens that ranged freely about the property. Sam kept the lines of trees irrigated and pruned. It was a productive grove; up to 2,500 field boxes of lemons and oranges were picked annually by a local packer. (Sometimes the price of harvesting the fruit nearly equaled its commercial value.) In the post-World War II era, such a self-sufficient, rural retreat was a craftsman's ideal.

California Design

When *California Design 4* opened in Pasadena on January 12, 1958, Maloof had four pieces, all built in the new workshop, on display. The text of the exhibition catalogue underscored the recent change in the relationship between hand craftsmen and the technological society in which they lived. Since industry easily supplied the vast majority of household items, it stated, the designer-craftsman was now needed only to satisfy certain demands that upscale consumers requested and mass production could not meet—specifically, qualities of "warmth" and "personal involvement." Moreover, many of the craft works on display had a new "integrity" and "timeless simplicity," characteristics that marked them as "outstanding in today's market."[64]

In a lead article prompted by the opening of the annual exhibit, "Some of the Faces behind 'California Design,'" the Sunday *Los Angeles Times* Home section took the opportunity to assess the state of the Southland's distinctive design culture. Noting the extraordinary level of local activity in art and design, critic Arthur Millier wrote:

> *The Greater Los Angeles area . . . is now the scene of a regional surge of the arts of design. This movement shares in and is inspired by the phenomenal growth in population. . . . Like the new Southern California which has literally burst upon us in the past three decades, our art movement is young in spirit. From being a provincial affair . . . it has become a movement of significance throughout the civilized world. . . . California Design has become a term touched with magic and spoken with respect . . . an artistic creation from Southern California, thanks to the adventuring spirit of this region, will generally be contemporary in style and young in spirit . . . not overburdened by the weight of the past . . . [our artists] create out of an incredibly flowering present. They live and work at the center of a new way of living. . . . Southern California's artists are not crowded into garrets or loft buildings. Their studios are surrounded by flowers and trees. They have homes and families. The outdoors is opened to them. They do not think or act in packs or cults. They are strikingly individual in their attitudes towards life and in their ways of working. These things, the climate and the expanding character of the region have all contributed to the contemporary growth of the arts in Southern California. . . . Los Angeles may yet become the art center of the nation.*[65]

In the same issue, under the heading "Southland Arts Invade the Home," a group of nine prominent furniture designers—"who have patiently worked to better the furniture industry here and provide constantly improved furnishings for American homes"—posed as a group, each next to one of his distinctive creations (fig. 67). Sam Maloof was the only designer-craftsman. The others, including Kipp Stewart, business partners Hendrick Van Keppel and Taylor Green, and Ernest Inouye, were well-known local designers for industry. The East Coast woodworkers he met at Asilomar would not necessarily have recognized Maloof's Los Angeles colleagues as his natural peers, but in Southland circles Maloof was still perceived as an outstanding designer of contemporary-style

Fig. 67 Leading Los Angeles area furniture designers, 1958. This group photograph was taken for a *Los Angeles Times* feature on Southland designers. Left to right: Kipp Stewart, Rex Goode, Maloof, Stewart MacDougall, Hendrick Van Keppel, Taylor Green, John Keal, Barney Flagg, and Ernest Inouye. Courtesy *Los Angeles Times*.

Fig. 68 Prototype upholstered hornback chair, about 1960.

Fig. 69 Credenza, about 1958. This large case piece shows Maloof's use of light-toned sapwood to add a decorative note to the otherwise unadorned surfaces of his cabinetry.

Fig. 70 Spindle-back settee, pedestal table, and chair, about 1958.

furniture rather than a creative woodworker. But the craftsman movement was then asserting itself locally, too, and drawing Maloof firmly into its orbit.

Concurrent with the *California Design 4* show at the Pasadena Art Museum was the first exhibition of the work of the Southern California Designer-Craftsmen, a hundred-member group formed in March 1957. Maloof was a charter member and later president. Held at the Los Angeles County Museum of Art (LACMA), it was a different type of display, focusing solely on one-of-a-kind, or limited-production craft objects.[66] It was planned to acquaint area consumers with the work of local craft artists, only a handful of whom were represented in the annual *California Design* shows. During the exhibition, several of the exhibitors gave workshop demonstrations, Maloof among them.[67]

Then as now, craft demonstrations were popular attractions. From 1955 to 1961, Maloof was a regular participant in the annual, three-day Padua Hills Arts Fiestas in Claremont, showing finished pieces, but also demonstrating joinery, hand shaping, and finishing to crowds of fascinated onlookers.[68] At the time, Claremont, with its prominent college art programs and colony of local craft artists, was one of the most significant craft centers in the United States. Indeed, so popular did these demonstrations become (they began up at the Padua Hills theater, but were subsequently relocated to Seal Court at Scripps College) that visitors spent little time viewing the paintings and sculptures on display. Eventually, Millard Sheets and the other fine artists simply eliminated the competition by banishing craftsmen from the Arts Fiestas. But, in the decades ahead, Maloof would be invited to demonstrate his woodworking skills in well-attended workshops across the country and Canada. Sharing his knowledge and experience with others was a vital part of his craftsman's philosophy.

In March 1958, *California Design 4* traveled north to promote Los Angeles County household wares in the San Francisco Bay area. The *Oakland Tribune* reviewed the display at the Oakland Museum, noting: "Although Scandinavia and the Orient have seemed to dominate the home furnishing design field for the past several years, much good design has been produced here in California." Of special interest to the writer was the work of Sam Maloof, whose pieces, he stated, "gain beauty through simple, graceful lines, hand rubbed finishes, pronounced wood grain, and use of exposed structural joints as important decorative elements." The museum's director had invited Maloof to display several additional works in a separate, solo exhibit in the newly inaugurated gallery shop. Entitled *Furniture by Sam Maloof,* the small exhibit was his first one-man show.[69] Taking these extra pieces into account, the newspaper critic noted the distinctive characteristics of his work: "the use of walnut in its natural state, waxed, and hand-rubbed finishes, simplicity of form, and curving, sculptural lines."[70]

Nineteen-fifty-eight was a highly productive year. Still working alone in his new shop, Maloof made 112 pieces for $20,637, and the local Upland-Ontario *Daily Report* (always a strong supporter) printed a short article on his industriousness, "Artist-Craftsman Stays Busy." While there was a downturn in demand for goods generally, the reporter noted, Maloof was "one manufacturer not plagued with dwindling orders." In fact, "the commercial artist-turned-carpenter is currently working to reduce a $6,000 backlog from numerous clients for his specially designed modern furniture."[71] After citing several of his recent clients—SAS, Gimbel's and Goldwater's, and Henry Kaiser's new Hawaiian Village development (designed and furnished by Welton Becket)—the writer cited Maloof's long working hours. But the hard work had paid off. He had made "a breakthrough in sales to a point where he could break even" and "established a luxury trade with a nationwide clientele." No other West Coast woodworker could make that claim.

New Designs

After moving to Alta Loma, Maloof acquired a camera that produced stereoscopic slides and began to photograph his latest designs outdoors to show to potential clients. Honed in the Army, his skills with a camera were considerable, and the images provide an excellent resource with which to study his work of the period 1954 to 1961.[72] Stored in a special leather attache case with a battery-operated viewer, the images proved especially useful in attracting private clients. After receiving initial telephone inquiries, Maloof would set up a series of afternoon and evening appointments, drive to addresses in the Los Angeles area and show the slides to homeowners or their decorators. The meetings generated numerous orders. The vivid, three-dimensional quality of the photographs was certainly a major selling point, but the artistic nature of the photographs themselves—the camera angles, compositional arrangements, and creative use of cast shadows and accessories such as fallen leaves, pottery, and woven rugs—proved delightful aesthetic experiences in themselves (figs. 68–70).

The stereos are also historically significant, for they record early designs that, during the 1960s, slowly vanished from Maloof's repertoire and remain generally unknown today. Among them are clean-edged, walnut desks with cork tops and slim, tapered legs, often featuring one or two drawers on one side, as well as low coffee tables with mosaic tile surfaces (always in monotones), boxy hi-fi cabinets with fitted radios, turntables, and speakers, and tall, table-like dining room buffets. But among the more than 200 stereo views, seating

Fig. 71 Double-back occasional chair with sculptured arms, about 1958. Only a handful of examples of this sculptural model were made.

Fig. 72 Low-back dining chair with spindles, about 1960. This popular model could be ordered either with or without arms.

Fig. 73 Wing-back side chair, about 1965. Walnut and leather; 30¾ x 27⅞ x 20⅛ inches; signed with shop brand "designed. made/MALOOF/California"; Sam and Alfreda Maloof Foundation. This design evolved from the spindle-back dining chair.

forms are the most common subjects—laced benches, dining chairs, side chairs, occasional chairs, office chairs, low-back counter stools, two- and three-seat, spindle-back settees, and upholstered sofas.

The slides record new designs as well as evolutions in existing models. For example, a new comfortable arm chair with a tall, two-tiered, angled back (called a double-back occasional chair in the workshop papers), which was introduced about 1958, appears in stereo form (fig. 71). So, too, does the evolution in dining arm chairs in 1955 when short spindles were added to the sculptured back rest, creating a more visually interesting composition (fig. 72). From this particular model, in 1957 a new sculptural form evolved—the so-called "wing-back" dining chair (fig. 73). As Maloof would frequently put it, "one chair begat another."

In the wing-back model, the large sculpted back rest (the upper edge flat, but the underside curved dramatically downwards), was not tilted, but attached vertically to the back posts and spindles. If four spindles were used, the back legs mounted straight upward, but if five were featured, the back posts splayed out as they rose. Angling the legs led to two arresting design evolutions, also seen in the stereos: upholstered, occasional arm chairs whose tall backs flared outward (introduced 1957; fig. 74), or those that tapered dramatically inward toward the top (1959–60; fig. 75). In the latter instance, a relatively thick, sculptured top rail drooped downward, visually balancing the strong, upward rise of the back. It is an expressive design, almost throne-like in form and very comfortable, but within three years, it vanished from Maloof's repertoire.

One of the most striking new features introduced in the mid-1950s—one that would evolve dramatically in years to come and help to define Maloof's mature style—is the flat, "sculptured" arm. It makes its first firm appearance about 1955 in a deep-seated, spindle-back occasional chair (fig. 76). Set rather high, in plan it looks like a graceful gull's wing; in elevation, it describes a gentle, sweeping curve on a slightly rotating axis. To create these flowing forms, Maloof first roughly cut them out of solid walnut blanks on his band

saw, following a pencilled outline made from a template. Then, using the power saw like a hand tool (and relying on a remarkable ability to keep the final, three-dimensional form clearly in his mind's eye), he slowly refined the shape by carefully pushing the block repeatedly through the vertical saw blade, gently twisting the wood as it was being cut to create its curvilinear form. (Although he didn't recommend it to others, he used this unorthodox band saw technique throughout his career, arguing that since he had no formal training in woodworking, he couldn't be blamed for breaking rules.) Once it had been cut out free hand, he shaped the arm more finely with chisels, rasps, and shavers, before attaching it to the chair frame and sanding it smooth (fig. 77).[73]

From their first appearance, the tactile qualities of Maloof's sculptured arm rests proved irresistible to customers. Their attractions were immediate and tangible. At the rounded ends, a clean ridge of wood automatically attracts sitters' hands and they begin to caress the nearby silken surfaces, stroking the smoothly shaped, sculptural transition between arm and leg. (For those familiar with Maloof's sculptured arms, the experience is emphatically sensual.) The early arms' plasticity, however, was relative—especially to Wharton Esherick, a dedicated carver and sculptor of wood. In the early summer of 1958, Maloof sent the Pennsylvania woodworker a set of his stereo slides for review. The older craftsman later returned them with a note: "I wish some of your things would have a little *more* sculptural quality."[74] In the years to come, Maloof would take Esherick's suggestion to heart.

Iran and Lebanon

In 1959 Maloof made only fifty-six pieces of furniture—exactly half the previous year's production. He had not been ill, or otherwise disabled, nor had there been a fall in demand for his work. Rather, for a six month period, he was out of the country, designing and making furniture in the Middle East. It was an unusual and adventurous sojourn. The previous year he had been contacted by industrial designer Dave Chapman, of the Chicago firm, Chapman, Goldsmith, and Yamasaki, Inc., and asked to participate as a technical and design assistant in the "Village Industries" program of the International Cooperation Administration (ICA).

Inaugurated in 1955, the ICA was an agency of the Department of State, and during the early Cold War era was intended to help craftsmen in underdeveloped—and politically nonaligned—countries increase their production of saleable designs, either indigenous or modern, and thereby gain needed income for themselves and their nations. While it was part of the global competition between the United States and the Soviet Union for hearts and minds of Third World peoples, it was nonetheless an appealing, philanthropic program for idealists. Believing that crafts were a "bridge to peace"[75] among cultures, uniting men "in the recognition of their common humanity,"[76] many leading American craft artists and designers willingly participated. Indeed, as Maloof himself later stated: "The craft language is truly universal. No matter where we may travel, craftsmen can converse through their mutual interest and shared

Fig. 74 Upholstered, double-, flared-back occasional chair with sculptured arms, about 1958. Walnut and wool fabric; 39½ x 27¼ x 27 inches; signed with shop brand "designed. made/ MALOOF/ California"; Sam and Alfreda Maloof Foundation. Not long after he made it, Maloof traded it for a radio, decades later repurchasing it for his collection.

Fig. 75 Tapered-back chair, about 1960. This tapered-back model could be ordered as an easy chair with sculptured arm rests, or as an office chair with low arms and a swivel base.

Fig. 76 Spindle-back occasional chair with sculptured arms, about 1958. In Maloof's words, such easy chairs, the seats set low to the ground, were designed "to sit well."

Fig. 77 Maoof shaping an armrest in his new workshop, May 1957.

experiences in crafts. This understanding transcends all barriers . . . the crafts make the world a universal family."[77]

At the outset of the program, five firms headed by leading industrial designers, among them Russel Wright, Walter Dorwin Teague, and Dave Chapman, had been assigned non-industrialized countries and contracted by the ICA to undertake surveys and determine local craftsmen's specific needs. All reported that the marketing of local crafts should be greatly improved if artisans were dissuaded from making poor copies of Western industrial goods. Maloof was already familiar with the overseas program. In 1958 his friend Richard Petterson had traveled to Taiwan with weaver Jack Lenor Larsen (whose textile designs Maloof then often used as upholstery fabrics), and ICA's technical assistance teams had been prominently featured in *Craft Horizons*.[78]

The Chapman firm had been assigned Iran and Lebanon, and its survey indicated a need for direct aid in the design and production of textiles and furniture. It had been a longtime dream of Sam's to visit his parents' birthplace, and since he was allowed to take his family with him, he jumped at the chance to visit his relatives in far-off Douma, his backlog of orders notwithstanding. But not long before the family was to leave, Maloof was suddenly informed that Freda, Sammy, and Marilou could not accompany him to Iran for the two-month stay. Given the current political turmoil, the Tehran post was deemed by the United States government to be too risky for dependents of American diplomats and contractors. However, they were welcome to meet up with him later in Beirut. Maloof almost canceled, but it was too late, and on February 9, the local *Daily Report* duly noted that "artist-craftsman Sam Maloof will follow the U.S. Marines into Lebanon with nothing more than a few hand tools as part of a U.S. foreign assistance program."[79]

He flew alone from Los Angeles to Chicago and then on to Washington, where he was briefed by ICA staff. The next day he landed in New York, where he visited Henry Dreyfuss's design office in Manhattan before going to the Museum of Contemporary Crafts. Here, he met Mrs. Webb, new director Paul J. Smith, and woodworkers Joyce and Edgar Anderson. A ninety-piece retrospective exhibition of Wharton Esherick's furniture and wood sculpture was on view and for the first time, he had an opportunity to examine the celebrated wood craftsman's work closely—including the sculpted, spiral staircase dismounted from his Paoli studio-home. In his travel diary, he noted: "Saw Wharton Esherick show—good. More sculpture than furniture. Staircase exciting." But there was a plaintive note at the end of the entry: "called Freda. Getting butterflies more than ever. Wish I could back out."[80] It was the first time he had been separated from Freda since their marriage, and, as he flew to London, the prospect of two months alone in a foreign land made him miserable.

He arrived in Beirut on February 15, the next day noting unhappily in his diary: "If there had been a plane home, I'd have left. Miss my family very much."[81] Embassy personnel introduced him to Abdul-Rahim Akram, owner of a new modern furniture factory where he would work after his Iranian sojourn. After visiting the up-to-date plant, he met up with his cousin Rogi and the two traveled north to Douma together (fig. 78). It was winter. The temperature was

below freezing, and as they drove through the mountains, it snowed, turning the pine forests into what he called a "fairyland." Maloof was wholly unprepared for the cold. He had expected a warm desert climate, like inland California, and had packed no winter clothing. Nonetheless, in his ancestral village, he was warmed by the enthusiastic welcome of relatives and family friends, all of whom wanted to hear how Nasif and Anisse were faring in far-off Chino. That night, in his diary, he confided: "like a dream—can't believe I'm here—the only thing that would make it perfect is my wife and children."

Flying on to Tehran, he joined his fellow team member, Roy Ginstrom, a Chicago weaver and a fellow conferee at Asilomar. Ginstrom had been in Iran already for a year working with local textile workshops and lived comfortably in a rented apartment. Maloof had expected to move in with him, but there was no extra room. Instead, he was booked into an anonymous, modern hotel. Alone in his room, he wrote home every day. But the time melted quickly away. Assigned an office with a drafting table in the United States Embassy, as well as a car and driver, he rapidly surveyed the local situation. To his chagrin, there was little useful wood in Iran—something Chapman planners had overlooked—but plywood was manufactured locally and square metal tubing was imported from West Germany. Responding pragmatically and creatively to the challenge imposed by these restrictions (metal-based furniture had been a Los Angeles specialty), he designed some fifty-two functional pieces—tables, chairs, and cabinets for a restaurant, and complete living room, dining room, and bedroom sets.[82]

Although the latter furnishings were intended to be manufactured locally for use by United States Overseas Mission personnel stationed in Iran,[83] the plans were available free from the Embassy to any Iranian factory that wished

Fig. 78 Village of Douma, Lebanon. Maloof's parents' native village in mountainous northern Lebanon.

to reproduce them. As established by Dave Chapman's firm, the problem was straightforward: design simple, modular furnishings that were attractive, durable, and easy to construct and maintain. So, functioning as the industrial designer he had once hoped to be, Maloof designed serviceable, contemporary-style goods for bureaucrats and their families.

Since he would be using square tubing, Maloof searched for a local metal shop that could fabricate chair and table legs, and bases and frames for dressers and cabinets. Sides and doors for the case pieces, and seating surfaces, were to be constructed from plywood, and back rests and chair seats were to be upholstered locally using a foam rubber base and colorful textiles produced under Ginstrom's supervision. On the outskirts of the ancient city, he found a suitable workshop. It had a tin roof supported by stone end walls, but since there were no sides to the structure, it was open to the winter weather. The laborers were a group of cheerful, but undernourished and shoeless teenagers whose feet were wrapped in torn sacking material. Language was no barrier. Sam had a Farsi interpreter, the boss spoke some English, and the workers communicated eloquently with their hands. The boys' poverty was heart-rending, and on his way to work he often stopped at the United States Army's post exchange in Tehran and bought them chocolate bars and candy.

According to United States Embassy regulations, at lunch time Maloof had to be picked up and driven back into the city to eat at his hotel and then, following local custom, take a two-hour siesta. It seemed such a waste of time, but he had no choice in the matter. Back at the shop in the afternoon, Maloof and the young workers fabricated the prototypes by placing lengths of tubing on full-sized drawings (side, front, and back elevations, as well as plan views) laid out on the floor, and then cutting or bending the tubing at the appropriate spot. It was a primitive, but effective way of doing things. No complex joinery was required: the components were subsequently welded together with an arc welder. (None of the youngsters shielded their eyes with welders' goggles, and Maloof was amazed no one was blinded.) Models of simple, contemporary design, the finished metal prototypes—they were painted matte black, white, gray, and coral—looked somewhat like Maloof's own work, although more sticklike and geometric in outline (fig. 79). Among the pieces he designed in Tehran was a tall rocking chair whose back posts extended upwards, like horns. In the 1980s and 1990s it would evolve into Maloof's most popular chair, viewed by collectors as a virtual signature piece.

William Goldsmith, a partner in the Chapman firm, later evaluated Maloof's work in Iran. (In his opinion, it proved to be one of the best programs developed by the ICA.)

Sam's experience [in Tehran] was characterized by infinite patience and resourcefulness to meet the contingencies which were always arising; a willingness to work night and day; a humility and understanding and empathy for the people he was working with. . . . Teaching the relatively unskilled craftsmen ways in which to cut, braze polish, weld, and finish must certainly have been a test of teaching skills as well as craftsmanship. The [furniture] line itself was

Fig. 79 Chair designed by Maloof in Teheran, 1959. Wood was in short supply, so he substituted square metal tubing.

something I've never seen duplicated. It did look like Sam Maloof's work, even though it was in metal. It was a very spare and economical design . . . without any unnecessary do-dads.[84]

In Beirut, he was happily reunited with Freda and the children, who arrived on April 25, 1959, accompanied by his sister, Eva Solomon. They all moved into a luxury apartment Maloof had located in an elegant neighborhood near the seaside. The landlord first charged a weekly rent equal to Maloof's full ICA lodging expenses (an exorbitant amount by local standards), but he later lowered it under pressure from Maloof's new Lebanese friends. During the second week in May, the Californians all traveled up to Douma. To the surprise of the local matrons, during the three-day visit Freda hitched up her skirts and rode a donkey Western-style through the terraced apple and olive groves. Since she was the first American woman to stay in the isolated village, they accepted the unusual behavior without complaint. A visiting English-speaking cousin from Beirut was asked by Maloof's relatives what profession Sam followed in America. He was unable to convey exactly what "furniture designer-craftsman" meant, so he told them simply that he was a carpenter. Their reaction (in Arabic) was one of sincere regret: "Ah, how sad that our uncle's son has not been successful in the United States and must work with his hands."[85]

In Beirut, Maloof worked at Akram's three-story furniture factory, the most modern in Lebanon. The owner imported walnut and other hardwoods from Europe, along with the latest machinery, and the plant operated its own wood-drying kilns, and plywood-making, upholstery, and finishing departments—a far cry from the primitive Tehran workshop. Here, Maloof encountered a very different consumer-manufacturer relationship. Instead of buying ready-made pieces, Lebanese homeowners typically brought color photographs of furniture scissored from glossy Western-European magazines (usually Italian) to the factory and asked to have the pieces copied. While the workmanship was usually excellent, the designs—based on two-dimensional images—left much to be desired: pieces were typically ill-proportioned, and chairs, their seats too wide, narrow, or high, were generally uncomfortable.

Like most Middle Easterners, the Lebanese loved ornate patterns, especially the compound curves and fancy veneering of neo-rococo furniture. Nonetheless, at the factory, Maloof drew up thirty-five full-scale plans from which simple, stick-like prototypes in walnut were produced under his direction. In outline, they were much like his own designs but lacked their subtle sculptural characteristics. After he left, they were put into production, proving popular with Beirut homeowners until the mid-1970s, when the factory was destroyed during the civil war.

During their two-and-a-half month stay in Lebanon, Maloof, Freda, Eva, and the children took numerous weekend side trips. They visited Amman, Jaffa, and the Roman ruins in the Bekka Valley. Maloof's ability to understand— if no longer fluently speak—Arabic proved extremely helpful. Finally, with Sam's work completed, the Californians departed Beirut on July 12, first journeying by bus to the Arab section of Jerusalem before flying on to Cairo, where they visited the pyramids and the Egyptian Museum. Maloof was thrilled to examine at first hand the graceful furniture of the ancient Pharaohs, including King Tut's bench. Elizabeth Gordon had been right. It was indeed similar to his own model. But as he later noted, "there isn't anything new under the sun, really. The Egyptians were using finger joints, dovetail joints, they were using box joints. Because of the scarcity of wood . . . they had to be very careful in their design [and not] . . . use an overabundance of wood. This is what I did when I first started out."[86] From Cairo, they flew to Athens for two days' sightseeing and then traveled on to Rome. Next stop on the tour was Geneva, followed by a flight to Frankfurt to board an airplane for Copenhagen.

In the Danish capital, Maloof and Freda visited the famous government-supported crafts cooperative, Den Permanente, to see the displays of contemporary furniture, glass, textiles, and ceramics—products then all the rage in middle-class American homes.[87] On the first day of the Asilomar conference, Den Permanente's director, Asger Fischer, had joined the wood panel's informal discussion and on day three, he had been a keynote speaker. Everyone had attended his talk. The Danish retail store—not unlike America House, Mrs. Webb's outlet for contemporary crafts in Manhattan—had been much praised by the Asilomar conferees as an ideal model, and after Asger's presentation, Maloof had picked up a copy of the store's 1956 catalogue which illustrated several of Hans Wegner's famous chairs.

From Copenhagen, the family traveled on to Malmo, Sweden, where Freda's mother's relations lived. After a week of Nordic hospitality, on August 4, they flew to London, visiting museums and tourist sights before boarding a trans-atlantic flight to New York. After a day in Washington, and two more in Chicago for a debriefing by Dave Chapman, the Maloofs finally returned to Alta Loma—and a backlog of orders—in mid-August.

But while Maloof had been out of sight in California, he had not been out of mind. Four of his furniture pieces, including a double-back chair and new tall, spindle-back settee (fig. 80) had been featured in *California Design 5*. Moreover, two chairs—one a wing-back model, the other an occasional chair—had illustrated an article that he himself had written for the *Los Angeles Times* just before he left for the Middle East. Published in the Home magazine in mid-July, it was entitled "'This is My Best.' Functional Beauty Shaped by Hand."

Sounding a by-now common ACC theme, and firmly restating his own viewpoint, Maloof declared:

There is still a place for the individual designer-craftsman. Today's designers of machine-made furniture have gained prominence because they have bettered the product offered to the mass market. But they are still designing for the machine and to fit the trends of the bulk of consumers. I believe the best results are achieved when the designer is also the craftsman. The two should never be separated, because they share equal responsibility. It is difficult for the designer to transmit his ideas to someone else. Thus in the mass market method, the machine craftsman must take part in the designing and, as a result, the designer often wonders if the finished product is actually what he intended. The designer-craftsman . . . isn't designing for a machine, but for an individual who seeks the finest quality of workmanship. People are becoming tired of the sameness of machine-tooled products. So the designer-craftsman is not obsolete; he steps in and fills a void that industry cannot satisfy. For me, it is not enough to be a designer only. I want to be able to work a piece of wood into an object that contributes something beautiful and useful to our everyday living. To be able to live and work with materials without destroying their natural beauty and warmth, to be able to work as we want—that is a god-given privilege.[88]

Additional Maloof designs were also used to illustrate a new book on modern art, *Art: An Approach* (1959), authored by Robert C. Niece, a design professor at El Camino College and the consulting curator for *California Design 6* in 1960. Along with functional pieces by fellow Southland woodworker Paul Tuttle and designer Charles Eames, Maloof's pieces (including a dining room set photographed in a glass-walled contemporary home) were selected to demonstrate four defining principles of "good design": *simplicity* (clean, uncluttered form), *appropriate form* (suitable for its function, not an exaggeration of it), *function* (considered in terms of both workability, and beauty), and *economy* (limited amount of materials and labor needed). Describing himself as untrained in either furniture design or woodworking, Maloof asserted his essential philosophy in the accompanying text: "When a designer is also the woodworker, he can feel out the piece as he goes along, making whatever changes from the drawing he desires. The object is to get a more perfect piece of furniture—not a perfect drawing."[89]

While Maloof was in Iran, New Yorkers also had an opportunity to see his work in the vast art exposition organized by Manhattan dealer Lee Nordness, *Art: USA: 1959*. Staged at the New York Coliseum in April, it was intended to expose the widest possible audience to current work in all media. In his own words, Nordness planned to "introduce Mr. Citizen to Mr. Fine Artist in the hope of making them everlasting friends."[90] With multiple works by more than five hundred painters, sculptors, printmakers, photographers, graphic designers, and craftsmen, the show was displayed in ten discrete sections. One of only three furniture makers among thirty-three craftspeople selected, Maloof was invited to contribute four pieces (including his spindle-back settee) to the Fine Art in Living section organized by Just Lunning, general manager of Georg Jensen, Inc.

In his introductory text in the catalogue, Lunning provocatively asked: "How does the hand craftsman fit into this machine-conscious, rapidly shrinking, space-conquering world? What is the value of one man's creative power compared to the might of industry with its ability to produce astronomical quantities and its precision approaching perfection?" The craftsman had an essential role in a mass culture dependent on machine production, he argued, for he answered Americans' growing hunger for the "humanistic." Given their recent exponential growth, Lunning concluded the handcrafts of the United States clearly were in the "early stages of a renaissance."

Crafts' New Identity

In a lead article published in a special issue of *Craft Horizons,* "U.S. Crafts in This Industrial Society," published at the time of the Coliseum show, editor Rose Slivka addressed a popular misinterpretation in the press about the recent "renaissance" of crafts. It was not a "revival," a nostalgic return to hand craftsmanship. Instead, she declared, "What has happened is this: the crafts have realized their own distinct, necessary and rightful place in [an industrialized society]—not in conflict with it, not absorbed into it—but existing within the larger structure, true to their own identity and to their continuity. The crafts and craftsmen . . . today . . . are filling a *new* need, meeting a *new* condition, and a *new* demand."

Slivka was a close friend of Jackson Pollock, Willem de Kooning, Franz Kline, and other abstract expressionist painters in New York, as well as art critic Harold Rosenberg, and her analysis of the state of crafts revealed her personal commitment to the artistic avant garde. As she later wrote, "the avant garde spirit of the time, expressed through painting and sculpture, enriched my vision of craft, its function and aesthetic range. It enlarged my ideas about the energy of materials and forms, the need of each artist to find his or her own way of working with materials, of trusting the events of process, and of recognizing the complex and expanding role of craft as art."[91] Perhaps more than anyone else, Rose Slivka led the movement to transform craftworks from utility-based objects of the 1950s to self-sufficient works of art in the 1960s and beyond.

In her ground-breaking article she firmly asserted that the craftsperson must be taken seriously, not as a maker of superior functional objects, but as a self-expressive artist. Although he was a "rugged individualist," existentially, the studio craftsperson was "alone," caught in a demoralizing "never-never land" between art and industrial design. Neither fine artists nor product designers

Fig. 80 Spindle-back settee, first exhibited in 1959. This two-seater, based on a side chair, employs tapered spindles whose widest dimensions fit into the small of the back.

Fig. 81 Drawing for cabinet with drawers, about 1960. This is one of twenty drawings Maloof prepared for a book that was never published. Reproduction by permission of Sam Maloof.

Fig. 82 Drawing for pedestal dining table, about 1960. Like exposed tree roots, the arched legs join a trunk-like pedestal support. Reproduction by permission of Sam Maloof.

accepted him as an equal. Moreover, government and industry refused either to support his independent existence, or to provide him a secure niche in the national economy. The ACC's purpose and challenge, Slivka declared, was to assist the craftsman by forcibly focusing the public's attention on "a persistent handcrafts culture sitting stubbornly, ineradicably in the midst of an industrial American society," and insist that this "enormous achievement" be an integral part of American life.[92]

Rose Slivka defined the typical American craftsman in ways that distinguished him from his European peers and more firmly allied him with contemporary fine artists. This new alliance represented a firm break with the consensus recently reached at Asilomar—that art and craft were different enterprises. The contemporary studio craftsman in the United States, she declared, was an intellectual, "the product of universities," who, instead of learning from peasant craftsmen, did his research in libraries, college workshops, and by traveling to countries with a strong, indigenous craft tradition. Indeed, the younger generation—many of them veterans benefitting from unprecedented access to higher education through the G.I. Bill—were "the best educated in the world, the most receptive to new ideas, the most eager to learn and absorb the riches of elder cultures, [and] the most intent in search of their craft continuity."[93] Moreover, they were imbued with the ideals of the workingman—his intimate knowledge and love for tools and materials—and his joy in working with his hands.

For Slivka, the ability of the designer-craftsman to control his product from conception to completion reaffirmed his "humanistic relationships," the moral connections—or lines of "responsibility"—that ran from the talented maker through the object invested with his creative impulse to the appreciative end user whose life was transformed for the better through its daily encounter and use. From her point of view, the craftsman in America was unique, because he was both artist and maker—not one or the other. As a result, the contemporary crafts (like abstract painting, generally adopting an experimental point of view and valuing ideas more than traditional qualities of craftsmanship) had become "a new American expression of creative power."[94] To all intents and purposes, her article was a clarion call for craftsmen to assert themselves as self-expressive artists, not functional object makers. From this point forward, both *Craft Horizons* and the Museum of Contemporary Crafts increasingly championed the nonfunctional.

"Contemporary Furniture As A Craft"

Although he did not conform to Slivka's vision of the university-trained craftsman-intellectual, Maloof was keen to share his "creative power" with a wide, literate audience. In September 1958, when he was approached by the executive editor of the Chilton Publishing Company of Philadelphia (on the recommendation of Conrad Brown) to write a book to be entitled "Contemporary Furniture as a Craft," he readily accepted the challenge. As originally conceived, the text was to be aimed at the "advanced amateur," someone who might be considering becoming a full-time designer-craftsman and would welcome Maloof's experience and advice. An essential component would be sequences of close-up photographs documenting his woodworking and furniture-making techniques. The contract stipulated a $400 advance (half paid on signing) and a delivery date of April 1, 1960. But once Maloof accepted the ICA's offer in the fall of 1958, the deadline was extended. After his return from the Middle East, "haunted" by the need to complete the text as well as reduce his back orders, he finally mailed the completed manuscript and photographs in late March 1961.[95]

Chilton was a publisher of craft books. After acquiring several titles from a competitor, in 1957 the company had published Daniel Rhodes's *Clay and Glazes for the Potter* and Oppi Untracht's *Enameling on Metal.* The firm was eager to expand its series for, as the editor of *Craft Horizons* noted, "in today's do-it-yourself culture, just about anything will sell that looks like a craft how-to book."[96] But to Maloof's chagrin and embarrassment, in October 1961, a new Chilton editor rejected the manuscript. The publisher now insisted on a do-it-yourself text for amateur woodworkers, replete with plans for simple projects. After agonizing over the situation, Maloof wrote to say that he simply could not rewrite the book with that end in mind. It was a difficult decision: he had already spent a thousand dollars on photography and, furthermore, the publisher now demanded he return his portion of the advance. (To do so, he had to borrow $200 from the bank.) He should not have been surprised by the rejection. *Craft Horizons* had noted: "Sign and symbol of the status of craft book publishing today . . . is the incredible fact that Chilton has no editor in charge of its program that knows anything at all about art, crafts, or good design."[97]

Maloof's unpublished book, dedicated to "my wife, Alfreda, whose faith in my work has been both a comfort and a challenge," was divided into eight chapters. Short texts, they were devoted to setting up and operating a shop, marketing, designing, wood turning (written by friend Bob Stocksdale), the material properties of different woods, finishing techniques, and the work of other individual furniture craftsmen. Maloof included numerous photographs of his newest pieces, as well as some twenty pen drawings of chairs, case goods, and tables (figs. 81 and 82). But the most interesting illustrations are the

workshop photos taken by Freda and Maloof's former Angelus-Pacific colleague, Harlan Chinn, detailing fabrication methods and stages in the production of various pieces (figs. 83–86). It is a magnificent archive; its informational value concerning Maloof's workshop practices is surpassed only by later commercial video tapes of Maloof at work.

Among the images destined for the book were several of Maloof's most recent designs that reveal a greater sculptural development: a pedestal support for a round table whose curved legs converge to join the trunk-like support post like tree roots; a square game table whose smooth plank edges were routed into a full half-round; and a tall side or dining chair with a strongly modeled, horn-like crest rail, introduced in late 1959 (figs. 87–89). (The progenitor of a long line of similar, evolving designs, after 1984 this model was called the "Texas" chair.) While increasing plasticity was a natural development for Maloof, the new sculptural quality of the "hornback" chair was prompted by the introduction of a new cutting tool that Maloof recommended in a section of his text on shop equipment—the Stanley Tool Company's flexible Surform rasp (figs. 90 and 91).[98] Designed to more rapidly and easily shape wood by hand, this device was marketed as a substitute for traditional cutting and shaping tools (such as files, solid rasps, and knifelike spoke shavers), and beginning in the early 1960s Maloof used it to increase the sculptural qualities of several of his new chair designs.

Another new design feature that appeared in 1960–61 was a radical innovation: a turned chair arm set unusually low, close to the side rail. Visually and structurally, it is linked to the adjacent lower cross rail of the back rest (fig. 92). In its placement and function, the Maloof low arm was unlike any other chair arm in the history of Western furniture. Pragmatically, it served a dual purpose. In Maloof's words:

the very low arm on some of my chairs acts as a handle, and, structurally, takes the place of a stretcher below the chair seat. The arm is used to lower yourself into and to raise yourself out of the chair. It also serves as a convenient means of moving the chair forward or backward from a seated position without having to grab the bottom of the chair seat. A stretcher below the seat would clutter the clean flow of my designs. . . . The low arm has the added advantage of being both comfortable and not interfering with the motion of your body, particularly your elbows. Furthermore, you can throw your knee over the low arm and slouch with abandon, and the chair will endure.[99]

Either straight or curved, for decades the radically low arm remained an essential component in his repertoire of chair designs.

In his chapter on designing, Maloof described his unique approach, one that relied on the acuity of his mind's eye. First, he wrote, "I conjure up a mental picture. Every piece of furniture that I have made was first preconceived in my mind before picking up a pencil or tool. This mental picture stays with me from the beginning of a piece to its conclusion. Most designers usually do a number of sketches. But I work better my way."[100] For standardized parts such

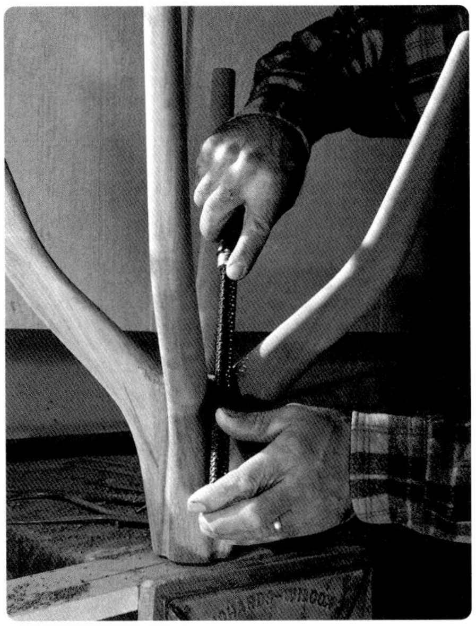

Fig. 83 Workshop photograph, about 1960. Half-circle cuts made in the side rails of a chair seat frame into which turned legs would be fixed.

Fig. 84 Workshop photograph, about 1960. The frames of chair seats were constructed using a tongue and groove joint.

Fig. 85 Workshop photograph, about 1960. Sam files the underside of a round arm that extends into a point.

Fig. 86 Workshop photograph, about 1960. Sam carefully sands a join on a low-arm chair.

Fig. 87 Workshop photograph, about 1960. The arched legs of pedestal supports for a round table.

Fig. 88 Square game table with wing-back chairs, about 1960. The solid edges of the table and drawers were given a half-round profile with an electric router—an example of the so-called "California round-over" style.

Fig. 89 Hornback chair with spindles and low, straight arms, about 1960. His "horn-back" chair was later called a "Texas" chair, due to the resemblance of its elongated crest rail to the horns of Texas longhorn cattle.

as chair backs or arms, he created plywood templates, or simple guidelines, whose silhouettes were pencilled onto solid blocks of walnut. He rejected the mechanical accuracy of jigs, and the templates—often numbered, or named after the person for whom he first made a design—were hung on the workshop walls within reach (figs. 93 and 94). Since he made everything to order, unlike other production cabinetmakers, Maloof did not stockpile ready-made parts.

As noted in the text, when all the components of a piece were cut out and shaped, they were assembled by dry doweling them together. The chair, desk, or table was then critically examined—in his term, "eyeballed"—from all angles. If it required "improvement," it could be taken apart and individual dimensions and proportions altered as necessary. Maloof's sense of "right-ness" in design was instinctive: "If the leg I have turned looks too heavy, I put it back into my lathe and turn it until it looks right to my eye. If an arm does not look right, a stroke or two with a spoke shaver remedies the fault."[101] The mental image of the imagined form was so clearly defined, it automatically guided his hand. Indeed, instead of calipers, Maloof simply used his thumb and forefinger to determine the correct size. As to the sources of his own designs, he stated firmly that he never copied or adapted someone else's work. Instead, each new chair or table was worked up from a design already in his repertoire. Since the Dreyfuss commission in 1952, it had been a matter of slow but steady evolution. The quotation selected as a chapter heading emphasized this cardinal point: "Is there anything whereof it may be said, see, this is new? It hath been already of old time, which was before us" (*Ecclesiastes* 1:10).

In 1960, while he was writing "Contemporary Furniture as a Craft"—and producing some seventy-three pieces—Maloof entered several of his new designs in museum shows. Two of his recent prototypes were displayed in

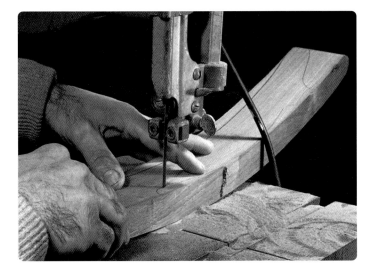

Fig. 90 Workshop photograph, about 1960. From walnut blanks, Maloof cut out the horn-like crest rails freehand on his bandsaw following outlines penciled from a standardized template.

Fig. 91 Workshop photograph, about 1960. The introduction of the Stanley Tool Company's flexible Surform rasp allowed Maloof to shape parts more rapidly and achieve greater sculptural effects.

Fig. 92 Upholstered double-back side chair with low arm, 1960. Maloof attached his low, handle-like arm to the back leg at a point level with the bottom rail of the chair back.

California Design 6—a spindled hornback chair with colorful red-orange leather upholstery (fig. 95) and a solid walnut office desk with tapered legs and five drawers. In *Crafts/Interiors,* the annual fall display of the Southern California Designer-Craftsmen in conjunction with local decorators at LACMA (he was a juror that year and also demonstrated woodworking at the show), he showed a game table and wing-back chairs as well as one of his new tall, tapering, double-back chairs (fig. 96).[102] A similar arm chair and a new pedestal table were likewise on view in New York in the MCC show, *Designer-Craftsmen USA 1960,* the first cross-country survey since 1953.

Subtitled "Designed and Handcrafted for Use," the show had been organized as an open competition. But from 1,992 submissions, the three-man jury selected only 114 objects.[103] To the jurors' dismay, much of the work was derivative and unimaginative. "Although much is said about the crafts as art," they wrote in their statement, "we saw disappointingly little work that had the sense of directed purpose and conviction which the arts express."[104] Moreover, few craftworkers had bothered to take into account the show's functional orientation and as a result, their pieces lacked requisite "discipline."

The MCC's new director, architect David Campbell, reported on the unfortunate situation in *Craft Horizons.* He began by noting that during recent years, the quality of craft work had increased steadily (along with the public's respect for its makers) and that both colleges and museums now regularly included crafts in their teaching and exhibition programs. So what was the problem with the limited numbers of works selected for *Designer-Craftsmen USA 1960?* The jurors? The open nature of the competition? Craftsmen's apathy? His conclusion: the increasing emphasis on exhibiting their work encouraged craftsmen to make a virtuoso artistic object, "the show piece."[105]

As a result, when a second or third exhibition called for submissions, the singular piece might already be on display, or otherwise reserved, leaving only lesser works available. While the problem was mostly restricted to one-of-a-kind object makers, "what to exhibit where?" was a question Maloof also regularly faced. If he was invited to participate early enough, he would make pieces specifically for the show. (Typically, they were purchased by patrons directly

Fig. 93 Workshop photograph, about 1960. Templates hang on the wall of Maloof's shop.

Fig. 94 Workshop photograph, about 1960. Plywood templates are used to outline the standardized shapes of chair legs.

Fig. 95 Prototype hornback chair with curved arms, about 1960. Walnut and leather; 37 x 21⅝ x 21¼ inches; marked with shop brand "designed.made/ MALOOF/California"; Sam and Alfreda Maloof Foundation.

Fig. 96 Maloof furniture in 1960 Southern California Designer-Craftsmen exhibition, Los Angeles County Museum of Art. Maloof was an early leader of this organization, formed to promote the sale of handmade crafts as furnishings and accessories in contemporary California homes.

Fig. 97 Spindle-back occasional chair with sculptured arms, 1955. Walnut and leather; 34 x 29 ¾ x 32 inches (refinished); unmarked; Sam and Alfreda Maloof Foundation. This was the only Maloof chair ever rejected by an exhibition jury.

from the exhibition.) Otherwise, he entered prototypes retained as showroom samples, or works originally destined for clients. As a result, the very same chair or desk design might be displayed more than once a year. But since uniqueness was never his objective, the repeat appearance was never a problem. The linkage of fine craftsmanship and functional beauty withstood all tests. Only once did a jury refuse one of his works, a spindle-back occasional chair whose sculptured arms were blunted at the ends (fig. 97). The rejection had stung, but Freda had put the galling experience into perspective: "Sam, it's good for the ego."

Chapter Four

EXPANSION

In mid-February 1961, the *Los Angeles Times* Home magazine focused on the work of California's "three most distinguished furniture designers." The feature article was of considerable interest to design-conscious Angelenos for, by this date, the city had become the nation's second largest furniture manufacturing center. "Distinct individuals," the men were bound together, the reporter wrote, "both by the remarkable qualities which stamp their creations and by the unyielding standards which they apply to their work." The subjects—each of whom had made a "definite impression in the field of furniture"—were Charles Eames, W. Wes Williams, and Sam Maloof (fig. 98). Eames was celebrated for his "brilliance in welding beauty and practicality," Williams (a beach and patio furniture designer) for his "wizardry with metal and canvas," and Maloof for "his excellence as both a designer and a master craftsman."[1]

The article, "Maloof: The Craftsman. Completeness without Ornamentation," featured a full-page color photograph of the woodworker sitting on one of his chairs in an Alta Loma vineyard (fig. 99). It is an evocative image: between rows of vines in late autumn foliage, six pieces of his furniture are arranged informally along a receding pathway. Eight-year-old daughter Marilou is seen in the distance, standing behind a wing-back chair. In the foreground, a smiling Maloof sports a colorful sweater acquired in Tehran, its pattern adapted by Roy Ginstrom from an ancient Persian design. One of the three photographs on the magazine cover included a view of a Maloof game table and two chairs in the same setting, the late afternoon sunshine throwing long shadows across fallen leaves. In California in the 1960s, photographing crafts outdoors was becoming a convention. By linking the handmade object with the spiritually uplifting natural world, the photograph disassociated it from the industrial culture.

The writer focused on the "organic concept" behind Maloof's unadorned work, equating his designs with nature's unalloyed grace:

When a designer-craftsman can give the back of a simple settee a gentle curve that is sheer controlled voluptuousness, or taper a chair arm into a flattened swell as organic as the human arm that will rest upon it, he has achieved the ultimate

Low-back settee with curved arms (detail), about 1967. Walnut and leather; Sam and Alfreda Maloof Foundation.

Fig. 98 *Los Angeles Times* article, "3 Southland Designers," 12 Feb. 1961 In the early 1960s Maloof was acclaimed one of Southern California's preeminent designers, on the level of Charles Eames. Courtesy *Los Angeles Times*.

in elegance, for the refined elegance of furniture is like the subtle elegance in nature. It is self-contained and it is complete: any ornamentation would be foreign, like silver sequins sprinkled on a rose. . . . One is not conscious of 'the technological age' when feeling and using his pieces . . . he has a way of joining structural members that is suggestive of a limb growing out of a tree trunk, or a human arm extending from its shoulder socket. Both limb and arm are coordinated parts of the whole, not independent elements. . . . The slight undulations in tree trunk ring patterns, the graceful twists and bends in branches—all are subtly repeated in Maloof's workshop.[2]

The following year, Maloof's work was again photographed outdoors for two feature articles. A *Los Angeles Times* photographer arranged a series of pieces by several different exhibitors in the Claremont Lively Arts Festival in the garden behind the woodworker's Alta Loma workshop, while the *Los Angeles Herald-Examiner*'s Pictorial Living magazine shot Maloof's tapered-back swivel chair upholstered in orange leather in *California Design 8* in a Pomona park.[3] In size and scope, the eighth exhibition of California-designed products was unprecedented. Instead of restricting participants to Los Angeles-area producers as had been the case previously, the 1962 show's new, permanent co-directors—Eudora Moore from Los Angeles and Elizabeth Hansen from San Francisco—opened the exhibition to designers, craft artists, and manufacturers from around the state. But selecting items of "domestic use and esthetic gratification"[4] for the vast display proved a herculean task. More than a thousand objects were shipped to depots in both Los Angeles and San Francisco for judging by two independent juries—one for crafts, the other for manufactured goods. In the end, some 750 works were chosen. Not only handcrafted objects (including architecturally scaled works) and mass-produced designs were featured, but such engineering marvels as a prototype helicopter for private use, an all-terrain, step-climbing vehicle, and two electric cars.

Arts & Architecture justified the widened scope on the well-rehearsed grounds of geographical determinism: "California is sympathetic to the ingenuity and daring essential to the formulation of new design concepts. Open landscape and warm climate encourage thinking on a large scale . . . [and a] youthful outlook frees Californians from restrictive traditions and stimulates the search for new forms to express contemporary life."[5] Novelties included objects and accessories for residential gardens, as well as those for ecclesiastical settings—altars, liturgical textiles, candelabra, even church doors. Since Moore and Hansen intended *California 8* to promote the sale of the Golden State's finest contemporary wares from coast to coast, the illustrated catalogue was circulated to department store buyers and consumer groups nationwide, as well as to professional associations such as the American Institute of Architects and the National Society of Interior Designers. Even foreign museums received copies. It was a high point in the show's history.

Not everyone was impressed with the number and diversity of products on display. A correspondent for *Craft Horizons* described *California Design 8* as more of a "marketplace" than an exhibition and therefore, he felt, "disorienting"

Fig. 99 Maloof posing in an Alta Loma vineyard with examples of his furniture, 1961. Courtesy *Los Angeles Times.*

to the museum-going public. In his opinion, there were only a "few good pieces"—a number of ceramic forms, wall hangings by Lillian Elliott, and Sam Maloof's furniture. But these select items, he declared, "had no chance against the mass of pedestrian work."[6] (Interestingly, the show was followed by the first extensive museum display of Pop Art, *The New Paintings of Common Objects*— an ironic celebration of "pedestrian" products.) Maloof showed six works in the 1962 *California Design* show: two different models of dining chairs; a cork-topped, pedestal dining table (one of the last with cork inserts to be publicly exhibited); a drop-leaf table with wood hinges; a square-backed occasional chair covered in tufted leather; and the colorful, high-back office swivel chair photographed in the park. They were among sixty-nine pieces he fabricated that year—down from eighty-six he made in 1961.

The decrease in production and annual revenue[7]—plus the burgeoning backlog of orders—prompted Maloof in 1962 to hire his first workshop assistant, Larry White. An eighteen-year-old art student at nearby Chaffey Junior College, White worked after classes, on Saturdays, and during summer vacation, eventually becoming a full-time employee in 1964 (fig. 100). For the first two years, he did little more than sand and oil works. (The extra pair of hands, however, proved immediately beneficial. In 1963, even though Maloof took three months off, production soared to ninety-five pieces.) Maloof proved a good teacher, patiently instructing him in his working methods and fostering a warm friendship with the young man. "It was an incredible relationship," White recalled in 1974, after he had left to start his own shop. "Sam is really a great guy—he really shared a lot with me—things that he didn't have to. When I first came . . . he was like a dad to me. He was concerned about what I was doing and he helped me a lot."[8] When other workshop assistants were hired in the late 1960s, White trained them in the manner in which he was taught.

In the fall of 1962, the theme of the Los Angeles County Fair's art exhibition was *Western American Crafts* and with seven works—including a leather-covered ottoman and a novel, pew-like bench—Maloof was a prominent exhibitor, recently winner of the Southern California Home Furnishings League's Gold Key award for his contribution to the field of modern furniture design. To celebrate the opening of the show, the *Los Angeles Times* ran a full page, color photograph of Maloof's pedestal dining table and four matching hornback chairs with turned spindles. Serving as a centerpiece on the table was a new design— a carved candelabra. Following the fashion of photographing crafts outdoors, the furniture had been temporarily set up on the sun-dappled lawn beside the Fine Arts Building (fig. 101).

Inside the exhibit hall, fairgoers could watch the woodworker demonstrating his shaping and joining skills in a popular, two-week workshop program, *Art in Action.* Among the twelve artist-participants were Sam's friends Paul Soldner, producing Raku pottery, and Bob Stocksdale, turning wood bowls. The program was repeated for several years. One season, a couple watched Maloof for over a half hour before the woman asked what kind of furniture he was making. "It's contemporary furniture," was the answer. "No, I mean what is it derived from, what kind is it?" she replied, somewhat annoyed. Maloof laughed

Fig. 100 Maloof and Larry White, his first
full-time shop assistant, in workshop,
about 1964.

and said, "it's Lebanese furniture." She then turned to her husband and declared,
"I told you it was."[9]

El Salvador

In early 1963, Dave Chapman's Chicago office asked Maloof to participate in
another ICA Village Industries program, this time in tropical El Salvador.
Fluent in Spanish, he was keen to visit Central America and agreed—but only
on condition that Freda and the children could join him for the three-month
sojourn. Not only did the design firm consent, but it even made Freda part of
the team of visiting American craftsmen. She was to assist local basket and doll
makers (fig. 102), while Roy Ginstrom (again the project director) worked with
weavers and ceramicist Robert Turner (likewise accompanied by his family)
with village potters. Artist Henry Glick had been hired to teach silkscreening
and, as he had in the Middle East, Maloof was to aid local furniture makers to
produce better designed, more saleable items.

The group assembled in San Salvador on July 6, and the Maloofs took up
residence in two rooms in the Pension Wagner, a small, downtown hostelry
built around an interior courtyard filled with tropical plants. Sammy and
Marilou and the Turners' two children became inseparable companions. For
their part, the two sets of parents entered into a lifelong friendship. While
Turner traveled to a village pottery outside the city, Maloof worked successively

Richard Gross photographs

More examples of fine furniture excellently designed and built by Sam Maloof which seems at home in park-like setting of Fine Arts Building at Pomona Fairgrounds. Note fine tapering of each element. Maloof also made the candelabra.

Fig. 101 Maloof furniture photographed outdoors at the Los Angeles County Fairgrounds, 1962. Courtesy *Los Angeles Times.*

with three different furniture shops, two in the capital, San Salvador, the other in a town some fifteen miles distant. One used only the simplest hand tools; another, with the addition of power tools, had been semi-modernized; while the third, Fabrica Capri, was equipped with up-to-date woodworking machinery. The most common material used by furniture makers in El Salvador was genisaro wood, a local species of mahogany. Poorly dried, it had such a high moisture content that finished pieces could not be exported to less humid climates lest they warp and crack.

In the most basic shop, the equipment was primitive, but the highly skilled and self-reliant workers employed simple, common-sense methods for clamping, gluing up, and joining. Maloof was impressed by their ingenuity, later writing: "So often the American craftsmen thinks that nothing can be accomplished without all the tools and inventions available on the market, or he may go to the opposite extreme and opt for antique hand tools. But while his attention is captured by tools and techniques, simple, direct ways of doing things are overlooked or forgotten. It is not a matter of nostalgia or romantic feeling for the past: the common-sense answer is the simplest one."[10]

Although restricted to hand tools, the craftsmen in this first shop turned out sophisticated work but in an outmoded, art deco style. For these non-industrialized craftsmen, Maloof designed and helped fabricate a complete set of modern office furniture in his own simple but elegant manner—an executive desk and swivel chair, credenza, and side chairs. As had been the case in Tehran, the pieces were fabricated outdoors on packed earth. When it rained (as it often did), the work-in-progress had to be quickly carried into the shelter of a nearby roofed shed (fig. 103). The finished suite was made of genisaro and unfortunately was later shipped to the Salvadoran consulate in New York. In the arid atmosphere of a Manhattan office building, the moist wood dried out rapidly and shattered.[11]

At the semi-modern shop outside the city, Maloof drew up plans for benches, low wood stools, and two different side chairs—one a version of his spindled, hornback model. Work on the various prototypes assigned to a craftsman and helper proceeded only during the weeks Maloof was on site. After he left, none of the designs went into production. At the next shop, the industrialized Fabrica Capri, Maloof planned a dining room set composed of a long table, six chairs, and a sideboard. Again, he was assigned an experienced woodworker and they completed the pieces, this time using native laurel wood instead of genisaro. An American woodworker visiting El Salvador later reported that the factory did indeed turn out work with a distinctive "Maloof" look. But the prototype dolls made by Freda were rejected. Familiar with Navajo Kachina figures, she produced examples that appeared too wild and expressive for official tastes. Unfortunately, toward the end of their stay in San Salvador, Freda became ill and Maloof sent her home two weeks early. Only when the others returned, did she go to a doctor—to discover she had contracted infectious hepatitis in San Salvador. She was immediately hospitalized and only slowly recovered her health.

From a personal perspective, Maloof's experiences as an ICA design and technical assistant were positive. He thoroughly enjoyed meeting and working

Fig. 102 Alfreda Maloof instructing
basketmakers in San Salvador, 1963.

with craftsmen from other cultures, admitting that he learned as much from
them as they did from him. But the political situations he encountered while
living abroad disturbed him deeply. As he later stated, "I've always been very
liberal in my thinking as far as social events go. To see what was happening in
Lebanon and Iran, and what was happening in El Salvador, made a profound
impact on me. Especially in El Salvador, the poverty that I saw, I'd never come
in contact with before."[12] Moreover, he clearly recognized that the intensive
militarization of the Central American nation would soon lead to civil war.

As for the ICA program itself, he was chagrined that there was little or no
followup after he and the others left. There were few, if any, attempts to improve
local production methods and market new designs. As a result, when the
Department of State later invited him to participate in two-year-long programs
in Nigeria and Sri Lanka, he refused. As a footnote to the San Salvador experience, some three months after he returned to California, the skilled craftsman
with whom he worked at Fabrica Capri appeared unannounced at his door in
Alta Loma asking for work. Maloof was not interested in hiring him, but he put
him up for several weeks and eventually found him a job with a Los Angeles
cabinetmaker. But the foreigner's arrival was a harbinger. Within months, more
than two hundred craftsmen from around the world would gather in New York
City, to meet Maloof and admire his work on display. They were not alone. In
1964 twenty-seven million visitors to the New York's World Fair had the opportunity to become familiar with Sam Maloof's life and furniture designs.

New York World's Fair

On April 22, under the direction of Robert Moses, former Commissioner of Parks for New York City, the 1964 World's Fair opened on 643 acres in Flushing Meadow, Queens—the site of the World's Fair of 1939. Dedicated in the new Space Age to "Man's achievements on a shrinking globe in an expanding universe," its themes were two-fold: Peace Through Understanding and A Millennium of Progress. The fair's symbol was the Unisphere, a 140-foot-high, stainless steel armillary globe encircled by three metal rings depicting the paths of Soviet and American satellites then orbiting the earth. Moses's goal for the fair, however, was not so much the facilitation of peaceful understanding among peoples, but the generation of sufficient profits from entry fees and pavilion rentals to complete the development of Flushing Meadow as a city park by adding a science museum, zoo, and botanical garden.

The official Bureau of International Expositions had not authorized the 1964 World's Fair. For one thing, the rules stated that a nation could only host such an event once in a decade, and just two years earlier Seattle, Washington, had been the site of a sanctioned fair. For another, to maximize revenues Moses planned a two-year venture—held from April to October in both 1964 and 1965.[13] (By decree, a World's Fair must open and close in the same year.) As a consequence of its non-official status, except for Spain, Belgium, Ireland, Sweden, Denmark, and Austria, the European countries, as well as the member states of the British Commonwealth and the entire Soviet bloc, boycotted Flushing Meadow. However, many Asian, African, and Latin American nations

Fig. 103 Maloof teaching woodworking in San Salvador, 1963.

did participate and Moses made up for the others' absences by inviting American states and corporations to build pavilions. In the end, 140 were constructed.

From industry's point of view, the 1964 World's Fair was a welcome opportunity to showcase the latest in technology and consumer products. Companies such as General Electric, International Business Machines, all the Detroit automobile manufacturers, Pepsi and Coca-Cola, Bell Telephone, DuPont Chemicals, and Westinghouse spent lavishly on ultra-modern buildings and displays. They were not alone in putting their best foot forward. Along with several other non-profit organizations, the American Craftsmen's Council capitalized on the international event. The organization not only set up an educational display in one of the pavilions, but opened a major survey exhibition downtown at the MCC, *The American Craftsman,* and, in honor of the fair, convened the First World Congress of Crafts at Columbia University. At all three locations, Sam Maloof was a prominent fixture.

In February 1964, the Pomona *Progress-Bulletin* proudly headlined the fact that "The World Will See Valley Man's Furniture." After recounting Maloof's background as a graduate of Chino High, a night student at Wiggins Trade School, and his employment with Harold Graham and Millard Sheets, the newspaper reported that his "glowing walnut furniture" would be displayed at both the ACC's display at Flushing Meadow and its larger museum exhibition in Manhattan. The Upland-Ontario *Daily Report* likewise detailed his upcoming shows in New York, disclosing that he was making eight to ten new pieces especially for them.[14] Actually, Maloof made fourteen works—eleven for the MCC show, one for the ACC display, and two more for another at Columbia University. He also had five more pieces for sale at America House, now relocated to 44 West 53rd Street, next to the Museum of Modern Art—a drop-leaf table and four spindle-back chairs.

The American Craftsmen's Council had been offered exhibit space in the Pavilion of American Interiors, a round, four-story, glass and steel building with two circular wings. Located at the upper end of the fairgrounds near the fountain-filled Pool of Industry, the structure housed displays by some 150 home furnishings industry representatives and interior designers. One prominent furniture manufacturer, Heywood-Wakefield, not only showcased its latest lines but also the modern designs it first introduced at the Chicago World's Fair of 1933. (The contrast proved startling.) On the second floor, the American Institute of Interior Designers (AID) and DuPont Chemicals (a major producer of carpeting and textiles for upholstery and curtains) co-sponsored fourteen model rooms, each of which had been furnished by regional AID chapters to reflect local decorating trends.

In terms of style, they looked very different than Millard Sheets's coordinated settings at the Los Angeles County Fair a decade before. By 1964, the visual unity and relative austerity of 1950s contemporary interior design had given way to period styles, along with the liberal use of opulent color, luxurious ornament, and rich surface textures. Even in the Los Angeles Hobby Room, decorated by members of the Southern California AID chapter, there were only faint echoes of the Southland's once-dominant modern design ethos.[15]

The ACC's display, *The American Craftsman,* was one of three editorial exhibits located on the pavilion's fourth floor. (The other non-profit exhibitors were the American Hardwoods Association and the art school of the Cooper Union.) Instead of an exhibition of objects, the display was composed of "photographic biographies" of five leading craftsmen representing different media—silversmith John Prip, weaver Alice Kagawa Parrott, enamelist Paul Hultberg, ceramicist John Mason, and woodworker Sam Maloof. *Craft Horizons* reproduced many of the images in a special issue devoted to the American craftsman, declaring that the photographic essays sought graphically to convey "the emotional, creative, and physical environment of five studio craftsmen, living and working in contrasting parts of the U.S.A., and facing the different problems of the material in which they work."[16]

In early 1964 photographer Lars Spears had spent a week living with the Maloofs, taking numerous candid shots of Maloof—"from sunrise to sunset"[17]—working in his shop with Larry White, visiting a lumber yard, playing with his children, attending church (where he read the scriptural lesson), and relaxing on the deck of the guest house. In varying sizes, the black-and-white images of the five craftsmen were affixed to curved, free-standing walls in the display, creating a visual collage of each artist's life and world.[18] But examples of their work were also included. Maloof's contribution was a tall, spindle-back side chair (fig. 104). (At the Brussels World's Fair in 1958, the situation had been different. Five woodworkers had contributed to an exhibit inside the official United States pavilion—Wharton Esherick and Paul Eshelman from Pennsylvania, and Californians Bruno Groth, Bob Stocksdale, and James Prestini.)

The American Craftsman

The five participants featured at the fairgrounds were also included in the thirty-person museum show in Manhattan, likewise entitled *The American Craftsman.* It was the most significant crafts show organized to date. A diverse display, it comprised 231 objects by the leading practitioners in various media, along with an additional eighty-nine pieces by contemporary American Indian and Eskimo craftsmen. Collectors of native crafts themselves, Maloof and Freda were thrilled to see the latter works. Among them were pieces by their good friend, potter Maria Martinez from San Ildefonso pueblo. (The establishment of the Institute of American Indian Art in Santa Fe in 1963 and recent promotional activities by the Indian Arts and Crafts Board of the United States Department of the Interior had done much to focus new attention on indigenous artisans, prompting their inclusion in *The American Craftsman.*) The range of artworks selected was broad: "from the strictly utilitarian object to the non-functional work of fine art . . . from devotion to traditional means of working to experimentation with new fabrication processes."[19]

Three furniture makers representing different generations and aesthetic philosophies had been chosen for the show: Wharton Esherick, Maloof—described as "one of the very few consummate designers and producers of furniture, an area that has been increasingly claimed by mass production techniques"[20]—and a relative newcomer to the crafts exhibition scene, thirty-two-year-old Wendell Castle. Trained as an industrial designer and sculptor at the University of Kansas (he had earned a Master of Fine Arts degree in 1961), Castle was then a professor of furniture design at the ACC-sponsored School for American Craftsmen (SAC) at the Rochester Institute of Technology in upstate New York. Initially influenced by Esherick's organically shaped work of the 1940s, in 1964 he was entering a more sculpturally daring phase.

Maloof had eight pieces in the museum show, the same number as Esherick, and twice as many as Castle. They included a long, drop-leaf dining table with wood hinges and eight shallow drawers nestled underneath the table top (fig. 105; still used in his own home); a Brazilian rosewood rocking chair (fig. 106; one of the first of its kind to be exhibited); a hornback side chair with low, curving arms; an upholstered chair with sculpted arms and crest rail; a spindle-back settee with sculptured arms (fig. 107); a tufted leather ottoman; a carved, nine-branch menorah; and a six-candle candelabrum—the latter two his most sculptural forms to date (fig. 108).

Esherick's contributions included several three-legged stools of different heights, along with other utilitarian wooden objects for kitchen and dining table—a round tray, turned bowls, a utensil board, a spoon made from cocobola wood, and a pair of salad servers in boxwood. Castle's four pieces (in the mid-1960s he made between thirty-five and fifty objects annually, about half Maloof's output) comprised a highly sculptured, cherry chest of drawers of dovetail construction, a rosewood piano bench with twisting legs, an oak chair with a leather sling seat, and a remarkable oak and walnut music rack. Esherick achieved great strength and rigidity in the rack's slender, curving uprights by using bent lamination, a nontraditional method he was vigorously exploring.

First World Congress of Crafts

In conjunction with the World's Fair and the MCC exhibition, from June 8 through 22, 1964, the First World Congress of Craftsmen in New York was convened during the ACC's national conference. Ferris Booth Hall at Columbia University provided the necessary meeting rooms, lounges, and dormitory facilities for all 942 attendees—250 from 46 foreign countries. Maloof and Freda attended the Congress, dining on opening night with 450 other guests at the Rainbow Room restaurant atop Rockefeller Center (two days later everyone was invited to a special supper at the Pavilion of American Interiors), attending lectures and panels, visiting with old friends and making many new ones among the foreign craftsmen, and enjoying various organized excursions around Manhattan and to the fair. As stated by the organizers, the conferees' primary objectives were "to highlight problems of world craftsmanship and communication, to exchange aesthetic and practical ideas, and to meet personally fellow artists and educators from all parts of the globe." During the Cold War, the international assembly's mission was to demonstrate "that men of all nationalities can work, play, and act together for a common purpose and their own happiness."[21]

Toward the institutionalization of these goals, under the leadership of Aileen Webb, on June 12 the attendees enthusiastically endorsed the founding of the World Crafts Council (WCC). A non-governmental organization and intended to be devoid of the era's ideological struggles, both political and artistic—it was established to strengthen common bonds between handcraftsmen in all parts of the world, to maintain or increase standards of excellence, create new markets, and, in the age of escalating mass production, to educate the broadest possible public to the value of craftsmanship.[22] Cyril Wood, director of the British Crafts Center, asserted that the unanimity of the founding members in embracing these ends was "an affirmation of faith that man does not live by atom bombs alone."[23] Influenced no doubt by the ACC's own commitment to the avant garde, from the outset the WCC aimed to promote the "art content" of crafts. As Mrs. Webb herself stated, the new council's "orientation toward the art concept in craftsmanship is a result of the belief that as world technology increases, there must be an outlet for the creativity of man."[24]

As had been the case at Asilomar in 1957—and the ACC's subsequent national conferences in Lake Geneva in 1958 and Lake Placid in 1959 (Maloof was unable to attend either)—the two-week Congress was organized thematically. The first week was devoted to Tradition and Progress; week two to Vistas of the Future. While sixty-four speakers and panelists addressed a variety of specific topics, the overarching theme was that of crafts in transition— from traditional designs based on local influences and practical needs to a new, revolutionary type of global art expression. In a prepared talk, Rose Slivka asserted that the era's pervasive international experience (caused by increased communications and travel) would not result in the "homogenization of cultural expression." Rather, the process of "internationalization" would produce even greater individuality as craft artists, reaching beyond regional and national cultures, took creative inspiration from sources worldwide. In one of the final panels, novelist Ralph Ellison described the present-day world as "an environment without walls," a virtual chaos of style, taste, and values. Yet from out of this inter-cultural disorder, he asserted, the artist could selectively construct his own integral reality that could be communicated effectively to others.

The most animated session, Vistas in the Arts, was also one of the last. Sam and Freda were in the audience. As an introduction, critic Harold Rosenberg (Rose Slivka's mentor) read a provocative paper in which he related the contemporary crisis in the arts to the present-day decline of the utilitarian crafts and their replacement by machine technology. Like contemporary abstract expressionist painting and sculpture—which, he declared, had discovered "the discipline for a continuous formation of individuality"—modern crafts were now imbued with "the gratuitous quality of art" and thus likewise could serve as a means for individual "self-creation." The artist-craftsmen in the audience warmly applauded the next speaker, poet Stanley Kunitz, when, expanding on Rosenberg's point, he declared that "only the artist stands completely committed to the thing he makes." Panelist Alan Schneider, a theater director, followed, noting that such a strong personal commitment often involves a critical stance toward society and as a result, the public tended to focus (usually negatively) on the artist's anti-establishment message, not the quality of its expression or its relevance.[25]

Fig. 104 Spindle-back side chair with sculptured arms, 1964. Maloof's single piece exhibited at the 1964 World's Fair in New York.

During the Congress, two afternoons were devoted to media-specific symposia. The well-attended sessions dealt with practical issues—tools, materials, and working methods. The topic for the furniture symposium was lamination, Wendell Castle's forte. The panel leaders were Finnish industrial designer-craftsman, Ilmari Tapiovaara, Donald McKinley, a woodworking instructor at Alfred University, and Castle. Maloof played a role, albeit secondary—he wrote up a report of the proceedings for the official record. In his written statement, Maloof noted that the technique of lamination was not new (after all, it formed the basis of plywood), but it was being utilized in a fresh and vital fashion by a number of younger furniture designer-craftsmen to achieve novel organic designs. In its latest form, he wrote, "lamination is a process of permanently bonding together several pieces of wood into whatever forms or shapes are desired . . . with the grain running in the same direction."[26] Castle had used lamination techniques to break away from the rectilinear character of traditional cabinetry, and indeed from the history of furniture itself. As he himself declared: "I believe that furniture should not be derived from furniture. This practice can only lead to variations on existing themes. . . . To me an organic form has the most exciting possibilities."[27]

Typically, to produce bowed or compound curved arms and legs, solid wood components were either steam bent or, more wastefully, bandsawn into the requisite shape out of large pieces of material. But by carefully gluing thin strips together (from one-eighth to one-quarter of an inch thick) and clamping them to a curvilinear pattern or jig, slender, expressively shaped components with a high degree of tensile strength could be effortlessly created. (Maloof himself would later adopt bent lamination for long, elegantly curved rockers on his rocking chairs.) Through slide presentations, Tapiovaara and McKinley discussed their own use of lamination, but the visual highlight of the symposium was an award-winning, twenty-five minute color film, *The Music Rack*. Sponsored by the acc and produced at the School for American Craftsmen especially for the wcc conference, it depicted the step-by-step process—from first sketch to final product—that Wendell Castle followed in fabricating a unique, gestural music stand (fig. 109). While it could certainly hold sheet music, the gracefully shaped showpiece operated as much in the realm of sculpture as musical performance.

The special edition of *Craft Horizons* published in honor of the mcc exhibition, the World's Fair, and the First World Congress of Crafts included an extraordinary eighty-one page "pictorial compendium" of recent work by 327 artist-craftsmen. Far more inclusive than the thirty-person show, editor Rose Slivka intended it to be a "self-revelatory document" of the "state of the craftsman's profession" and the "individuality of its practitioners." Among the plethora of photographs Slivka selected, experimental work predominated. Within the array of one-of-a-kind, avant-garde works, Maloof's graceful, understated—and thoroughly practical—hornback chair looked decidedly out of place.

In her lead article in this special issue, "The American Craftsman/1964," editor Rose Slivka focused on artist-craftsmen like Castle—"those who make one-of-a-kind objects of superb expressive quality"—rather than designer-craftsmen like Maloof who produced work on commission from a repertoire of evolving designs. Released by industry from the obligation to provide functional items to satisfy the needs of consumers, she wrote, the new artist-craftsman was free to be an "object-maker"—with only himself to please. But to turn traditional crafts into expressive artforms, she noted, the artist first had to restore to the handmade object its objectness—"its intrinsic material self." Just as contemporary painting was about painting, so a pot, Slivka asserted, was to be about pottery—not the function of containment.

By experimentally "probing the limits" of a fresh, new language of craft, she argued, the American artist-craftsman of 1964 had expanded not only the materials, but the very vocabulary of art itself. Slivka admitted this "energizing presence" in American craft was youthful—just seven years old—and had originated in the media of ceramics (which she described as a new "hybrid art" of painted and textured surfaces on dimensional, plastic forms) and weaving (especially free-hanging, sculptural constructions).[28] Within this rhetorical framework, Peter Voulkos's manipulated pots, Lenore Tawney's woven forms—and Wendell Castle's laminated furniture-sculpture—were on the cutting edge

Fig. 105 Drop-leaf dining table with drawers in Maloof home, about 1964. Many of Maloof's dining tables of the 1960s incorporated shallow drawers for storing cutlery and table mats discreetly located beneath the table top.

of craft-as-art. As Maloof himself was forced to admit during the Congress, his chair designs were no longer in the vanguard; they had assumed the status of classics.

The program at Columbia University included a series of small exhibits. The most popular was devoted to the work of foreign attendees. The other six, organized by panelists in the different media sessions, focused on new directions in materials and technologies. The furniture display had been arranged by Wendell Castle. It was composed of several of his own pieces employing lamination, examples of the work of his students at the School for American Craftsmen, and a spindle-back chair and pedestal table by Maloof. Among Castle's contributions was a music stand and a wood and leather rocker whose bold, curvilinear design (fig. 110) echoed the tubular steel armature of a lounge chair designed in the 1920s by Le Corbusier, the leading French modernist architect.[29] However, Castle had distanced himself from the austerity of his modernist sources by substituting sculpturally shaped, laminated wood for stainless steel and, in an anti-modernist stance, carving a decorative date "1963" onto a plaque on the front stretcher. Maloof and Freda visited the display during the opening reception. It was jammed with fellow conferees. As he looked at the audacious, non-traditional designs next to his own, more conventional furniture, Maloof remarked aloud, "Boy! This sure makes my stuff look dated." An unidentified voice in the crowd immediately behind him replied drily, "Just wait a few years, Sam, and see whether you feel the same way."

As had been the case at Asilomar seven years earlier, Maloof found the spontaneous discussions at the informal get-togethers most fruitful. Between the organized sessions, at meal times, and after hours, groups of American and overseas craftsmen gathered in the hallways, lounges, and stairwells of Ferris Booth Hall and talked about the common issues that united them into a worldwide community. He was quoted on the subject in *Craft Horizons*: "To me, informal gatherings of craftsmen in informal bull sessions [is] always the most stimulating and gratifying part of a conference when ideas, thoughts, the ways of working and living are discussed. Here people who work with their hands exchange photographs of their efforts—and at this First World Congress of Craftsmen it was all the more interesting to meet, talk with, and see the work of craftsmen from other countries."[30]

Exhibitions and New Designs, 1965–73

In January 1965, the *Los Angeles Times* Home magazine devoted an issue to the theme of wood in contemporary home designs. The cover photograph revealed an open, spacious interior with a plank ceiling supported by upward sweeping, laminated pine beams. Architectural styles were changing, and in contrast to the boxy 1950s house with its flat roof and glass and steel walls, a less austere style of residence was emerging in the Los Angeles area, one in which soaring interior spaces and natural wood surfaces—both inside and outside—were principal features. In the mid-1960s, Maloof's walnut furniture proved ideal complements to this so-called traditional Western wood house,[31] and to underscore that point, the editors of Home magazine included an article, "Wood

Fig. 106 Brazilian rosewood rocking chair, about 1963. Note on this early example the relatively short, solid wood rocker units.

Fig. 107 Prototype spindle-back settee with sculptured arms, about 1965. Walnut and leather; 38½ x 45½ x 22½ inches; unsigned; Sam and Alfreda Maloof Foundation.

Comes Alive in Fine Furniture by Sam Maloof." It was illustrated by close-up photographs of his joinery that revealed contrasting grain and figuration patterns in the wood, as well as a full page, color image of three different chairs with orange leather upholstery photographed outdoors in a eucalyptus grove. The jungle-like setting adds an air of mystery to the provocative image (fig. 111). (The cameraman for this latter shot was Richard Gross, a principal photographer for the *California Design* catalogues and a leading advocate of the craft-in-nature aesthetic.)

The accompanying text noted that "people say his work has a 'Scandinavian' look, but Sam is quick to point out that it originated several years before the Danish invasion, when designers were still wavering between Traditional and Modern."[32] While there were natural affinities between Maloof's work and mass-produced Scandinavian furniture, the one was certainly not a direct reflection of the other, and it irked Maloof to have his far more elegant and craftsmanly pieces compared to the factory-made imports whose perennially changing designs were far more showy. The Upland-Ontario *Daily Report* emphasized this stylistic independence: "his furniture can only be described as 'Maloof' and not characterized as Danish, Venetian, or some other style."[33]

While Maloof was attending the wcc conference, Eudora Moore had written to him in Alta Loma about the forthcoming *California Design* show, the ninth in the series, scheduled for 1965. Given the logistical problems of organizing the first state-wide exhibit in 1962, co-directors Moore and Hansen had decided to make the annual event a triennial one, open to work made during the three preceding years. In her letter, Moore wrote that she wanted Maloof to be "importantly represented." Since he stood "at the top of [his] field," she said, an exhibition of California design would not be "complete" without "a major submission."[34] Maloof entered seven non-juried pieces into the 787-object show,[35] including chairs, tables, a new shoe bench design, a menorah, and the Brazilian rosewood rocking chair—priced at $400—which he had exhibited in *The American Craftsman*.

Early Rocking Chairs

Maloof had made his first rocking chair in late 1958, before departing for the Middle East. A gift for Freda, it was a spindle-back arm chair to which solid, bandsawn rockers and a stretcher system had been added (fig. 112). Although he had no proof that a brace was needed, he added a support structure beneath the upholstered seat. He employed such strengthening devices until 1975. While a rocker had been among the pieces he had designed in Tehran and built in Beirut in 1959, the first to be exhibited was a model shown in 1963 at an exhibit in Corona Del Mar.[36] Maloof's interest in developing this particular chair form had been piqued two years earlier, when Henry Dreyfuss had written him a note enclosing a report, "Kennedy Kicks Off a Rocking Chair Boom," clipped from the front page of the *Wall Street Journal*. It stated: "Makers and sellers of rockers report brisk business since the president's physician said rocking was relaxing. North Carolina's P. & P. Chair Co., which is geared to produce 250 rockers daily, says its order backlog has zoomed from nearly nothing

Fig. 108 Maloof carving a candelabrum, 1965.

Fig. 109 Music stand by Wendell Castle, 1964. This ground-breaking curvilinear stand propelled studio furniture into the realm of sculpture. Reproduction courtesy of American Craft Museum.

Fig. 110 Rocking chair by Wendell Castle, 1963. This inventive, laminated and carved rocker with a leather sling seat was the hit of the small furniture display at the First World Congress of Craftsmen. Private collection. Reproduction courtesy of Wendell Castle Studio.

to four weeks of work since the president was photographed in one of its $25 rockers."[37]

In his note, Dreyfuss had asked, "Sam. Why don't you design a rocker and send one to Kennedy?"[38] The celebrated designer had a personal interest in the project: Dr. Janet Travell, the therapist who treated the president for his chronic lower back problems and advised rocking, was one of the Dreyfuss firm's advisers on ergonomic design. Maloof indeed constructed a chair and contacted the White House, but the transfer of the gift was still incomplete when Kennedy was assassinated in November 1963. However, three presidents of the United States—Ronald Reagan, Jimmy Carter, and Bill Clinton—were to acquire Maloof rockers. After 1980, they would become Maloof's best-known designs, but they were introduced slowly. In the 1960s there was little demand. One each was ordered in 1963 and 1964; four in 1965; two in 1966; and five each in 1967, 1968, and 1969. These early rockers featured deep, upholstered seats; high, sculpted or curved arm rests; tall, straight backs with turned spindles (sometimes upholstered backs were ordered); and a sculpted crest rail. They also typically included backposts with hornlike extensions, as well as stretchers beneath the seats (fig. 113). Made in solid, rather than laminated wood, the relatively short, bandsawn and Surform-shaped rockers were attached to the legs with dowels, the joins sculpturally modeled.

Music Rack

In 1965, Maloof introduced another design—a music rack (fig. 114). It was first featured in a two-man show in May at Museum West, an exhibition space recently established by the ACC in San Francisco's Ghiardelli Square. Administered by Elizabeth Hansen of *California Design* fame, Museum West hosted some ten ACC-organized shows a year. Among the first, *Maloof/Parrott* featured sixteen pieces of Maloof's furniture along with an array of woven fabrics by Alice Parrott, the Santa Fe weaver with whom he had exhibited at the World's

Fair.[39] Music racks were woodworkers' showpieces. Wharton Esherick had been among the earliest to create one in 1953. (Maloof had seen his curvaceous version at Esherick's retrospective in New York on his way to the Middle East; fig. 115.) One of Castle's laminated music stands had been memorialized in the film shown at Columbia University in 1964, while a similar design had been featured in the "pictorial compendium" published in the special issue of *Craft Horizons* devoted to the American craftsman. A three-legged, duet version by Northern California designer-woodworker Arthur Espenet Carpenter had also been reproduced in that issue.

Maloof's rack actually had started out as a long-armed book support designed in 1964 for his painter friend Emil Kosa Jr., who enjoyed reading in bed. The two attended an exhibition opening in Los Angeles one evening, and Kosa, a previous client, asked Maloof to solve a problem. "Sam," he said, "I'm the laziest man in the world. When I go to bed, I love to read, but I have to hold the book in my hand. Can you design me a book holder, so that all I have to do is turn the pages."[40] The arm of the book rack had been unusually long, but within a year, the form had evolved into an elegant, tripodal stand with arched legs similar to those of his pedestal tables. The horizontal arm could be adjusted for height, while the sheet music holder—a double version soon debuted—likewise could be tilted to suit individual needs (fig. 116).

In late January 1966, Maloof included the new design among eight works he submitted to a three-man studio furniture show, *Esherick/Maloof/Castle,* organized by the University of Chicago's Renaissance Society and displayed in Goodspeed Hall. With the music rack, he sent two different settees and benches, and a spindle-back dining chair and pedestal table (fig. 117). (It was not the only Chicago venue to show Maloof pieces that year. In a promotion of California products, the Carson-Pirie-Scott department store exhibited three of his works from *California Design 9.*) The Renaissance Society exhibition opened simultaneously with a startlingly different display that also featured Wendell Castle's work, but not Maloof's—*Fantasy Furniture* held at the Museum of Contemporary Crafts in New York.[41]

The new directions in artistic woodworking heralded by this widely acclaimed, five-man show were wholly antithetical to Maloof's functionalist philosophy with its amalgam of fine craftsmanship, traditional joinery, and formal beauty. While semi-functional, the fanatsy pieces—expressively carved, painted, or incorporating found industrial parts, and containing symbolic or metaphorical content—represented a novel desire to produce sculptural furniture forms that were, in organizer Paul J. Smith's words, "capricious or whimsical," even "macabre."[42] One of Castle's pieces was a cherry blanket chest shaped like a large, bulbous piece of fruit supported by a stubby, sculptural base. The unusual container form had been constructed using stack lamination, a method of building up mass larger than the dimensions of a log through gluing boards horizontally to create irregular forms and then carving the final shape. Borrowed from contemporary wood sculpture, it was a method that allowed Castle to reject rectilinear construction and one that greatly facilitated his development as a furniture sculptor.

Fig. 111 Three Maloof chairs photographed in a eucalyptus grove, 1965. Courtesy *Los Angeles Times.*

Fig. 112 First Maloof rocking chair, 1958. Originally made for Freda, this prototype was later sold to a visiting client. Maloof soon replaced it with a newer version, marked especially for her.

Fig. 113 Adult- and child-sized spindle-back rocking chairs, 1968 and 1969. Adult: walnut and wool fabric; $44\frac{7}{8}$ x 26 x $42\frac{1}{8}$ inches; embossed "48 6–68 Alfreda Maloof"; child: walnut and leather; $28\frac{1}{4}$ x $21\frac{5}{8}$ x 29 inches; unsigned; carved on rear of headrest "Aaron." In 1968 Maloof made the large chair for Freda and a year later, fabricated the small one for his three-year-old grandson, Aaron.

Along with five other unsold works from the University of Chicago show, Maloof's peripatetic music rack traveled in late March to Buffalo to appear in another exhibit, *Craftsman-Designer-Artist,* staged at a national conference, The Role of Crafts in Education. Sponsored by the United States Office of Education, the meeting was held at the New York State University at Buffalo. (In 1965 Maloof had been asked by the ACC to serve on the conference steering committee and he traveled to New York several times to attend meetings. His involvement in the planning process marked the true beginning of his long-time service to the Council.)

The Buffalo display included work by twenty of the conference participants (in all, some fifty had been invited), among them Maloof and woodworker Don McKinley, then a craftsman-trustee of the ACC.[43] (The show stopper was ceramicist Robert Arneson's notorious polychrome Funk sculpture of an unflushed toilet.) Another attendee was Jonathan Fairbanks, the recently appointed curator of American decorative arts at the Boston Museum of Fine Arts. Equally outgoing and congenial, and sharing a mutual dedication to fine woodworking, Maloof and Fairbanks began a lifelong friendship that would have lasting effects.

Conversation at Esherick's

After the conference ended, Maloof and McKinley traveled by car to Paoli, Pennsylvania, to visit Wharton Esherick's home and studio. It was Maloof's first visit to that legendary architectural landmark which he had first seen illustrated in a 1951 issue of *House Beautiful.*[44] En route, however, they stopped in Rochester, New York, where the Californian had been invited by Wendell Castle to give an illustrated talk to students at the American School for Craftsmen. Later, settled in Esherick's house, Maloof, McKinley, and the seventy-eight-year-old furniture maker spent the better part of a day talking about their personal histories, working habits, and philosophies. The informal discussion was actually one of five similar conversations organized by the ACC in the spring of 1966.

That year, the Council had asked fifteen distinguished artist-craftsmen-designers from across the nation—representatives of the so-called first generation of the New American Craftsman—to meet and converse about the changes they had witnessed over twenty years. The dialogues were taped, transcribed, and later published in *Craft Horizons.*[45]

When the visitors arrived at lunchtime, Esherick met them outside his front door and showed them through the remarkable house. Maloof admired the famous carved staircase, the shaped wooden door pulls (a source of inspiration for his own unique examples), the floor-to-ceiling wood sculptures, and asymmetrical furniture prototypes. After lunch, Maloof began the conversation by observing that few of the craftsmen attendees at the recent Buffalo conference actually made a

Fig. 114 Maloof with a single music rack, about 1969. Sam's adjustable sheet music stand was first introduced to the public in 1965.

Fig. 115 Carved music rack by Wharton Esherick, 1957 (based on his 1953 original). Courtesy Wharton Esherick Museum.

Fig. 116 Double music rack, about 1969. Maloof's sheet music holders were shaped like open books.

living from their work. "People are so afraid to go out and try what they were trained to do," he said, "they take up teaching as security, and the practice of craft is a fringe benefit." The iconoclastic Esherick agreed that teaching was "overdone." When asked to instruct students, the older woodworker would gruffly answer, "I make, I don't teach." Maloof felt the same way: "I've been asked to teach and have said 'no, thank you.' What happens instead is that classes— from UCLA, Los Angeles State, Long Beach State—call up and ask, 'Can we come out and see what you're doing?'" During these class visits, he was often queried: "Can we ask a question, or is it a secret?" He always replied: "There are no secrets in joinery. It's a matter of figuring it out. . . . I just picked it up, and I'm still learning."

At another point in the discussion, the pragmatic, fifty-year-old Maloof noted: "Wharton, there aren't too many people making furniture—really making a living at it like we are. I think the reason is they can't produce enough to make a living. They treat a chair like a painting or a piece of sculpture, working on it for three, four months. But you can't do it this way. You've got to turn these things out; you can't afford to sell them for a thousand dollars." McKinley then raised the possibility that objects carefully crafted by hand tools were now an anachronism: "maybe things made by hand should be just like art." In a well-known retort (its blunt language edited for public consumption), the irascible Esherick lambasted the notion of technical purity in woodworking: "This thing you call handcraft, I say, 'Stop that thing.' I use any damn machinery I can get a hold of. . . . Handcrafted has nothing to do with it. I'll use my teeth if I have to. There's a little of the hand, but the main thing is the heart and the head. Handcrafted! I say, 'Applesauce! Stop it!'"[46]

The conversation then turned to the issue of working with wood. Maloof noted that Esherick had never "overextended" his material, made it "do what it doesn't want to do," and asked whether the older man objected to younger, more experimental woodworkers like Wendell Castle who, through stack lamination, forced wood to its physical limits in their goal to achieve novel, organic shapes. The retort revealed the widening divide between older cabinetmakers and the new generation of artist-craftsmen who no longer revered natural materials: "what did he make it out of wood for, then, if he's only after form? There's no beauty of wood there." The published transcription concluded with Maloof's comment to Wharton Esherick: "You have to find your own personal way as a craftsman. I recall vividly what you said to me after the ACC conference at Asilomar: 'Keep doing what you're doing.' That's always stayed with me. You can only do so much and earn so much, but this is secondary. To do what you want—this is the important thing." The elder woodworker concurred: "If you don't have joy, are not enthusiastic with what you're doing, no matter how much dough you've got, you're no good."[47]

The Evans Chair

During the taped conservation, when the subject had shifted to the retention of prototypes (which, for financial reasons, were often sold to visiting clients), Maloof had remarked that a woman who had visited the recent *Esherick/Maloof/*

Castle exhibition in Chicago had asked him to design a dining chair not unlike a tall version on display, but without spindles and with a lower back rest. The visitor, Mrs. J. Burgen Evans, was a keen admirer of Maloof's graceful designs and wished to order a set of twelve chairs for the dining room of a new home she and her husband were building in suburban Northfield, Illinois.[48] Maloof had agreed, but instead of sending a measured drawing of the proposed new model, he made a finished prototype with an upholstered seat and shipped it to her. Evans was ecstatic, and in March 1966 she ordered a full set for $2,700 through the Chicago design firm, Watson & Boaler. These were among 133 pieces he fabricated that year. Before they were shipped in October, Maloof lined them up outside his workshop and took a photograph (fig. 118). It proved to be one of the most important designs Maloof introduced in the 1960s.

In retrospect, he was sorry not to have kept the prototype for it was the first of a long line of chairs with low, sculpted back rests—called Evans chairs after the original client—which, as they evolved over three decades, would become perhaps his favorite chair design. Actually, two prototypes had been fabricated. One, worked on by Larry White, had straight, low arms (fig. 119). The other, finished by teenage Sammy (who had now taken his grandfather's first name, Slimen, to distinguish himself from his father), came with downward curved arms and was actually the model shipped to Chicago. The main feature of the design is the sculpturally shaped back support which, like the taller, spindled models from which it evolved (fig. 120), spans the width between the backposts. Over the years, it would be given an ever-increasing sculptural definition, and would become the most organically shaped of all of Maloof's chairs (fig. 121). Maloof also designed a settee based on the low-back chair for the Evans house (fig. 122). Originally, the two-seater incorporated a central support post and legs. Later versions daringly dispensed with these features.

Cradle Hutch

In 1966 yet another new model made its debut—the so-called cradle hutch or cradle cabinet (fig. 123). Repeated only five times, it remains Maloof's most unusual design, combining as it does both rectilinear and curving components. Many at the time declared it his most attractive creation.[49] The cradle hutch was literally a showpiece, its design prompted by an invitation to submit a special work to a thematic exhibition—*The Bed,* a twenty-seven piece show mixing historical and contemporary pieces organized in 1966 by the MCC.[50] As the woodworker later recalled, he agreed to the request to fabricate a new piece, but didn't begin the project until Director Smith telephoned several weeks before the deadline. Under pressure, he decided to make something that not only met the criterion for the exhibit, but would prove immediately useful at home afterwards.

Slimen had recently married and his wife, Kathryn, was expecting a baby. The young couple were living in the guest house and Maloof decided to make an ingenious, space-saving cradle-cum-storage unit for his grandchild. (His own son's first bed had been a dresser drawer in the Plaza Serena house.) "Now, most

Fig. 117 Dining chair and pedestal table, about 1966. Since Maloof rejected metal hardware, the leaves of the table were attached by wood hinges through which an invisible brass rod was inserted.

cradles are so low that mothers break their backs putting the baby in and taking the baby out," Maloof later recalled. The challenge, then, was to design something more ergonomic and functional: "'Why not bring the cradle up to the mother? And why not put drawers under it for the baby's clothes?' . . . Then I thought. 'Why not enclose it completely in a cabinet, with storage space for blankets up above the open cradle?' This is the way the cradle hutch was conceived."[51] While he had formulated an image of it in his mind, Maloof wasn't sure what the finished piece would really look like until he completed it in two weeks of hard work. While it proved a resounding success on view—it was one of six in the cradle section of the show—the most sensational piece was a bed made by Douglas Deeds from 673 welded beer cans.

Six-and-a-half-feet-high, four feet wide, and eighteen inches deep, the cradle-storage unit was among the largest case pieces he had yet constructed. There is a Shaker lightness and simplicity to the classic proportions and harmony of parts. Since utility was always uppermost in Maloof's mind, later versions included pull-out diaper changing boards and rear cabinet doors (fig. 124). In 1976 a free-standing design with pedestal end supports appeared (fig. 125). A more popular cradle, by 2000 some eleven examples had been ordered. With its ten curved ribs, the swinging unit looked like the hull of a small vessel, its planking removed. Indeed, the cradle had a keel-like strip running lengthwise underneath, gunwales to which the ribs were attached,

Fig. 118 Set of low-back dining chairs with curved arms made for Mrs. J. Burgen Evans, 1966.

Fig. 119 Prototype Evans dining chair with straight arms, 1966. Walnut and leather; 29¾ x 20¾ x 21½ inches; signed with shop brand "designed . made/MALOOF/ California" and embossed: "3–66." This first prototype for the so-called Evans chair—like several other popular designs, named after the original client—had horizontal arms.

Fig. 120 Spindle-back low-arm dining chair, 1964. Walnut and wool fabric; 39⅝ x 21 x 19¾ inches; signed with shop brand "designed . made/MALOOF/ California" and embossed "3 3/64." Sam and Alfreda Maloof Foundation. At the suggestion of the client, Maloof adapted the shaped crest rail of this tall chair for the back rest of his Evans chair.

Following pages:

Fig. 121 Low-back side chair, 1987. Walnut and ebony; 30½ x 21¾ x 23½ inches; inscribed "No. 5 1987 Sam Maloof f. A.C.C." Collection Slimen Maloof. Within two decades, the sedate Evans chair had evolved into one of Maloof's most sculptural seating forms.

Fig. 122 Prototype low-back settee, about 1967. Walnut and leather; 29¾ x 43¼ x 20¾ inches; unmarked; Sam and Alfreda Maloof Foundation. The original Evans chair was the basis for this double settee. Later, when he began to use wooden seats, Maloof dispensed with the central legs and support post.

and, like a Viking ship, towering prows fore and aft. When orders for such pieces were received, Maloof stopped work on other projects to complete them quickly. Babies didn't wait for back orders to clear.

More sculpturally conceived, subsequent cradle hutches included cutout pulls and shaped wooden latches in place of turned drawer and door knobs. As conceived, the overall design was multi-purpose. When the infant outgrew it, the hutch could be used as a room divider, at parties the cradle serving as a large bread basket, the changing board as a cheese server.[52] If desired, the cradle unit could be removed altogether and open shelves added. The design prompted another, unique case piece—a tall storage cabinet incorporating a fall-front desk (fig. 126).

In May 1966, Maloof displayed pieces in two West Coast shows: *Design: Wood* at Museum West and a one-man display at the Egg and I, an innovative restaurant and crafts showcase located across the street from the Los Angeles County Museum of Art and founded by artist-collector, Edith Wyle. Maloof exhibited sixteen works, including a rosewood music stand and a new 1966

Fig. 123 Prototype cradle hutch, 1966. Since it was raised, a mother could comfortably and safely place the infant in the swinging cradle unit without having to bend down. Collection American Craft Museum. Reproduction by permission of Richard Di Liberto Photography.

Fig. 124 Subsequent version of the cradle hutch, incorporating a diaper changing board and rounded cutout door and drawer pulls. Reproduction by permission of Jonathan Pollock.

design evolution based on it—a double-sided print rack or dictionary stand incorporating a drawer beneath its top ledge (fig. 127). The craft pieces that Wyle acquired for the upscale, egg-based eatery (among them Maloof's music stand) eventually formed the basis of the collection of the Los Angeles Craft and Folk Art Museum that she and her husband, aerospace engineer Frank S. Wyle, helped to establish. The Maloofs and the Wyles became close friends, and in 1967 the woodworker designed dining room and occasional furniture for their contemporary-style glass, wood, and stone residence set in a forest in North Fork, California, a home and furnishings lavishly featured in *House & Garden*.[53]

Locally, Maloof remained a well-known and respected figure. Amenable and civic minded, he readily assisted area groups and organizations in a variety

of activities. During 1967, for example, he held a fund-raising open house for Alta Loma High School, and gave talks on furniture design at the LaVerne Lion's Club, the San Bernardino County Art Association, the Pomona Kiwanis Club, the Chino Valley Women's Club, and the Scripps College Fine Arts Foundation. He even contributed a walnut podium to the auditorium of nearby Upland High School. In August, he loaned a chair and writing desk to the exhibition *Seven Decades of Design* held at Long Beach State College (fig. 128). The roster of his fellow participants reads like an international who's who of progressive design: Michael Thonet, Gerrit Rietveld, Mies Van Der Rohe, Alvar Aalto, Eero Saarinen, Hans Wegner, Frank Lloyd Wright, and the Pasadena Arts and Crafts designers, Greene and Greene. Maloof's pieces were a hit. According to a local reviewer, trend-setting contemporary chairs by Charles Eames and designers for Herman Miller, Inc. were contrasted, in her words, "with the superb, one-of-a-kind chairs by Sam Maloof, one of the Southland's widely respected designer-craftsmen."[54]

"A Visit with a Master Craftsman in His Home"

Maloof's reputation as a local hero perhaps peaked in September 1968, when an issue of the *Los Angeles Times* Home magazine was devoted to the woodworker and his remarkable residence. Since the mid-1950s, the latter had slowly blossomed into a total artistic environment filled with art and crafts, both native and contemporary, American as well as international. But tastes in furniture design were changing, and it was one of the last times the long-supportive magazine treated the woodworker in any depth.

Emblazoned with the headline, "Sam Maloof. A visit with a master craftsman in his home," the cover featured a photograph of Sam from the back, taken by Richard Gross, reading a book in an upholstered rocking chair, a design described inside as "a classic in its own time" (fig. 129). He is sitting in his redwood-sided living room, a large Paul Soldner pot resting on the carpeted floor. In essence, the lavishly illustrated article was a visual house tour, the first of many similar journalistic treatments. It began:

Sam Maloof designs and makes fine furniture. For the past 20 years he has lived and worked in a six-acre lemon grove in Alta Loma, at the base of the San Gabriel Mountains. This house is famous among designers and artists because it is filled with his furniture and collections and because it fits him as a shell fits a mollusc. It's not so much a structure as an experience, and to feel it best you must go through it with Sam, just in from the shop, still dusted with sawdust, lean and intense, and delighted as you are to exchange ideas.[55]

An opening, two-page photograph revealed a dining table and chairs, a rosewood music stand holding an open book, and a large photo print of the cradle hutch situated in the glass-fronted room that originally had started out in the mid-1950s as a carport, then, when enclosed, became the master bedroom, and now in the late 1960s functioned as a music room–office where Freda kept the business files.

Fig. 125 Free-standing cradle, 1980. Maloof introduced this free-standing version of his swinging cradle in 1975. Reproduction by permission of Jonathan Pollock.

A wide-angle photograph on a following page revealed the latest addition to the house—a twenty-by-thirty-six-foot master bedroom lined with redwood boards and featuring a central clerestory and exposed beams (fig. 130). Constructed at right angles to the original structure, this new bedroom wing was reached by a short corridor. Since most bed chambers were wasted space, Maloof had decided to turn it into a large living room with the bed (which had no headboard or frame) placed in the center. In front of a wood stove located against a free-standing wall, hornback chairs and a pedestal table were informally arranged on a colorful kilim rug. On the table top and on wall shelving, and the ceiling beams, Sam and Freda had placed pre-Columbian ceramic figures, Indian baskets and pottery, and other decorative objects. Adding to the warmth of tones in the room were throw pillows with Alice Parrott textiles, hanging lampshades covered with Jack Lenor Larsen fabrics, and brightly patterned Navajo rugs and blankets.

The Maloofs' collection of art and crafts was eclectic and ecumenical. Since 1950, Maloof and Freda had traveled to Santa Fe almost every summer, often adding new pieces to their historically significant collection of Indian textiles, pottery, and jewelry. During his travels to the Middle East and El Salvador, Maloof had acquired indigenous art; he also regularly purchased pictures, pottery, and other crafts from artist-friends in the Claremont–Padua Hills area, as well as objects by fellow designer-craftsmen nationwide. Sometimes he traded work. However, only his own furniture was on view in the home. (Since he had severed his connection with Kneedler-Fauchere, and neither had nor wanted commercial gallery representation, his house served as his principal showroom where visitors could see pieces in daily use.) Another photograph in the article had been taken outdoors, revealing a new front patio enclosed on three sides by the evolving dwelling. It was an evocative image. Above large plant-filled pots on the ground, sand-cast bronze bells by Paolo Soleri hang from a beam, framing Maloof and Freda in the background. With its natural materials, artistic decorations, and personalized design, the rural workshop and home represented an ideal that many in the tumultuous counterculture of the late 1960s sought to emulate—the "craftsman lifestyle."

Objects: USA

In the summer of 1968, before the pictorial house tour was published, Lee Nordness, organizer of *Art: USA: 1959* invited Maloof to show eight pieces in the opening show of his new Manhattan crafts display space, Forms and Objects.[56] Maloof agreed and among the works he shipped east in August were a rosewood rocker and a music rack. (All the pieces were later acquired privately by Samuel Curtis Johnson, usually called Sam, a fourth generation of the Johnson Wax Company empire.) Earlier that year, Nordness had given Wendell Castle a critically acclaimed, one-man show in his former painting and sculpture gallery and even had added him to his regular roster of artists—the first craftsman to be inducted into a New York art dealer's stable. Along with others selected for the inaugural exhibit at Forms and Objects, Maloof was also invited to join Nordness' stable.

Fig. 126 Desk hutch, about 1970. Walnut; $71\frac{5}{8} \times 43\frac{7}{8} \times 21\frac{3}{4}$ inches; unmarked; Sam and Alfreda Maloof Foundation. Maloof made this monumental storage unit for his own home where it was used in the dining room. Note the carved latches that secure the cabinet doors.

While arranging the crafts show, the dealer asked all the exhibitors how they wished to be categorized. In analyzing their responses, he discovered the term craftsman was viewed by most as "not dignified enough," while artist-craftsman was "redundant" and artist was "pretentious." Maloof's preference was straightforward: "I always call myself a woodworker, and let it go at that." Nordness's solution to the nomenclature problem was simple: refer to all those on his roster according to their specific craft—potter, furniture maker, painter, etc.[57]

During 1968, with Paul J. Smith as a consultant, Nordness was building an extensive corporate collection of contemporary crafts for S. C. Johnson & Son, Inc., the Wisconsin manufacturer of wax products. It was the second collection he had created for art-conscious Johnson Wax, whose headquarters in Racine had been designed in 1936 by Frank Lloyd Wright. In 1962 the Manhattan dealer had assembled a cross section of recent American painting which, as the company-sponsored exhibition, *Art: USA: Now*, had toured Japan and Europe before traveling to museums across the United States. In 1968–69, after the national tour was over, the firm donated all 102 works to the Smithsonian Institution's National Collection of Fine Arts, now the Smithsonian American Art Museum (SAAM).

For eight months, Nordness and Smith criss-crossed the country, seeking works in all media from both established and emerging talent. Money was no obstacle, only numbers, for from the outset, the Johnson Collection of Contemporary Crafts was envisioned as an exhibition that would tour nationally beginning in the fall of 1969. In the end 308 objects were acquired. But unlike the previous collection of contemporary paintings, it was not an inclusive survey, balancing traditional and avant garde pieces. Instead, it focused on one-of-a-kind, experimental artworks. As a writer in *Craft Horizons* put it, the new corporate assembly of crafts included: "the bizarre, the misshapen, the caricature. The func part of function. The spectacular, the exciting, the chic. The useless. The experimental, the mistaken, the discarded. The found, the lost, the free. The pure. The multi. The involved." In other words, "the newest directions and inventions of the creative leaders in the major medium categories."[58]

In their search for works, Nordness and Smith stopped in Alta Loma and commissioned or purchased seven traditional pieces from Maloof—the most selected from any craftsman. The works included two Evans chairs; a settee based on that 1966 design; a rosewood music rack; a small, drop-leaf, pedestal table; a two-door rosewood chest with dramatic graining; and the cradle hutch featured in *The Bed.* (Grandson Aaron had already outgrown it.) In late February 1969, Maloof crated the works and shipped them cross country by commercial van line. The driver reached Manhattan after dark and, parking his vehicle on a street in Harlem, checked into a hotel for the night. In the morning, he discovered the truck had been broken into and Maloof's chairs, settee, and music stand—their crates situated just inside the back doors—had been stolen. The thieves had even tried to make off with the original cradle hutch, but it had proved too heavy to carry and was found abandoned on the sidewalk two blocks away. Maloof was not informed of the loss until mid-May, and with no time

Fig. 127 Double adjustable print rack, about 1966. The rack could also hold a dictionary or other book. Reproduction by permission of Jonathan Pollock.

to fabricate replacements in time for the show, his contribution was reduced to the three remaining works—hutch, table, and chest.

Objects: USA opened on October 3, 1969, at the National Collection of Fine Arts (now SAAM) where it proved to be the most popular exhibition yet held at the museum. By the time its twenty-three city national tour ended on November 30, 1971, it had attracted an astonishing 530,000 visitors—the largest audience hitherto exposed to contemporary crafts. (In the fall of 1972 it began a two-year European tour.) In the history of the studio craft movement, the show's importance cannot be underestimated. In the mind of the public, not just the ACC, but the Smithsonian Institution and the wider museum world had anointed nontraditional craft objects (those representing "the func part of function") with the prestige commonly attached to contemporary painting and sculpture. The Council's decade-long campaign to blur, if not erase, the boundaries between art and craft had largely succeeded.

With *Objects: USA, Craft Horizons* boasted that American crafts had now "taken a seat beside the fine arts."

Craft products command attention in the same way that a painting or sculpture does. They can hang on a museum wall or be placed on pedestals for aesthetic contemplation. Craftsmen who have joined the movement away from the merely functional, who have taken note of the changing times, and who have something contemporary to say are not only paying their bills regularly nowadays, but are often to be found in universities at the center of a coterie of disciples. . . . Craftsmen have made it. Status symbols can be woven in unusual fabrics and blown into weird glassy bubbles. They can be hammered into silver, carved in laminated wood, fired in slabs of clay. And such up-to-the-minute examples will not only be displayed enthusiastically, but will actually be purchased by museums, big-name collectors, and with-it banks. Nearly everything that has happened in the fine arts—pop, op, abstract expressionism, hard edge, funk, porno—is happening in the crafts today. The border line between the arts and crafts is, in fact, as precarious as that between madness and genius.[59]

Fig. 128 Writing desk and spindle-back chair with low arms, about 1967.

But the writer sounded a cautionary note: while new directions defied tradition, tradition in turn "challenges change." With the inclusion of a handful of functional forms (to demonstrate the superior quality of handmade objects over factory goods), the writer felt the show would help bridge the widening gap between tradition-minded craftsmen and experimentalists, effecting an accommodation between what he called the "necessarily useful" and the "necessarily useless." But in the late 1960s, the separation remained intact. While respecting his skills as a designer-woodworker and his pioneering role, the younger, more radical studio furniture makers following the footsteps of Wendell Castle viewed Sam Maloof as an elder statesmen, not a trend-setting figure on the cutting edge of craft-as-art.

Among the 267 artists represented in *Objects: USA,* only thirteen were woodworkers—Esherick, Maloof, Castle (who also displayed work in plastic), George Nakashima, William A. Keyser, Bob Stocksdale, Jere Osgood, Thomas Simpson, Harry Nohr, Arthur Espenet Carpenter, Lee M. Rhode, Daniel Loomis Valenza, and J. B. Blunk. Woodcraft was still among the least popular of craft media, and in contrast to many well-known ceramicists and weavers, only a handful of practitioners like Maloof enjoyed national reputations. But times were changing. In September 1968, *Craft Horizons* had noted that there was growing interest on the part of younger craftspeople, especially in the more experimental aspects of the medium.[60]

In the show, objects by Castle, Blunk, and Simpson best represented new directions in woodworking. With its elongated, wandering shape, Castle's carved biomorphic, stack-laminated desk was an especially strong sculptural statement, only vestigially functional (fig. 131). For his part, Blunk, a reclusive Northern Californian who lived in the midst of a national forest, contributed a ten-foot-long, monolithic seating sculpture that had been vigorously shaped and carved with a chain-saw and gouges from a large redwood root structure (fig. 132). No other object in the show had such a powerful, sculptural presence. Simpson's anthropomorphic painted cabinet, *Man Balancing a Feather on His Knows,* on the other hand, had something to "say" (fig. 133). A bizarre, whimsical figure standing on two feet (its stave body contained a storage unit), in the anti-establishment artist's words it condemned the "nonfunctional dehumanization" of the contemporary environment.[61] But with their disciplined resolution of form, clear functional purpose, and timeless designs, Maloof's three pieces held their own. Within the cacophony of experimental work, they conveyed what one commentator would term "the tranquility of a philosopher."[62]

The lavishly illustrated, 360-page catalogue, *Objects: USA* (1970), was the first crafts coffee-table book. Not only were all the works in the collection reproduced, but a candid photograph of each maker also appeared, personalizing the illustrated objects. Also included were narrative entries describing either the individual's oeuvre or his artistic intentions, short resumes, and often personal statements. A bit defensively, Maloof declared: "I am a furniture designer and woodworker, perhaps in the traditional manner, where craftsmanship and joinery are of prime importance, and also where design is of equal, if not more concern."[63] The book also included an extended, ground-breaking essay by Lee Nordness. Reviewing the history of American crafts from colonial times to the postwar studio movement, it was the first in-depth report on the context, motivations, and achievements of the new artist-object maker.

Clearly, Rose Slivka's writings had influenced the author's point of view. For Nordness, as well as the editor of *Craft Horizons,* proper terminology was essential. From his standpoint as an art dealer, "handcraft" was a pejorative word, carrying with it a "parasitic multitude of connotations ranging from therapeutic to folksy." He preferred "object." It was a neutral and unpretentious term. Thus, following Slivka's lead, he decreed the contemporary artist-craftsman was best defined as an "object maker."[64] (In 1968 the MCC was in full agreement,

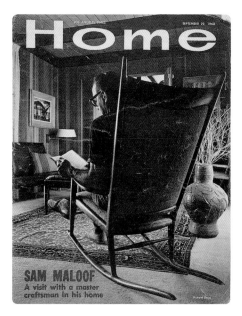

Fig. 129 Cover for *Los Angeles Times*
Home magazine, 29 September 1968. The
issue featured a visit with Maloof in his
home. Courtesy *Los Angeles Times.*

Fig. 130 View of the Maloof master bedroom, 1968. Since the house functioned
as a showroom, potential clients could see
Maloof furniture in daily use. Courtesy
Los Angeles Times.

confounding the public's desire to categorize works as either art or craft in its
provocative, open-ended exhibition, *Objects are . . . ?*)

According to Nordness, there were three different sorts of object makers,
defining divergent directions within the craft movement. *Industrial designers*
created drawings and prototypes for objects to be mass produced by machine,
while *production designers* were tradition-bound craftsmen, like Maloof, who
reproduced their own functional designs, often with workshop assistants. The
studio object maker, however, represented the ideal. He was "an artist who
works alone and with complete freedom . . . in a studio creating objects satisfying only his standards of technique and aesthetics."[65]

But a crucial question remained to be answered: were nonfunctional craft
objects the only candidates for fine art status? "Can a chair ever be a work of
art?" he asked. In responding, Nordness revealed the avant garde's bias against
usefulness. The more functional an object, the Manhattan art dealer asserted,
the more its utilitarian nature overshadowed its aesthetic "presence"—the quality that defined it as an independent work of art. Moreover, since production
craftsmen like Maloof responded to the external needs of clients—not their own
subjective impulses—they lacked the "spark" that animated true artists. "Passion
is one of the most salient ingredients of art," Nordness declared, "it will not
flow or spark on demand or for reward."[66] But passion was an essential ingredi-
ent in Sam Maloof's workshop routine. Passion for his materials, tools, and
techniques—and for satisfying others' needs—invigorated him daily. Work
offered a renewal of energy, spiritual as well as physical. "Whatever I'm working
on, I get excited," he later wrote, "It does not matter whether I have done the
same piece many times. I still can't wait to get out to the shop in the morning."[67]

Aside from handcraft, Lee Nordness objected to another word long attached
to objects and favored by craftsmen in the 1950s—"design." In his view, it was
associated with production work, not art. Painters and sculptors, along with
Rose Slivka, firmly rejected the term, instead substituting "form." For the sake of
clarity and consistency, he argued, the craftsmaker intent on creating artworks

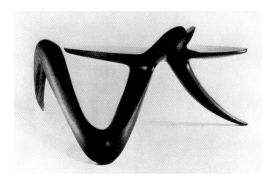

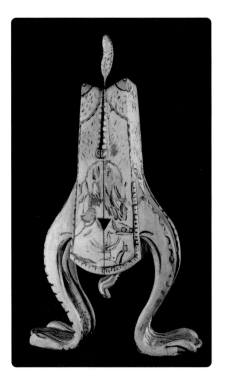

should eliminate such "unstable" words as "design" from his working vocabulary and employ expressions more applicable to sculpture than replicated products. He believed such verbal prescriptions would help eliminate the dichotomy between function and non-function that, in his view, now plagued the crafts field. But "design" was fundamental to Maloof's creative identity: his shop invoices and personal letterhead were boldly printed "Sam Maloof / Designer-Woodworker," and from the late 1950s to 1971, his pieces were "signed" with a brand that read "designed.made / MALOOF / california" (fig. 134).

New Workshop Assistants

In July 1969, before *Objects: USA* opened in Washington, Maloof and Freda traveled to Albuquerque, New Mexico, to attend the annual assembly of the ACC's Southwestern membership, one of six geographical groups organized by the Council. At the general meeting, the attendees officially elected him the region's new craftsman-trustee to serve on the Council's board for a three-year term. It was his first official position with the national group, and he traveled to New York three times a year to attend board meetings. (When Freda accompanied him, the couple often stayed in Aileen Webb's Park Avenue apartment. While she liked Maloof, Mrs. Webb simply adored Freda.) The Southwest region encompassed California, Nevada, Arizona, New Mexico, and Hawaii (each state organization had its own chairman), and apart from annual general assemblies to discuss ways to promote crafts regionally and hear Maloof's reports on ACC matters, yearly conferences were held in different states featuring demonstrations, lectures, and exhibitions.

The national Council on the other hand, hosted biennial meetings in various regions to which all members were invited. But in the 1970s, the nationwide movement began to splinter into independent guilds or societies that were either geographically or medium-based. For example, in 1972 craftsmakers in the San Francisco Bay area formed the rather anarchic and communal Baulines Guild whose annual, roadside crafts fairs—virtual counter-culture circuses—attracted considerable public attention and sales.[68] (Woodworker Arthur Espenet Carpenter was among the leading members who helped instruct younger craftsmen.) But Maloof was "too darned busy" to join a guild, even a wood-working one. Moreover, he was disappointed to see the movement fragment into insular, media-related groups such as the Society of North American Goldsmiths and the National Council for Education in the Ceramic Arts.

When the Maloofs returned to Alta Loma from the Albuquerque meeting, they faced new developments on the workshop front. After only two years at Chaffey College, in the summer of 1969, Slimen decided to quit school and work full time for his father. He had virtually grown up in the shop: from the age of ten he applied the oil finish to new pieces and wove the leather thong seats of curved benches. Since the summer of 1967, he had been working part time as a paid employee, getting hands-on instruction from Larry White (fig. 135). Like his own father before him, Maloof had wanted his son to com-plete college. But it was the Age of Aquarius, and the call to "drop out" and "do your own thing" proved too strong for Slimen to resist. Initially, Maloof was upset by the decision, but Slimen argued that he was simply following in his footsteps. "Dad," he said, "you're the first hippie I ever met. You quit your job to do what you want without considering the financial consequences."

In the summer of 1969, another assistant joined the workshop team, Paul Vicente, a friend of Slimen's from Chaffey (fig. 136). One day Vicente had brought a stereo cabinet he was making to the workshop to use Slimen's finish-ing sander. Maloof was so impressed by the young man's workmanship that he invited him to join the shop. For his part, when Vicente encountered Maloof's work, he was stunned. "When I first saw his furniture," he later recalled, "I said aloud, 'This is the way furniture should be made. This is what I had in mind.' It was unbelievable. It was as if I had visions or ideas and here they were."[69] Yet another worker was added to the rolls at this time—Maloof's nephew, Nasif. Nasif had been living with Maloof and Freda since 1966, after his father, Maloof's brother Jack, died. The working relationship among the assistants was informal, but effective. Paid by the hour, the three new workers, all initially trained by White, tended to work haphazardly. But if one wasn't there, the others would be. But by the end of 1969, for personal reasons, Larry White decided to branch out on his own and left to set up his own independ-ent studio in Santa Cruz. (White's departure had an immediate impact: from 152 pieces in 1969, production dropped to 106 the following year.)

Six months after Vicente was hired, in 1970, Maloof was awarded the first grant in the Apprentice/Master Craftsman program of the Louis Comfort Tiffany Foundation. He had strong, if ambivalent, views on apprenticeship. For one thing, it was really much more efficient simply to hire an employee and train him to do specific tasks. "Let's face it," he has stated, "there are headaches: there are times when you wonder what on earth you are doing spending your time working with a young trainee. It takes so much energy."[70] But there were

Fig. 134 Shop mark used by Maloof from the late-1950s to 1971. Sam regularly employed this brand to sign his work before delivery to clients. It was placed out of sight—on the underside of seat frames and table tops, and in desk drawers.

Fig. 135 Slimen Maloof working in his father's shop, about 1966. In high school, Sammy began to use his great-grandfather's first name, Slimen (Solomon), to distinguish himself from his father.

compensations, especially when former assistants, like White, later established their independent reputations. From a moral point of view, as a successful craftsman, and one indebted to the ACC, he felt a strong obligation to share his professional insights with a younger generation. If that wisdom is not imparted, he argued, it would disappear. "What I know is available for the asking," he later wrote, "If nothing else, sharing my experience and knowledge may save a struggling craftsman hours of frustration . . . and give him time to deal with other matters. I think this is what life is all about: giving of yourself."[71]

Although many would-be woodworkers begged Maloof to be taken on for free, he insisted on paying his young workers the minimum wage; otherwise he would feel obligated to them. (After two years' employment, the biweekly check that Freda issued was then predicated on what the shop earned annually. But each man also received a small bonus for every piece of completed furniture on which he worked.)[72] Maloof was never interested in hiring trained assistants: "I prefer a young man who has not had experience. I would rather teach him my way of working than have him filled with ideas that he has gotten from an instructor in a school."[73] He also preached what he himself had practiced in Harold Graham's shop in the mid-1930s: "I tell him that I want him to always observe out of the corner of his eye, no matter what. If a young man is intent on learning, he will have eyes in the back of his head."[74]

A congenial working relationship was of prime importance and would remain a consistent condition throughout Maloof's changing workshops (fig. 137). "Compatibility and a sense of respect between the master and the apprentice is very important," Maloof has written. "If I do not respect the young person who works with me, and vice versa, the relationship is a failure from the start. This is the main criterion with which I select an apprentice. I am more concerned with him as a human being than what he has done in the past. If we are not compatible, then it does not matter how much knowledge or ability he may have. The workings of an apprenticeship should be like those of a happy marriage."[75] As had been the case at Vortox when he started in 1934, Maloof observed the character and personality of new assistants during a three-month probationary period, when they were put to work sweeping the floor, washing windows, and simple, repetitive sanding.

In the late 1960s and early 1970s, when the counterculture was at its height, woodworking was viewed by many individuals disenchanted with "the system" as a romantic and mystical way of life. Innumerable people—mature professionals, as well as young students—wrote beseeching letters or made a pilgrimage to Alta Loma, seeking to be inducted into what many considered the cult of woodworking. According to Maloof, during 1969–70, there wasn't "a week that two or three of them have not come to my shop. They usually say, 'I want to be a woodworker. Can you help me, or hire me?' I've had engineers and former teachers—not all of them art teachers, either—ask to be trained. They want to work with their hands." Freda noted: "Usually, young people want to come and they want to start right at the top. They want to start to design. They want to be woodworkers. And they think they can just jump in and do it."[76]

Maloof recalled one young, would-be woodworker who in 1971 had brazenly passed himself off at a job interview in Seattle as a former Maloof employee. The interviewer—a friend of Maloof's—was suspicious and called Maloof on the telephone to ask whether the young man standing in her office, Mark Singer, indeed had worked for him. "I never heard of him," was the answer, "Let me talk to him." "Well, I haven't worked for you yet," Singer said, "but I'm going to work for you. I'm coming down to Southern California and I'm going to camp on your doorstep until you hire me." "Please don't," Maloof replied wearily, "because I don't need anyone." Two weeks later, he showed up, a pack on his back. His brashness notwithstanding, Maloof took a liking to him and allowed him to stay at least for lunch. Later, after dinner, Maloof finally convinced him to leave, but he called once a month. His persistence paid off and in January 1973, he was hired. In the close quarters of the sanding room (a twenty-by-twenty-foot addition built onto the west end of the workshop), his personality caused considerable conflict. In fact, in May 1974, it led to Slimen's angry departure and shortly afterward to Nasif's leaving. Singer, too, soon left. Eventually, grateful for Maloof's forebearance over his youthful behavior, Singer established a reputation—and a fortune—as an entrepreneurial furniture manufacturer with factories in the Far East. With his father's help and blessing, in mid-1974 Slimen set up an independent studio in an old house on land Maloof had added on the western side of his original property. Although the son had quit the workshop, he had not left the grove and the compound still remained very much a family preserve and enterprise. Like their father before them, Slimen's children, Aaron and Amy Rebecca, grew up around Maloof's shop, while their mother worked closely with Freda. Since childhood, Maloof had prized family togetherness and to have three generations living in the oasis-like setting seemed idyllic.

First Major One-Man Show

On February 15, 1970, Sam's first major one-man show, *The Designer-Craftsman Furniture of Sam Maloof,* opened at the Museum of Art in Long Beach, then housed in a former mansion. Consisting of fifty pieces—a full array of forms—it was imaginatively installed in the ground floor rooms. Chairs, stools, and benches hung from the ceiling at odd angles by thin wires, while others were placed randomly on the floor (sometimes upside down). One chair was displayed in exploded, or disassembled form. However, tables, desks, chests, and music racks were displayed more conventionally. Museum staff had placed "Do Not Touch" signs on pieces, but Maloof insisted they be removed. He wanted visitors to handle his tactile creations.

The exhibit was highly popular, garnering a number of local press reports. The Long Beach *Independent-Press Telegram* declared that "if 'Designed by Sam Maloof' is burned into the base of some of your furniture, you not only have an exquisite piece of contemporary furniture but you may well have tomorrow's finest antiques." After citing various awards and honors—among them his appearance at the World's Fair—the writer described the family compound and noted how "working in all design media and having a good wife's approval" had given him the "daring" to devote his life to a creative—if not financially lucrative—business.

Maloof was quoted in the paper as saying that "good furniture must convey a feeling of function but also must be appealing to the eye." Moreover, he declared, "I never make conversation piece furniture . . . [and since] I'm not subject to the manufacturing syndrome, I don't have change for the sake of change. I just keep on improving."[77] His work caught the attention of Bernard Kester and Susan Peterson, Los Angeles correspondents for *Craft Horizons*:

California's master of handcrafted furniture . . . continued to present theme and variation of a relatively simple structural form, masterfully realized in subtle wood grain of oiled finish. . . . Chair leg, arm, and back blended effortlessly together through Maloof's beautiful joinery. Many of the pieces were shown to display their undersides, disclosing the clear resolve with which he concluded his forms. Table leaf hinges of wood became important sculptural details for a utilitarian concern. The spare line of the chair and seating unit disclosed Maloof's sense of disciplined form and his reserve for materials. Nothing in his work was self-conscious; nothing was experiment that had not been resolved.[78]

Although The Oakland Museum (which had recently acquired an Evans settee)[79] requested the Long Beach show, it did not travel and its impact beyond the Los Angeles area was slight. However, Maloof pieces were included in five other exhibitions in 1970, four in California and another in New Jersey—the ACC traveling show, *The Excellence of the Object.*

Teaching

Although Maloof previously had turned down teaching positions, in the spring of 1970, he officially taught a course to fill in for a friend on sabbatical leave.

Fig. 136 Sam Maloof and assistant Paul Vicente, 1978. Paul worked for Maloof from 1969 to 1978.

Fig. 137 Sam's workshop, 1981, from left to right: Mike O'Neil, Slimen, Spring, Maloof, Nasif Maloof, and Mike Johnson.

Design in Wood was part of the curriculum at California State University at Northridge. Treating it as a master class, he instructed the upper-level students individually, on a tutorial basis, setting them two practical problems: design a chair to be fabricated in six weeks and to be sold for $150 ensuring a reasonable profit; and design and construct a side table and chair. Every week he critiqued the group's work. The students were impressed by his business-like manner, focus, incisive observations—and skill. One wrote: "He amazed us all when he cut the arms of a chair [freehand] on the band saw. We were overwhelmed." (Nonetheless, he advised them against employing this unorthodox and dangerous method.) Another described him as "one of the truly powerful teachers I have ever had the joy to work with," while student-woodworker Joseph Bavaro recalled: "The attention that Sam gave to each piece of furniture has had a profound impact on how I deal with my own work."[80] By popular demand, Maloof agreed to repeat the classes in 1971 and 1972. Dextra Frankel, gallery director at California State University at Fullerton, summed up his influence—formal and informal—as a teacher: "He has made a remarkable impact on students of furniture design. His work has been the prime example for so many years for so many students, and his working life and the ability to make a living from his craft has encouraged students to do likewise—and at the same time make no compromises in aesthetic ideals."[81]

In July 1970, Maloof gave the first of six annual, three-week workshops at the Penland School of Crafts in North Carolina. (His legendary series of summer workshops at the Anderson Ranch Arts Center near Aspen, Colorado, began in 1975.) The school could only pay transportation costs and room and board, but Maloof had met the director, liked the seriousness of the summer program, and thought it would be fun for him to spend time with Freda in the rugged Appalachian setting. Moreover, as a successful furniture craftsman, he felt obligated to pass on his knowledge and experience, even to amateurs of all ages and walks of life. His charismatic personality, openness, and willingness to share fully made a deep impact on both students and fellow staff and for years he maintained contact with them. In the 1970s Maloof also "instructed" individuals who dropped by his workshop unannounced and asked questions while watching him work. "I have people who come all the time," he explained, "I feel if they've taken the time to drive out this far, then I can take a little time to talk with them."[82]

California Design XI

In the spring of 1971 Eudora Moore staged the last of the series of triennial *California Design* shows. (The 1974 version was an historical exhibit, *California Design 1910,* for the first time disclosing an earlier manifestation of the designer-craftsman movement in the Golden State.) The eleventh and final craft and product display was held in the spacious new wing of the Pasadena Art Museum and included 350 pieces selected from six thousand submissions. Proving to be the most popular of the series, on opening day some 4,300 visitors showed up, while during its six-week run, it attracted over 70,000 exhibition-goers. But the mix of half unique, handcrafted pieces and half mass-produced designs—suitable in the early, trend-setting days of the program—was no longer viable.

Avant garde *Artweek* described *California Design XI* as a "safe" show, with too much attention devoted to manufactured goods and to work in plastic. Revealing the tenor of the times, among the craft items on display, the reviewer lamented the absence of "irreverent, erotic, anti-establishment, and protest art."[83] Ceramics professor Susan Peterson reviewed the show for *Craft Horizons* and concluded that "our work *is* at a crossroads," for ambiguity and conflict reigned. "One finds," she wrote, "a current state of flux, to say the least, in the mood of California craft—out from Pop, into Pop, it's too straight, where is Funk, the conceptual enters and struggles to go, size and scale, miniature, minimal. Is it art, can it be? Sure, some day. Yes, some pieces, by some people."[84]

The showstopper was a sculptural doorway by Duane Brown. The design was a complicated motif—an enormous, three-dimensional floral element—composed of Fiberglas-covered shapes carved from foam rubber. Intertwined when the door was closed, the "petals" unlocked like a giant puzzle when opened. (At the time, Maloof's friend, furniture designer Kipp Stewart, was also experimenting with plastic-coated, shaped foam sculpture.) Another far-out piece was a "womb-room" by Jack Hopkins. Categorized as "environmental furniture," Peterson described the unique construction in *Craft Horizons* as "hideous in statement."[85] But it was overshadowed by displays of more traditional wooden furniture. In fact, Maloof's success had sparked a number of local imitators and followers from whom less observant clients sometimes ordered "Maloof" pieces.

From Peterson's point of view, two furniture designers dominated *California Design XI:* "There's no better way to make chairs and desks of wood, than lovingly, the way that Sam Maloof does," she wrote, "nor the for-production without-peer way Charles Eames does, and both men, represented here, are indicative of the most elevated possible concepts in furniture. After these guys come everybody else."[86] Later in the year, area residents were able to test her conclusions about his achievement in a fifteen-piece exhibition, *Sam Maloof: Contemporary Furniture,* organized by the Edward-Dean Museum of Decorative Arts in Riverside, California. Among the more complex designs on display were a music rack, dictionary stand, and rocking chair. As always in his work, aesthetics and serviceability were perfectly balanced. As Maloof himself stated to a reporter in November 1971, when lecturing in Hawaii: "If any arts have lasting beauty, they must certainly exist in utilitarian objects created by people aware of the materials, forms, and colors, and surfaces that please the eye and the body—and consequently live on through the years, growing more mellow and beautiful as time passes."[87]

Woodenworks

In 1971 Sam Maloof had been invited by Lloyd Herman, administrator of the soon-to-open Renwick Gallery at the Smithsonian Institution in Washington, D.C., a new federal museum dedicated to showcasing American design and craftsmanship, both past and present, to participate in a landmark exhibition,

Woodenworks: Furniture Objects by Five Craftsmen. Co-organized by the Minnesota Museum of Art in St. Paul, the show was to be one of eight inaugural displays in the recently restored historic edifice, the original home of the Corcoran Gallery of Art.[88] To reveal a variety of approaches to studio furniture making, Herman had also selected Wharton Esherick, George Nakashima, Arthur Espenet Carpenter, and Wendell Castle. Except for the recently deceased Esherick, whose works were selected from his estate, each was asked to contribute ten pieces representative of their production over the years.

Maloof fabricated an entire suite of pieces, promising them all to Freda once the exhibition ended: a rocking chair with turned spindles and a stretcher system, but with a novel, all-wood seat; a tall occasional chair with a new form of sculptural spindle, one with a flat face, rounded back, and curved profile; a round, drop-leaf table and "steer" horn chair; a shoe bench with strongly modeled, integral handles; a double music rack; a vertical desk with a lift top; and a reprise of the original sculpted-back dining chair design (figs. 138–143). Instead of using his well-known brand mark, he manually inscribed each piece with his name, the year, and "Renwick Gallery" using an electric burning pen that Bob Stocksdale had recently given him. Once he mastered the technique— and he employed the pen for the rest of his career, numbering pieces sequentially each year—his inscriptions clearly demonstrated the calligraphic skills he had developed in high school (fig. 144).

On January 26, 1972, Maloof and Freda attended an opening reception for both the Renwick Gallery and *Woodenworks*. The second of three such soirees, it was an elegant affair. The invitees—Washington notables, museum officials from across the nation, cultural attaches from local embassies, as well as artists and designers—were attired in formal evening dress. As his guests, Maloof had

Fig. 138 Rocking chair, 1971. The rocker was among his first chairs to have a solid wood seat, made from a single plank of walnut, saddle-shaped to fit the sitter's anatomy.

Fig. 139 Occasional chair, 1971. A new type of spindle represented not only a therapeutic, but an artistic advance.

Fig. 140 Drop-leaf pedestal table and "steer-horn" chair with low, round arms, 1971.

Fig. 141 Shoe bench with drawers and carved handles, 1971.

Fig. 142 Lift-top desk with drawers and cabinets, 1971. Maloof made ten pieces especially for the landmark 1972 exhibition, *Woodenworks,* at the Smithsonian American Art Museum's Renwick Gallery.

invited early clients, the Langens from Greenwich, Connecticut, plus ten of his recent summer workshop students from Penland. Prior to the reception, they all crowded into the small Washington apartment of another young woodworking friend where they would stay the night.

Their host drove Maloof and Freda to the reception in his battered Volkswagen Beetle. Both doors were broken and had to be wired shut from the outside, so when they reached their destination, to the surprise of other arriving guests, the driver slid out of his open window onto the street to untie the passenger side door to allow the Maloofs to disembark. As usual, the nonconformist Maloof had refused to wear a shirt and tie, and as he mounted the grand stairway to the special dinner for the exhibitors and museum officials in a side gallery on the second floor, Freda was mortified to see a visible rip in the pants of his unpressed corduroy suit. (Since Nakashima refused to attend—explaining he was allergic to black tie gatherings—and Carpenter remained in California, the tuxedo-clad Castle was the only other woodworker to dine with Maloof.)

At dinner, Maloof was seated next to Mrs. Dillon Ripley, the wife of the Secretary of the Smithsonian who was hosting the event. The menu included Cornish game hen *roti* Corcoran, *haricots verts* Taylor (named after SAAM director, Joshua Taylor), and *mousse au chocolat* Ripley. The room was airless, the heat almost unbearable, and the other men, dressed in tuxedos, perspired. Mrs. Ripley, dressed in cool chiffon, declared Maloof, attired in his loose-fitting cotton suit and turtle neck shirt, the most comfortable looking of all. Afterward, the twenty-four dinner guests filed into the Grand Salon, newly decorated in High Victorian style and crowded with guests sipping champagne while a harpist played in the background. Dressed in boots, patched jeans, and

Fig. 143 Low-back dining chair with round arms, 1971. Walnut and leather; 30 ¼ x 20 ¾ x 19 ¼ inches; inscribed "No. 82 OCTOBER 1971/RENWICK .SMITHSONIAN/SAM MALOOF"; Sam and Alfreda Maloof Foundation. This low-back chair was a reprise of Maloof's original, 1952 dining chair and was one of the first pieces of Maloof furniture to be signed, numbered, and dated using an electric burning pen.

Fig. 144 Sam Maloof inscribing a chair frame, 1982. In a cursive script, each completed piece was marked with its chronological number within a given calendar year and the woodworker's name. In 1977 he began to include the initials of his employees who had also worked on the piece. Reproduction by permission of Jonathan Pollock.

bandannas, Maloof's incongruous, long-haired group of former Penland students let out a collective cheer when their proud teacher strode into the room.

The show was highly popular, helping to attract crowds of visitors to the new facility. (Eight thousand showed up on the first Sunday the Renwick was open.) Largely ignorant of the studio furniture movement, local audiences found the custom pieces on display exciting, and Maloof received numerous letters requesting copies (prices were available at the front desk) and others expressing heart-felt admiration for his work. In retrospect, the display was essentially conservative, revealing well-established trends in studio furniture making and—Castle's stack-laminated pieces notwithstanding—conventional approaches to materials and joinery. One local reviewer remarked that Castle's fanciful, abstract shapes reminded visitors of literal forms. A carved, free-form cherry table, she wrote, seemed to many to be "resting on the bodies of huge writhing slugs," while a large, lidded jar looked like an elephant foot topped by an "impacted wisdom tooth." Maloof's more traditional designs, on the other hand, were reported to appear much like the kind of modern furniture one might find in a high-end, retail store.[89]

In California, the Cucamonga *Times* proudly informed Maloof's neighbors that with the Smithsonian show, he had reached "the big time." The woodworker, the reporter noted, could himself be considered "a hippie," since twenty-five years earlier, he had left a good job to do what he wanted to do. For his part, Maloof reported that many young people likewise were currently "turning back to the 'blue collar' jobs where they can actually use their hands." It was not just a "fad," he added; they were "serious." However, he continued, a woodworker needed more than a hammer and a saw to become a cabinetmaker; he had to see the entire process through, from start to finish. The best way to learn the trade was not through college programs, but rather during hands-on apprenticeships. While anyone could learn to use machinery, design, on the other hand, could not be taught; it had to come "from within." "Either you have it, or you don't," Maloof cautioned the readers, "you can't teach it." Looking at his own designs in *Woodenworks,* Maloof was pleased to report that they had held up over the years, and still "looked good."[90] The local newspaper printed several photographs, including one of Maloof sitting on an early spindle-back bench with a copy of *Objects: USA* on the seat beside him.

In a short review of the show, *Craft Horizons* noted it focused on the modern use of traditional materials and skills, and, contrasting the work of different individuals, presented a variety of solutions to problems in furniture design. While the correspondent was pleased by the "surprise and delight" of Washington visitors to the tactile qualities of the smooth-edged work on display, she was also distressed by their unbridled enthusiasm: it "reinforced a realization of how really few Americans are aware of such craftsmen's existence in our country."[91] In terms of written explanations, the writer was gratified that the organizers had allowed the participants to express in their own words their individual philosophies of woodworking, both in wall panels and in the exhibition book.

Like the lavish publication for *Objects: USA,* the heavily illustrated *Woodenworks* catalogue—which soon sold out—included candid photos of the participants, descriptive biographies, detailed resumes, and a series of personal commentaries. Esherick was quoted on his initial impetus to build furniture: "I was impatient with the contemporary furniture being made [in the 1930s]— straight lines, sharp edges, and right angles—and I conceived free angles and free forms; making the edges of my tables flow so that they would be attractive to feel or caress." For his part, Nakashima stated that craftsmanship "is not only a creative force, but a moral idea . . . design is only something [with which] to realize a way of life."

One of Carpenter's quotes affirmed his sincere belief in the utilitarian basis of crafts: "I don't think there's any need for the crafts to pretend they are doing more than making beautiful things for function. There's no need for us to make a chair that you can't sit in. There are many craftsmen that do make chairs that you can't sit in, and that's all right, but you sell it as a sculpture, you don't sell it as a chair. You sell it as an idea of form." Castle was quoted on the subject of his decidedly sculptural, yet still serviceable seating: "I feel my chairs are comfortable even though I don't spend a lot of time thinking about that part of it. . . . I spend more time thinking about how I am going to suspend this thing in air to hold a person."[92]

In Maloof's case, the editors found it difficult to discover unpublished quotes, for over the years he had repeatedly refined a series of well-known, summary statements. However, they located several, less familiar ones in the transcription of an interview Maloof taped in June 1970, with Glenn Loney, a Brooklyn drama professor and former client, that had been the basis for an article Loney had written for *Craft Horizons* in August 1971.[93] They mostly referred to the stimulus behind the inauguration of new designs, including the music rack and the cradle hutch.

Flat Spindles, Wooden Seats, Half-lap Joints, and Hard Lines

Two of Maloof's pieces in *Woodenworks* featured important recent advances in design. The unusual, flat spindle employed on the occasional arm chair had been introduced in late 1970. Like many of his inventions, its genesis was purely practical.[94] A client, plagued with lower back problems, had asked him to make her a tall-back chair with special lumbar support. He agreed, but instead of first sketching a shape on paper, he had gone directly to the band saw and free-hand cut from a piece of stock a long slat whose profile was a gentle S-curve. The compound curve was based on pure intuition and experience, not Henry Dreyfuss's new science of ergonomics. (The latter was formally codified in the *Humanscale* seating guide, whose rotating dial provided designers with precise height, depth, and angle measurements for a full range of chair types to suit people of large, average, or small builds.)

Since he always used his own body as a universal model, Maloof simply sat down and positioned the bowed form against the small of his back to judge the therapeutic value of the spindle. Satisfied with how it felt, he made a template from it and fabricated a set of seven curved spindles with flat faces, inserting them in an existing chair design. From the front they looked like arrow back slats on traditional Windsor chairs. But he fashioned them in a much

Fig. 145 Front view of flat spindles on an occasional arm chair, 1984. The flat, curved spindles introduced in late 1970 provide excellent back support, matching the compound curve of the spine.

Fig. 146 Workshop photograph, 1978. Maloof is seen adjusting the angle of a set of flat spindles at the back of a chair seat during the fabrication process. Reproduction by permission of Jonathan Pollock.

more sculptural manner, rounding the sides and backs of the thick supports for the area of the lower back and tapering the ends where they joined the seat and crest rail (figs. 145 and 146).

In a later interview, Jonathan Fairbanks queried him about the new spindle: "Didn't you try it against her back to see if it was going to suit her?" Maloof replied: "No, just my back. That's the way I design, Jonathan. I just do it by feel and by eye."[95] The invention proved so visually attractive and comfortable that he soon adapted it for most of his tall-back chairs, including rockers. The first of the latter to be ordered with flat spindles was completed in March 1971. The precise curvature of the slats—and their alignment along the rear of the

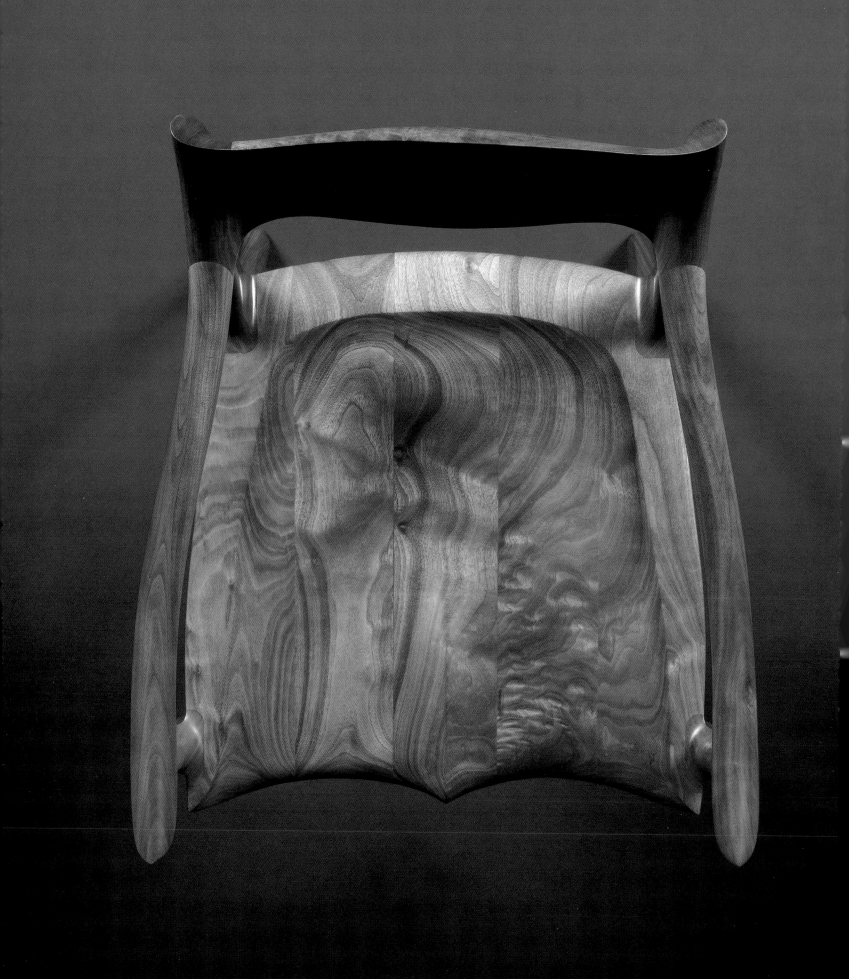

seat—were adjusted according to the height or tilt of the chair back. But in each case, it proved a therapeutic advance, as well as an aesthetic one. Slowly, less comfortable straight spindles began to disappear.

Although the slats on the rocking chair in *Woodenworks* were turned ones, its contoured, all-wood seat was a recent innovation, dating from September 1970. Although wooden seats had long been commonplace in chairs by Nakashima, Carpenter, and Castle, in Maloof's case they were novelties. For twenty years, he had inserted upholstered seats into wood frames, fixing them to corner blocks. Maloof's early wooden seats were relatively thin planks with supportive saddle-shaped surfaces to which legs were attached using his conventional joinery. But by the mid-1970s, Maloof had increased the seats' thickness and sculptural character by fashioning them from five separate pieces of wood whose edges, glued and doweled together, were cut at slight angles to create a subtle curvature. The more solid seats, with their deeper, sculpted saddles and front, bandsawn cutouts for thighs (fig. 147) assisted in the development in 1974 of Maloof's inventive half-lap, or dado-rabbet joint that structurally integrated legs and seats into a strong, seamless, and sculpturally pleasing unit.[96] The precise origin of his signature-style joint is obscure, but in 1973 Slimen had experimented with a deep-set dado join on a wood seat rocking chair he had designed, and Maloof himself had already begun to strengthen his conventional leg joinery with an integral, connecting device. But the new feature was not fully developed until 1975 (figs. 148 and 149).

Both the rocking and occasional chairs in *Woodenworks* also included new surface design features—emphatic ridges that Maloof termed "hard lines." The hard line had originated accidentally. Sometime in the late 1960s, Maloof was working on an Evans chair, shaping the area where the inside of the back leg met the crest rail. Pressing hard on his gouge, he cut too deeply, creating a trough in what was otherwise to be a gently rounded zone.[97] Running his thumb over the unintentional edge, he liked the feel of it and instead of smoothing it out, he deepened and extended the short declivity so that it suggested the curl of a wave, repeating it on the opposite side. Visually, it accented the join and added greatly to its tactile qualities. The concave swirl soon appeared in similar places on the backs of other chair models—including rockers—becoming an increasingly emphatic, evolutionary feature that even appeared on spindles (figs. 150 and 151).

In the early 1970s, the hard line began to extend down the back leg from the crest rail to the seat and to appear on the front in two places—where the arms met the back post and along the sides of low arms and underneath, meeting at a point at the tip (figs. 152–154). It had no practical purpose; it was purely aesthetic, providing a delightful, palpable contrast with soft, adjacent half-round shapes. Eventually, like a continuous line drawing, it would run throughout a chair, traceable with fingers along the arms, up and down the legs, across the seat front and the top of the back support. Indeed, as he worked on rough shaping an assembled chair, Maloof often sketched it on the bare wood. Serendipitously, the original error had turned into a positive feature, one that accented the subtle, sculptural quality of his furniture and demonstrated the

Fig. 147 Low-back chair seen from above. The varied grain patterns in the separate pieces of walnut that comprise the wooden seat make this example from 1987 visually dramatic. See fig. 121.

difference between the designer-craftsman's workmanship of "risk" and that of the factory worker's machine-based industrial certainty.

World Crafts Council 1972

In August 1972, the Maloofs traveled from Alta Loma to Istanbul to attend the general assembly and conference of the World Crafts Council. Maloof had been appointed head of the American section of the wcc and he was among seventy-three craftsmen from the United States (the largest national contingent) to make the overseas trip. The celebrated English woodworker John Makepeace was among the 240 conferees from thirty-nine countries and Maloof was delighted to meet him. Years later they would collaborate on a book project. Aside from the formal meetings and media sessions, the Maloofs enjoyed the local tourist attractions, visiting the Grand Bazaar, Topkapi Palace, the Blue Mosque, and Hagia Sophia, whose scintillating mosaics reminded him of Millard Sheets's own architectural wall decorations. *Craft Horizons* later published a group photograph of American craftsmen and their spouses during an organized yacht cruise on the Sea of Marmora. Sam and Freda were joined on this trip by California friends Paul and Virginia Soldner, among others. The magazine also noted that after the conference, many of the Americans traveled further afield, Paul J. Smith to North African destinations and Rose Slivka to Athens.

The Maloofs had intended to go east, to Iran, and then back to Israel. But Jack Lenor Larsen invited them and San Francisco jeweler, Ramona Solberg, to join him and a friend from Paris on a ten-day odyssey in Afghanistan and Maloof and Freda agreed. They stopped first in Tehran where Maloof wanted to contact the men with whom he had worked during the ICA project in 1959. There was a cholera scare at the time and the authorities at the airport insisted arriving travelers take pills to ward off the disease. At the hotel, in reaction to the drug, Freda became deathly ill, but the crisis fortunately soon passed without lingering effects and the group traveled on to Isfahan, Shiraz, and Persepolis. When they flew into Kabul, Maloof thought that Afghanistan looked like New Mexico, but he was shocked at the poverty of rural people and couldn't really enjoy the countryside through which they journeyed by Land Rover. Writing later to potter Bob Turner, he commented: "It makes one want to cry out at the stupidity of our country where we know the cost of the bombs we drop [on Vietnam] in one week would feed a country such as Afghanistan."[98] Maloof vigorously opposed the war in Southeast Asia and during Richard Nixon's second inauguration ceremonies in late January 1973, he had planned to join an antiwar protest. But while jurying a show in Philadelphia he became ill and had to return home.

Clients and Commissions, 1962–1973

While exhibition reviews and press reports provide the most visible evidence of Maloof's activities during this period of expansion, lesser known commissions from homeowners and organizations daily sustained the workshop. In the early 1960s, Maloof received several substantial orders for ecclesiastical furnishings, presenting the woodworker with unprecedented design challenges. Constructed in a modern architectural style, new Los Angeles-area churches and synagogues of the time required non-traditional liturgical and other furniture to coordinate with their unadorned soaring wood, stone, or glass-walled interiors.

In 1962, the year of *California Design 8,* Covenant Presbyterian Church in Inglewood requested a set of cherry chancel furniture—a communion table, pulpit, chairs, and benches, as well as designs for pews to seat 450 worshippers. The same year, the architectural firm, Victor Gruen and Associates, ordered furnishings in walnut for the new Leo Baeck Temple in Beverly Hills. It was a large order: lecterns for rabbi and cantor, choir stools, reading table, and six upholstered chairs for the bima, plus fifty-two pews and 358 individual upholstered seating units. To manufacture the pews and seating he designed for both institutions, Maloof subcontracted the work to a commercial cabinetmaker, Stanislaus Mill and Manufacturing of Anaheim.

Fig. 148 Dado-rabbet leg joint during fabrication process, 1979. Sam perfected this interlocking, socket-like joint during 1974. Glued and fitted together, it was made more secure by inserting a screw through the leg into the solid seat. An ebony plug then covered the hole, adding a decorative accent. Reproduction by permission of Jonathan Pollock.

Fig. 149 Finished dado-rabbet joint on a low-back chair, 1981. Reproduction by permission of Jonathan Pollock.

Mr. and Mrs. Irving Stone were members of the temple, and in 1962 approached Maloof to design furniture for their new Beverly Hills home. After discussing the couple's needs, he drew up plans that he presented one evening. But the wife of the wealthy, best-selling novelist expressed such shock at the price he quoted, that he angrily rolled up his drawings and left—only to be stopped at his car door by a now-soothing Mrs. Stone. The celebrity commission proved to be a welcome one, garnering him important media attention. The Stones wanted two sets of walnut dining room furniture for adjoining spaces, one more formal than the other—plus a breakfront cabinet and bookshelves.

The "informal" dining table was a so-called "square round," pedestal model measuring fifty by fifty inches (to which a twenty-inch, extra leaf could be added); the chairs were tall, spindle-back models with low arms. For the adjacent area dining area, Maloof made a long rectangular table to accommodate eight upholstered chairs with low arms and sculpted crest rails. According to the *Los Angeles Times* Home magazine, which featured the interior of the home, Maloof and Mrs. Stone collaborated on the "finely-tuned, high-keyed" color scheme.[99] At the time, Southern California decorators preferred strong, citrus tones, and yellow and orange dominated the eleven-foot-high, terrazzo-floored principal rooms. For the upholstery, Maloof selected a bright yellow wool fabric by Knoll with a textured weave. Once decorated, the residence was featured on a tour of architect-designed homes by the regional chapter of the American Institute of Architects (AIA), further advertising Maloof's furniture to a discriminating audience.

In 1964, the year he exhibited at the World's Fair, Maloof was asked to design furniture for the sanctuary of the Sun Valley Community Methodist Church. It was a challenging commission. While the budget was limited, there were no restrictions on design. After sketching ideas and making small wooden models to judge their effectiveness, Maloof produced a simple lectern, a daring architectural pulpit (fig. 155), and an unusual altar and communion rail. Believing that the cross should be the "Christ-centered hub of the church," he created an elemental, fourteen-foot version which rose dramatically out of the middle

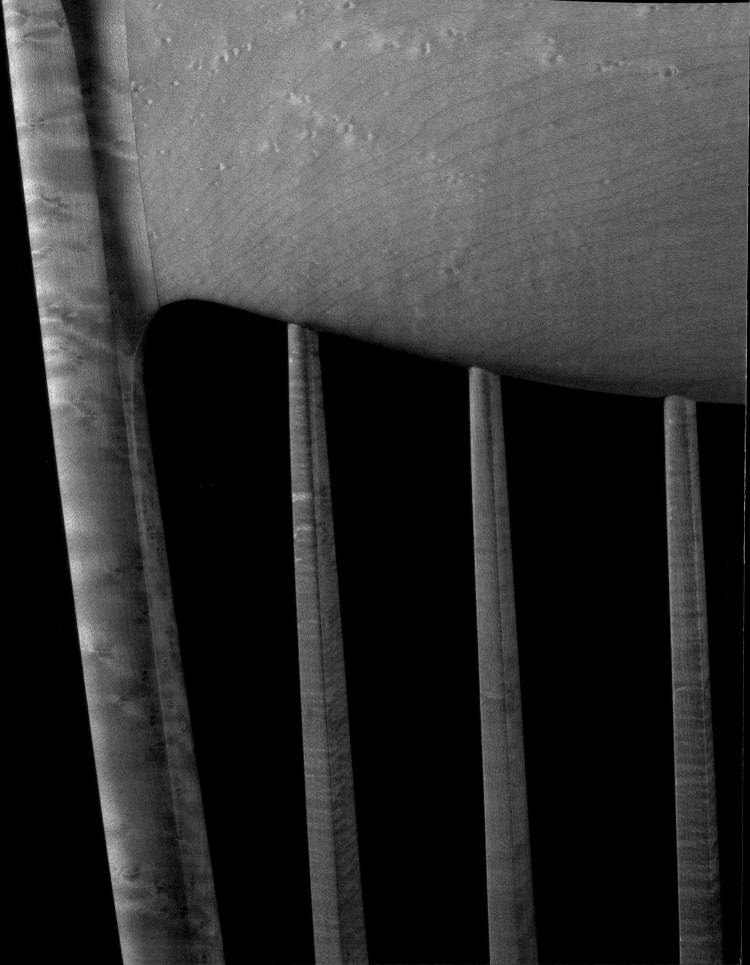

Fig. 150 Occasional chair seen from the back. Dating from 1984, this fiddleback maple chair reveals Maloof's increasingly sophisticated use of the sculptural "hard line." The sharp ridge swirls around the tip of the headrest and then drops straight down the narrow back post. Another hard line emerges out of the soft curve where the bottom of the headrest is faired, or smoothed into the back post. The defined line also appears on the tapered spindles, turning them into four-sided forms. See fig. 179.

of a round altar that, inventively, was completely encircled by a simple communion rail. The commission later earned him a craftsmanship award from the Pasadena AIA chapter.

In the secular world, in 1966 he designed a suite of furniture for the executive lounge and reception area of Interpace Corporation in Parsippany, New Jersey—sofas, side and coffee tables, wood screens, a dining table and twelve chairs, and a wall-mounted buffet. Millard Sheets had planned the firm's new offices and recommended his one-time assistant, now a national celebrity with the World's Fair display behind him. In the mid-1960s, for the reception areas of major corporations, interior designers generally ordered reproductions of classic steel and leather pieces by Bauhaus designers or simple, block-like upholstered seating. However, the president of Interpace wanted all-wood furniture. At the outset, he had asked Maloof to make several pieces out of rare woods, but Maloof resisted. "I would prefer to use exotic woods for contrast rather than to design something that is contrary to my way of thinking and working," he wrote.[100] Although he rarely assented to mixing woods, he inset several Interpace pieces with Carpathian burl and another with rosewood and ebony.

Two years later, a local institution, Claremont Men's College, ordered a large conference table and twenty chairs with sculpted arms and black leather upholstery for its board room, as well as a suite of furniture for the lounge. The finished table proved so heavy that it took eighteen men to carry it upstairs, and when it was pushed along the carpeted hall through the board room door, it left an indentation that was still visible more than twenty years later.

On a lighter note, in 1969, among the 152 pieces he fabricated that year was the first of a series of twenty-eight, straight-backed rocking chairs that were presented to retiring members of the Los Angeles chapter of the Young President's Organization. The idea was the brainchild of Robert Dickerman, then chairman of the under-forty group of business leaders and a private Maloof client. For his own home, Dickerman ordered a massive, twelve-foot-long dining table requiring three pedestal supports, plus ten matching dining chairs with hornlike, vertical extensions (similar to those on rocking chairs), and a long sideboard—all in solid English brown oak, a rare and expensive material. Other major clients of the time included Harry and Lynn Altman of Beverly Hills for whom in 1969 Maloof likewise made an elegant dining room set for their new California-style home, as well as pedestal and side tables, chests, and chairs—but all in walnut.

In 1972 Maloof created a one-of-a-kind chair in rosewood. It was a rare instance in his work of a unique design. The client was Jan Hlinka, principal violist for the Los Angeles Philharmonic Orchestra. The musician had appeared at the workshop unannounced one day, explaining to Maloof that a mutual friend had promised for years to bring him by the grove, but since he hadn't, he had taken the initiative—and could Maloof please make him a special musician's practice chair and a double music rack in Brazilian rosewood.[101] Since he had to sit upright, he needed a seat with good lower back support that would neither restrict his arm movements, nor his ability to spread his knees or move his hips while he played.

Fig. 151 "Hard line" on the back of a head rest. After 1969, sculpted ridges on otherwise smooth surfaces became a distinguishing features of a Maloof chair. Reproduction by permission of Jonathan Pollock.

Fig. 152 Side view of low-back chair, about 1982. The hard line developed along the outer edge of the arm flows into the sculptured curve and then down the back leg to converge with the sharp edge of the seat. Reproduction by permission of Jonathan Pollock.

Fig. 153 Outside view of unfinished chair arm with hard lines marked, about 1982. Maloof marks the placement of the hard lines. Shop assistants then begin the laborious process of fairing the join and shaping the hard line. Reproduction by permission of Jonathan Pollock.

Fig. 154 Outside view of low-back chair arm, about 1982. Like the ridge of a wind-eroded sand dune, the hard line defining the inner edge of the ovoid arm mounts to the tip. Reproduction by permission of Jonathan Pollock.

After considering the practical problems, Maloof developed a design based on a simple folding chair that incorporated the low, carved back rest of an Evans chair (fig. 156). The legs, like those of a metal folding chair, were arranged in a triangular fashion. It was an early example of an all wood chair; the seat a solid piece of contoured rosewood. Both Maloof and Slimen worked on it and when finished, Hlinka insisted it be signed with both their names. The inscription, engraved with the burning pen, reads: "No. 71 December 1972/ For Jan Hlinka/Sam Maloof/and/Slimen Maloof." Two years later, at the musician's request, a storage chest for sheet music was added. After Hlinka's death, his widow, recognizing the importance of the pieces, returned them to Maloof.

In January 1973, the month *Woodenworks* opened, Los Angeles businessman John C. Elliott (a financial backer of *Art & Architecture* magazine under John Entenza's editorship) commissioned Maloof to make forty pieces of furniture for his Hawaiian residence, Muolea, on Maui. The extensive order included a wide variety of designs, some in teak and rosewood, but most in walnut, for dining, living, and bedrooms—standard pieces from his repertoire, but also new wall and floor lamps, and a custom radio/hi-fi cabinet. That same month, former clients from Corona del Mar, Mr. and Mrs. Edker Pope, visited the Maloof home on a Sunday afternoon, quietly admired the furniture and collections, and when leaving, placed an order for a rosewood rocking chair. Later that evening, they telephoned with an unusual request—would Maloof consider making an entire houseful of furniture in rosewood for them?

A year later, Maloof shipped forty-three pieces in Brazilian and East Indian rosewood (purchased through his major local supplier, Penberthy Lumber Company) to the Pope's dramatic, seaside residence, including a unique oval, 40 by 72 inch dining table. Another, rectangular dining table measured 44 by 72 inches. But when it was finished, the scale didn't look right, so he made another top that, at 39 by 74 inches, satisfied his innate sense of "rightness." He also created a set of six novel bar stools, small-scaled Evans chairs with long legs, curved arms, and tactile hard lines, along with a one-of-a-kind piece—an upholstered chaise lounge. But while he liked the rich color and graining of rosewood, he didn't enjoy working with the material—he was allergic to the fine dust it produced. Neither the workshop's exhaust fans, nor a breathing mask could keep it out of his lungs.

In early June 1973, after returning from the seventh national ACC conference in Fort Collins, Colorado (where Maloof and Wendell Castle conducted separate workshops) and traveling through "Indian country" with the Turners, the Maloofs celebrated their twenty-fifth wedding anniversary. (While they were away, KCET public television station aired a color film, *Sam Maloof—Woodworker*, produced and directed by station manager Maynard Orme. Among other subjects the film documented the construction of a cradle hutch.) In their parents' honor, Slimen and Marilou organized a surprise party with three hundred guests and a live band playing Middle Eastern music. Intrigued by the event, the Cucamonga *Times* later sent a reporter over to the house to interview Sam.

"Known to the world, but a secret in his own community," the writer began, "who would guess that tucked in the midst of a six-acre lemon grove on

Highland Avenue lies Maloof's creations—the show place home (which has become a regular feature in the *Los Angeles Times* Home magazine) and his exquisite furniture." Entering the Maloof "environment" was a "total experience," she continued, for the "cloistered home" was like an "oasis," totally sheltered and separate from "the rest of the world." The woodworker admitted that from the outset, he had a "total conception" of what he wanted to achieve with the meandering design, simply adding a room when so "motivated." Filled with his furniture and Indian crafts (together, the subject of an exhibition in March of that year at the Chaffey College museum and gallery), the residence was "famous among artists and designers," if not his neighbors.[102]

Almost a year later, the Maloof house and compound was the subject of another journalistic treatment, this time in an article he himself authored for *Perfect Home* magazine. It was a paen to the craftsman lifestyle. "We live and have our workshop in a quiet lemon grove with a house that cannot be seen from the side of the road," he wrote.

A tall stand of eucalyptus trees runs across the front entrance. We like the good earth and I take care of the five hundred lemon trees and my wife, Alfreda, spends much of the time in her garden. . . . Our house of glass and wood is close to the earth, and I continue to add rooms when we feel it needs expanding and our furniture overflows and we begin to feel crowded. We have filled it with paintings by artists who are friends and we have ceramics by California potters in every room. We like to visit Indian country in the Southwest and have brought back mementoes from those trips. I suppose the house represents a great deal of creative energy. . . . There is a sense of security in living on the land, and while you may not make as much money as others feel they need, there are other needs which are satisfied. But you have to seek these things out; it takes time. After twenty-five years, I know now, as I believed long ago, that the very best way to live is doing something you love, in the surroundings you built for yourself and your family.[103]

In Praise of Hands

Maloof moved effortlessly not only between his adjacent shop and home, but between his Alta Loma oasis and the wider world. During the second week of June 1974, he and Freda traveled to Toronto, Canada, to attend the biennial conference of the World Crafts Council held at York University. Among twelve hundred conferees from fifty-six member countries celebrating the tenth anniversary of the founding of the wcc (the Australian contingent was the largest), the Maloofs shared a simple dormitory room, as they had at Columbia University in 1964. At the general assembly, their friend Aileen Webb, now eighty-two years old, resigned her presidency of the world body, handing over her duties to Lord Eccles, responsible for establishing Britain's Crafts Advisory Council. During the ceremony, he exclaimed to the packed audience: "What a patron saint, you've had!" But for her part, Webb wanted simply to be viewed as the movement's "grandmother, with all of the pleasures, and none of the responsibilities." Along with the other delegates, she attended workshops and demonstrations, watched craft films, and listened to lectures and presentations. Maloof gave a talk on his furniture and participated in the half-day, general North American workshop in which one thousand conferees joyfully "got to work and did things with their hands."[104]

The First World Crafts Exhibition, *In Praise of Hands,* was installed concurrently at the nearby Ontario Science Center. The culmination of three years of planning, the epoch-making show (a wide-ranging display of six hundred

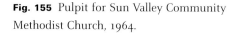

Fig. 155 Pulpit for Sun Valley Community Methodist Church, 1964.

objects from fifty countries, all made since 1970) was intended to be "a panorama of the world's crafts as they are practiced today in the largest metropolitan centers and the smallest, remote villages."[105] While craftsmen belonged to one universal family, organizers recognized they nonetheless were divided into two separate branches: those from the developing world and those from industrialized societies.

To organize the bewildering diversity of handmade objects (ranging from traditional New Hebridean dance headdresses to Harvey Littleton's latest, hotworked glass sculptures), they were grouped thematically in the exhibit: apparel and adornment; the home; utility and embellishment; play; and ritual and celebration. Sam Maloof, one of three Americans exhibiting in the eleven-piece seating subsection of the home (the others were Wendell Castle and Jon Brooks), contributed a new walnut rocking chair combining the new flat spindles and plank seat, but retaining the stretchers. During the three months the extraordinary display was on view in suburban Toronto, more than 750,000 visitors passed through it, seeming to confirm the assertion by wcc secretary general, James S. Plaut, that "the world appetite for crafts is at present insatiable."[106]

The lavish exhibition catalogue, *In Praise of Hands: Contemporary Crafts of the World,* reproduced Maloof's latest rocker and contained essays by Plaut and philosopher Octavio Paz, both exalting the creative use of the hand in the face of the increasing industrialization of work. Plaut noted that youth in the developed, Western countries had rebelled against the dehumanization fostered by technology and automation. "Dropping out" of their mechanized society, they had rediscovered the virtues of life before industrialization—living independently off the land, shaping their own environment, and reasserting handcraftsmanship as a vital and estimable endeavor. As a consequence of this widespread phenomenon, he declared, "the industrial society's dismissal of the craftsman as a nonconformist, irrelevant eccentric has been laid to rest."[107] The inherent curiosity of this new generation of American and European craftspeople also had resulted in a renewed appreciation for the traditional handwork of non-industrialized peoples. In turn, this had led to a growing national pride in indigenous crafts (which now found a ready market in Western countries) and attempts by Third World governments to preserve local crafts traditions facing extinction from mass production goods.

In "advanced societies," however, the opposite held true: there was an obsession with rejecting the past and creating wholly new forms of self-expression. As a result, Plaut declared, the exhibiting craftsmen of New York, Tokyo, and London were evincing the pathology of fine artists—an egotistical craving for public adulation and prestige. Rejecting the concept of craft, they aspired (self-destructively in his view) to be contemporary artists, not craftsmen. However, he cautioned, "we know that craft becomes art only in the hands of a master, and not because it is so *wished,* but because it is so *done.*" He argued that throughout the unbroken history of craft, there was but one constant: the purpose and the use to which the maker's product was put. For Plaut, the value of the First World Crafts Exhibition (truly the first fully to integrate the crafts of industrialized and non-industrialized societies) was its ability to emphasize the universality of craftsmanship and to raise the hope that, through the creative use of his hands, man might remain master of his world.[108]

For his part, Octavio Paz eloquently underscored the point that in making things, craftsmen continuously shifted back and forth between function and beauty, in the process creating sensory delight for those who used or touched their objects. But the modern world, still separated along lines of art and industry, was blind to this integrative pleasure: "the religion of art forbids us to regard the useful as beautiful," he wrote, "the worship of usefulness leads us to conceive of beauty not as a presence but as a function." Since man's relation to craftwork was corporal, the affective impact of handmade objects was transpersonal, directly expressed through touch. Thus, on a daily basis, users implicitly communed with makers. In Paz's view crafts were local, not national, and thus helped protect mankind from the artificial uniformity broadly imposed by new technology. Preserving, instead of eliminating, differences, they sustained what the philosopher termed "the fecundity of history."[109]

The fact that many young people in the Western world were resurrecting time-honored trades such as pottery and cabinet making, he further asserted, revealed a healthy rebellion against the Western world's quasi-religious belief in progress and the "quantitative vision" of man and nature. For him, crafts mediated between the twin poles of art and industry. "Between the timeless time of the museum and the speeded up time of technology," he wrote,

craftsmanship is the heartbeat of human time. A thing that is handmade is a useful object, but also one that is beautiful; an object that lasts a long time, but also one that slowly ages away and is resigned to so doing; an object that is not unique like the work of art and can be replaced by another object that is similar but not identical. The craftsman's handiwork teaches us to die and hence teaches us to live.[110]

It was an inclusive, humanistic philosophy that Maloof fervently supported. But it was one that the American craftsmen's movement, with its emphasis on originality and self-expression, generally considered naïve and reactionary.

In the mid-1970s, advertisers were keen to exploit the public's new awareness of the uplifting values inherent in the word "craftsmanship." After returning to Alta Loma from Toronto, in a letter to Robert Turner, Maloof wrote that the Genessee Beer Company of New York had recently asked to use his furniture in their print advertisements. By association, the firm wished to assure consumers that their brew "was well crafted, too."[111] A teetotaler, Maloof righteously—and rightfully—refused the request. His legacy as a craftsman had a higher goal.

Fig. 156 Double music stand and musician's chair, 1972. Brazilian rosewood; stand: 44½ x 51 x 30½ inches; chair: 29 x 24 x 18¾ inches; inscribed "No. 71 December 1972/For Jan Hlinka/Sam Maloof/and/Slimen Maloof." Sam and Alfreda Maloof Foundation.

Chapter Five

ACHIEVEMENT

In June 1975, Sam Maloof, cited for his "outstanding leadership and expertise in the crafts during many years of accomplishment," was one of seventeen craftspeople (both living and deceased) to be installed as a fellow in the ACC's new Collegium of Craftsmen.[1] He took great pride at being among the first class of inductees. From that date forward, he signed all his newly completed pieces with his burning pen: "Sam Maloof/ f.A.C.C." The following year, he was nominated and elected by the membership of the ACC (numbering some 33,000) to be a full trustee, joining a twenty-five member board, chaired by Barbara Rockefeller, that included craftspeople Jack Lenor Larsen and Brent Kington, as well as his former client, Samuel C. Johnson. Continuously reelected after the end of each three-year term, he served until 1992, heading the committee on fellows. No other craftsman maintained such long ties to the board, and he took his duties seriously, in the face of administrative expediency, firmly supporting the viewpoint of practitioners in the field.

Nineteen-seventy-six marked the nation's bicentennial—and Maloof's sixtieth year. The intense public focus on America's past sparked a resurgence of popular interest in the country's traditional crafts and folk art—everything from Paul Revere silverware to Hopi pottery. In cabinetry, Colonial era and Shaker furniture attracted widespread attention, and many younger woodworkers, searching for greater "honesty," rejected modern power tools and reproduced Windsor chairs and other pre-industrial designs with the hand saws, chisels, and jack planes of their artisan forebears.

In its groundbreaking book, *The Craftsman in America,* the National Geographic Society explored the intricate links binding the present with the past, and in the field of furniture making cited Sam Maloof, George Nakashima, Wendell Castle, and Arthur Espenet Carpenter as heirs to a rich historical legacy. Maloof's workshop and home were illustrated, and he was quoted on the phenomenon of college students and professionals abandoning conventional careers for the economically uncertain, but spiritually rewarding, life of the craftsman. They were searching, he said, "for something that began with the beginning of civilization—working with their hands."[2] *U.S. News and*

Rocking chair (detail), 1982. Walnut and ebony; Sam and Alfreda Maloof Foundation.

World Report likewise commented on the "comeback for handicrafts" in a "mechanized" America, and as a well-known exemplar of fine craftsmanship, Maloof was again quoted on the current, "do-it-yourself approach." "People are tired of conformity," he asserted, "a handmade piece . . . has more meaning than one bought in a store." But there were other reasons many consumers turned away from factory-made goods, he noted—the shoddy workmanship and poor design of much merchandise.[3]

During the bicentennial year, Maloof was invited to exhibit in a number of shows, the most significant of which were *American Crafts '76: An Aesthetic View,* organized by the Museum of Contemporary Crafts in Chicago, and *California Design '76,* staged at the Pacific Design Center in Los Angeles.[4] Both surveys revealed current ideals and trends in crafts. The former was based on the curators' widely accepted premise that the best contemporary craft objects fulfilled "the same vigorous aesthetic expectations we set for painting and sculpture." Mostly non-traditional pieces, the works displayed were described as "objects of human, expressive, and formal value rather than . . . craft products or merchandise."[5] UCLA art professor, Bernard Kester, served as consultant, helping to select works by fifty-nine craftworkers, including pieces by three woodworkers—Maloof, Wendell Castle, and Southern California newcomer, John Cederquist.

For the catalogue, Kester wrote an extensive essay on the artist-craftsman movement. It had begun after World War II, he wrote, with university-trained veterans. Seeking to build "a new life-style of self-worth," they had turned to working with their hands as a means of achieving "personal integration and independence."[6] Kester had chosen two pieces by Maloof, one of the returned veterans—a free-standing version of his laminated cradle (introduced only the year before) and a 1976 all-wood rocker with flat spindles that dispensed with the stretcher system. In the essay, he succinctly described his friend's achievement:

With exquisite joinery and fine hardwoods as the basis of structure and design, Sam Maloof over the years has crafted individual furniture pieces and sets which have earned him a national reputation for consistent excellence. His works reflect appropriate simplicity of line where capacity for human comfort has been translated into lean, spare form, where the supple grain finish and the details of construction (each peg or hinge) become satisfying visual/tactile components in the form. His work has been linked to the Shaker tradition, perhaps because of its structural economy and clarity and the timeless quality of design.[7] (fig. 157)

For its part, *California Design '76* was a special bicentennial year review, not a continuation of the series inaugurated in 1954. Two juries, one for crafts, the other for manufactured products and industrial prototypes, reviewed six thousand submissions (actual objects, not slides), selecting only one in fifteen for display. The vast number of entries was a sign of California's current pre-eminence in the nationwide crafts scene. Indeed, no other state had such a high percentage of practicing craft artists. With its numerous undergraduate

and graduate craft programs—many of which pioneered in the inclusion of woodworking—the extensive public university system had played a key role in establishing California as the leader in training artist-craftspeople.[8] Indeed, a comprehensive questionnaire sent to all 375 exhibitors revealed that the vast majority were university-educated art majors, many with master's degrees.

Kester and Dextra Frankel helped select the craft objects, and reviewing them, organizer Eudora Moore noted a recent phenomenon: a movement away from creating "monuments" (i.e., "works for all time") to celebrating "the act of doing."[9] In California, a younger generation regarded the creative process as a joyful end in itself, the resulting product simply as its record. The works displayed were generally raucous and energetic—in the parlance of the time, "funky." Alongside more conventional craftworks in the survey show, there were neon sculptures, an enormous environmental fiber construction, a colorful, crocheted "body covering," and all manner of mixed-media jewelry and non-traditional ceramics. Among the more inventive wooden works on display was an asymmetrical, bent-laminated *Captain's Chair* by Michael Cooper, its turned peg-leg sliding down a canted, deck-like platform. Except for an increase in humorous and metaphoric content—and a new emphasis on experimenting with mixed media—no stylistic or design trends were visible. A recent craft revival—papermaking—made a strong appearance, but, as a sign of the regional resurgence in woodcraft, there were more turned wood pieces and handcrafted, sculptural furniture on display than had been the case in any previous *California Design* show. The lonely trail that Maloof had blazed in the early 1950s had now become a well-traveled freeway.

The experience of organizing the show and talking with the participants prompted Eudora Moore to produce an illustrated, sociological study, *Craftsman Lifestyle: The Gentle Revolution* (1978). The text was based on taped interviews with select craftsmen who over the years had participated in the *California Design* shows. From their recorded statements, she drew a series of conclusions: those who consciously chose to become craftspeople did so for the joy, freedom, and personal commitment it offered; they viewed process as more important than product (with the result that their art and lives were "seamless" creations); they loved nature, and identified with the unity of all things; and they always elevated quality above quantity, considering it a reflection of their personal life, rather than simply a feature of their work. The "craftsman lifestyle," she deduced, was one of "doing."[10] As to why California had become a paradise for those working creatively with their hands, she cited the hedonism inspired by the benign climate and the broad support offered by the state's system of higher education.

Sam Maloof was one of eleven furniture makers and wood turners featured in the book, and was described as holding "a special place in the craftsman's world," not only as a successful role model, but for his generosity to young craftspeople and organizations that benefitted the craftsman's cause. After commenting on the Maloofs' remarkable home, brimming with arts and crafts, the author let the woodworker speak for himself:

I always feel that a person who's able to build what he designs is one step ahead of the next guy. This is the nice thing about working the way craftspeople do when they actually design and make things. People say it isn't really necessary to be able to draw, although I think it is. I don't make drawings of a lot of things—but I have a drawing in my head. . . . I try to make things aesthetically pleasing; but, if it isn't really functional, people will 'oo' and 'aah' over it in an exhibit but they won't buy it. I think this is the problem today. So many people are trying to do something different [but] . . . I think it often gets tricky instead.[11]

Moore's book was not the only one of the era to analyze the contemporary craftsmaker and his goals. In *Tradition and Change: The New American Craftsman* (1976), Julie Hall tried to impose order amid the confusion generated by the ongoing—and sometimes rancorous—art versus craft debate. She identified the issue of function as a primary cause of the friction, noting that "there was pressure on the craftsman on every side to abandon the making of anything functional in order to prove he or she is involved in the making of art."[12] To help clarify the situation she established a classification system. At the outset, she made a clear distinction between "production" and "nonproduction" craftsmen, subdividing the latter (previously simply typified as artist-craftsmen, or object makers) into distinctive categories based on the character of their work. They included *fine craftsmen* (those concerned with decorative arts traditions of elegance), *abstractionists* (emphasizing formal values), *imagists* (employing whimsical dream imagery), *icon makers* (creating personal totems or contemplative, fetish-like pieces), *advocates* (expressing personal identity, or social or political awareness), and *monumentalists* (those making large works for public spaces).[13]

While production, or utilitarian craftsmen, she noted, made up only a small part of the contemporary movement, they were nonetheless fundamental to any attempted definition of modern crafts. Throughout history, such individuals had risen to the challenge of making objects that simultaneously "served" and "graced" daily life. In their functional wares, their present-day counterparts continued to elevate "quality of life" over "necessities of living." Although she devoted only a single chapter to production craftsmen, Hall characterized their work as simple and understated, informal and unaffected, neither luxurious, nor ornamental, and lacking superfluous decoration. Nor was it overly intellectual. Indeed, the best production crafts had an inherent dignity and restraint emanating from "honest service" that could be fully appreciated by anyone "with eyes and hands and the time to touch and see."

The author described Sam Maloof as "totally committed to the tradition of production crafts." His work was functional, honest, avoided fussy detail, and his output—"in the thousands"—was steady and impressive. Believing that trends and fashions were ephemeral and only classic design and good workmanship endured, Hall stated that once he had developed a satisfying prototype, he employed it "indefinitely."[14] Like other production craftspeople, including George Nakashima, he evinced a love for rural living, enjoying his closeness to nature. By contrast, furniture makers Wharton Esherick, Wendell Castle, and

Arthur Espenet Carpenter were excluded from the "production" category. Instead, often concerned with surface decoration or elegance, they were classified as "fine" craftsmen. Tommy Simpson and J. B. Blunk, on the other hand, were placed, respectively, in the "imagist" and "monumentalist" sections. While there were a number of omissions among established woodworkers, as well as well-known practitioners in other media, *Tradition and Change* was the first book since *Objects: USA* to represent the full range of contemporary crafts.

The Decade: Change and Continuity

As part of the bicentennial fervor, the ACC assembled thirty-two leading craftsmen in New York in April 1976, under the rubric *The Decade: Change and Continuity,* to participate in two recorded, round-table discussions. With more than a quarter century of experience as a self-supporting, production craftsman, Maloof was invited to join the panel on The Future and the Past. Among others, his fellow panelists included Aileen Webb, Rose Slivka, Paul J. Smith, Jack Lenor Larsen, and Elena Canavier, co-ordinator of the newly established crafts programs of the National Endowment of the Arts. (Federal support for the crafts now signaled a fundamental acceptance of the field's independence from the fine arts.) Like the conversations recorded in 1966, the discussions were subsequently transcribed and printed in *Craft Horizons.*

The decade since Maloof and Don McKinley had met with Wharton Esherick to tape their observations about the woodworking field had seen enormous changes. An ever-expanding crafts movement had gathered such momentum by the mid-1970s that it seemed to be the wave of the future. Studies showed that more than sixty million Americans regularly engaged in some sort of handcraft, while another thirty million wanted to join them. On a smaller, but still explosive scale reflecting soaring interest, in the four years since it was founded in 1972, the membership of the Handweavers Guild of America had grown from three thousand to twenty thousand.[15] There were important sociological reasons for the swelling numbers of independent craftspeople. The early 1970s were characterized by economic recession, political turmoil, and civil unrest, and to many Americans increasingly disillusioned with "the system" (and especially its manifestation in the continuing Vietnam War), craft offered attractive social and cultural alternatives. Viewed as a peaceful, anti-industrial lifestyle, by 1976 craftmaking was the nation's fastest growing profession and business.

Under the direction of Rose Slivka, among other issues of the day, the panelists addressed the following questions: had the various liberation movements—Black, women's, gay, and back-to-the-earth—increased the number of craftspeople? Had the traditional separation between the fine arts and crafts disappeared? and, portentously, given the enormous popularity of handmade objects, were craftworks in danger of becoming commodities, produced for profit?[16] It was just the sort of free-ranging, give-and-take that Maloof enjoyed. Canavier began by noting that while California was still the crafts leader, the movement was truly a nationwide phenomenon. Someone asked: what was the root cause of the explosion? Museum director Smith had a simple answer: "Traditionally, crafts were associated with making something for everyday experience. Today, there is a reversed need: it's a totally psychological one . . . coming out of a humanistic requirement: People want to make something from beginning to end and feel that." But, as another panelist put it, it was one thing for an idealist to turn to crafts as a spirit-nourishing diversion, but another altogether to make it a paying proposition. Maloof voiced his agreement, stating that it had taken him years to earn a decent living, something the hippie generation couldn't seem to understand. Before he made a penny, he noted, he had to pay out $800 a week in salaries and overhead costs. He simply couldn't convince the young utopians who flocked to him for advice that woodworking was a serious profession demanding years of hard work and self discipline—with no guarantee of success.

In California, Maloof complained, "there are fairs, mall centers, and all, and the work [displayed] is horrifying. Yet thousands of craftspeople follow these fairs and, rather than progress, the work has regressed." Given the general public's enthusiasm for the handmade, even badly made objects found buyers. "What do we do about that?" he asked rhetorically. As someone who had devoted decades to mastering his tools and materials, and subtly perfecting his prototypes, Maloof was angered that poor workmanship and bad design was financially rewarded. He felt "clothes' line" arts and crafts fairs demeaned the true craftsman's product, obscuring its quality. As a new ACC trustee, one of his principal goals was to help young people become skilled craftsmen, not ill-disciplined amateurs satisfied with hawking wares outside shopping malls.[17] He was not alone. Eager to raise standards and ensure quality control, the ACC soon established American Craft Enterprises (ACE), a marketing subsidiary that organized high-quality, juried shows for both wholesale buyers and retail customers across the nation.

Please Be Seated

The day before the panel met, Maloof and Freda had been in Boston, attending the opening of an unusual exhibition at the Museum of Fine Arts, *Please Be Seated.* A temporary display that would evolve into a permanent fixture, it was composed of twelve chairs, settees, and benches, all of which had been commissioned from Maloof in 1975 by Jonathan Fairbanks, curator of the museum's newly formed American Decorative Arts Department. Since public seating was needed for the elegant, antiques-filled galleries (where factory-made benches would be sorely out of place), Fairbanks had convinced the museum to acquire examples from contemporary studio furniture makers, securing $10,000 in matching funds to begin the program. Familiar with Maloof and his work since the 1966 crafts education conference in Buffalo, he contacted him in Alta Loma. Maloof agreed to participate, eventually responding by generously creating a dozen pieces for the sum—many more than expected—including an all-wood rocker that in 1981 was hailed as one of the august museum's 105 masterpieces (fig. 158) and a high-back settee with flat spindles (fig. 159).[18] (The rocker was one of the first to incorporate the new Maloof joint.) After their initial collective showing to announce the program, the individual pieces were distributed

Fig. 158 Rocking chair, 1975. This example is the earliest of Maloof's rockers to incorporate a wood seat and dado-rabbet leg joint. Given the strength and beauty of the joinery, Maloof dispensed with the obtrusive stretcher system beneath the seat. Courtesy, Museum of Fine Arts, Boston. Purchased though funds provided by the National Endowment for the Arts and the Gillette Corporation, 1976.112.

throughout the galleries, in Fairbanks's words, "making the connection between past and present come alive."[19]

The public's response was enthusiastic. Few visitors had ever sat on museum quality, handmade furniture and they reacted with such delight that not only was the continuity of the innovative program ensured (three years later, pieces by Nakashima, Frid, Castle, and newcomer Judy McKie were acquired), but a new policy of collecting contemporary crafts was inaugurated.[20] The initial success of *Please Be Seated* also prompted the museum, through research and exhibitions, to become a leader in documenting new directions in studio furniture.[21] For Maloof, it resulted in a deluge of orders. Sore-footed museum goers not only experienced the remarkable therapeutic support of his chairs, but also their intrinsic, sculptural artistry, and many telephoned or wrote—from as far away as England—requesting examples of their favorite models.

Blind visitors also benefitted greatly from Maloof's seating. Unlike other museum displays, they could touch the pieces, caressing the shaped joints, and following the hard lines as they rose out of soft forms to run as clean ridges along arms, legs, and seats only to blend ineffably back into smooth, continuous surfaces. For Fairbanks, a painter in his own right, Maloof's furniture provided a welcome opportunity to explain to the sightless the difference between clearly defined and diffused shadows in painting. "If they can imagine in their mind what they feel on that sharp edge and soft edge," he later told the woodworker, "they can sense by their fingers what the eye sees. . . . By feeling your furniture, the blind could actually 'see' light and shadow."[22]

Jazz musician Ray Charles was another blind person who established personal contact with Maloof through touching his work. In the mid-1970s, the singer-pianist was visiting the Claremont home of Maloof's friend and client, attorney and jazz aficionado, Herbert Hafif. The Frank Lloyd Wright-influenced house was filled with Maloof furniture, and when Maloof and Freda were invited to dinner, Hafif said to Charles, "Here, I want you to see it." With Maloof nearby, the celebrated musician explored various chairs and tables, feeling the smooth undersides, and running his hands over the hard lines and sculptural joins. "My, you are a fine craftsman," the jazzman responded warmly, "this is

Fig. 159 Settee with flat spindles, 1975. This tall-back settee is among the earliest to be fitted with flat spindles. Courtesy, Museum of Fine Arts, Boston. Purchased though funds provided by the National Endowment for the Arts and the Gillette Corporation, 1976.113.

Fig. 160 Low-back chair (detail), 1980. Sam's joinery is so organic that different components are often only visible through changes in the color and texture of the wood. Reproduction by permission of Jonathan Pollock.

absolutely beautiful." Several years later, they met again and Charles vividly recalled the tactile experience. "This is exactly what I want my furniture to do," Maloof commented, "I want people to feel it, I want them to touch it. By touching, by feeling, I want them to sit. . . . I think a lot of times people can tell more by feeling than by seeing."[23]

Increasing Activities

As a trustee of the ACC, and a widely respected craftsperson, in the late 1970s Maloof markedly increased his activities on behalf of the crafts movement. In February 1977, for example, he was invited to show eleven pieces in a one-man exhibit at the Contemporary Crafts Gallery in Portland, Oregon (six sold, including a double print rack), and also gave a fully subscribed woodworking demonstration. He expected the same number of attendees—thirty-five—to show up for a lecture he delivered afterwards, but an astonishing 500 arrived, many of whom had to be turned away. In a subsequent letter to Maloof, Elena Canavier explained the reason. It wasn't a matter of simply rising interest in the crafts, she explained, rather, "it was your work and your continued endeavor to better the state of crafts that draw the crowds and sales. You are one of America's most beloved and respected craftsmen."[24]

The Portland area press responded enthusiastically to the show. "Maloof is not aloof," one writer decreed, while another described him as "unusual"—but only in the sense that his work seemed not to have gone through typical phases of experimentation in different styles. Instead, the reporter noted, from the outset he had selected designs that, with minor modification, had satisfied him ever since. "Maloof furniture has a fluid contemporary look," she wrote, "reminiscent of Swedish Modern in the tapering legs and contoured chair backs." But while his chairs with slender spindles were "Shaker-like" in appearance, overall, his work had "a fluidity of line, a deep-seated proportion" that was all his own. His fine cabinetmaking skills were described as truly impressive: "Maloof's work can endure any amount of microscopic critical inspection," she continued, "His flawless and imaginative joinery is one of the principal aesthetic pleasures of his work. Some joints are nearly invisible; others are deliberately emphasized by the conjunction of wood grains, dovetailing, or a line of contrasting details" (fig. 160).[25]

In April, Maloof was back in the Northwest, lecturing to students at the University of Washington. In June, he and Freda were on the move again, traveling East to attend the ACC's eighth national conference held in Winston-Salem, North Carolina. Several of his pieces were on display in the concurrent ACC Fellows' exhibition and during the formal sessions, among other friends who presented talks, he listened to his one-time mentor, Millard Sheets, lecture on crafts in modern architecture. For the first time, he met Joan Mondale at the conference. The wife of the vice president of the United States was herself a potter and a strong supporter of the crafts. Afterward, the Maloofs traveled across state to the Blue Ridge Mountains, where Sam gave a two-week workshop at Penland and Freda indulged her love for black-and-white landscape photography. Later, in August, the couple drove from Alta Loma to Snowmass, Colorado,

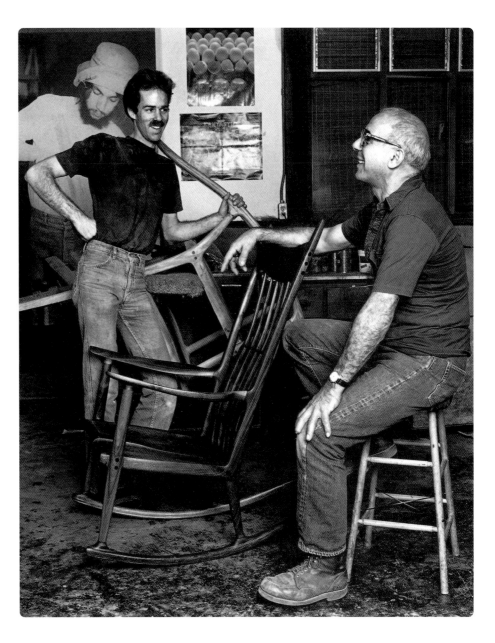

Fig. 161 Sam Maloof and assistant Jerry Marcotte in the sanding and finishing room, 1979. Marcotte was employed between 1977 and 1984. Teenage Slimen Maloof appears in the enlarged photograph on the wall behind. Reproduction by permission of Jonathan Pollock.

where Maloof participated in an NEA-sponsored workshop with Wendell Castle at Anderson Ranch Arts Center.

In October, the "self-taught dean of furniture makers"[26] traveled to Ogden, Utah, to attend the ACC's Southwest regional meeting, showing slides of his work and discussing how his family and apprentices were involved in his business. The following month, the peripatetic woodworker and his wife again flew East for slide talks at Dartmouth University in New Hampshire (at Walker Weed's behest) and at the respected Philadelphia Craft Show (where his exhibited cradle and rocking chair found ready buyers). From there, it was on to Manhattan for the November ACC general and board meetings (as usual, Aileen Webb provided Maloof and Freda accommodations), before returning to home and work. Even with all these outside commitments of time and energy, Maloof, his stamina unflagging, was able to reduce his backlog by fifty-two pieces, train a new shop assistant, Jerry Marcotte (fig. 161; hired in August 1977), and even start construction on a second story atop his sitting room/den, opening up a

Fig. 162 View of the Maloof sitting room, 1981. In 1977–78, Maloof renovated his one-story sitting room. Note the tree trunk post supporting the ceiling beam. Reproduction by permission of Jonathan Pollock.

Fig. 163 Front entryway to the Maloof home, 1982. Maloof embellished it with his famous slatted, entry gate made from strips of redwood cut into wavy patterns to create a play of light and shade. Reproduction by permission of Jonathan Pollock.

section of the ceiling to create an atrium-like space with a wraparound interior balcony reached by a side stairway. That year he also began the distinctive entryway to the front patio with its celebrated gate composed of wavy, band saw-shaped redwood slats (figs. 162 and 163).

Nineteen-seventy-eight proved to be another busy year. In early January, in his role as an ACC Trustee—and a senior spokesman for the crafts movement—Maloof testified in Los Angeles before a Congressional subcommittee headed by United States Rep. John Brademas, then drumming up public support across the country for a White House Conference on the Arts that he was proposing in the Congress. (When he had introduced his bill, Brademas had entirely over-looked the crafts—a blunder the ACC was quick to point out.) Among Maloof's suggestions: expand artists-in-schools programs, commission more art for Federal buildings, and increase grants to full-time craftsmen. Later, he attended a February ACC board meeting in San Francisco, timed to coincide with the opening of a Peter Voulkos retrospective, and then traveled south with the group to Los Angeles where they were honored with a dinner by the Wyles. The next day, Maloof invited them all to breakfast and a workshop tour in Alta Loma. In early June 1978 (leaving some sixty chairs in various states of completion behind in the workshop), Maloof and Freda attended the ACC's Southeast regional meeting in Berea, Kentucky, where the woodworker gave an illustrated lecture and a demonstration at Berea College. Afterward, the couple flew to New York and caught a plane to London on the first leg of the trip that would take them to Stockholm for a week's visit with Freda's relatives and then to Rome for an important, four-day stay in early July.

Vatican Seminar: Craft Art and Religion

In 1977 Maloof had been among one hundred American craftspeople invited to submit work for an exhibition to be held at the Vatican the following year during a seminar entitled Craft Art and Religion. His adjustable, double print rack was among forty-four works chosen for display and he was also one of two exhibitors asked to speak—artist-blacksmith Brent Kington, a professor at Southern Illinois University and a fellow ACC Trustee, was the other. The July seminar, co-sponsored by the Vatican and the Smithsonian Institution, ran from July 9 to 13, 1978, and was supported by the ecumenical Committee for Religion and Art in America (later renamed Friends of American Art in Religion). Terence Cardinal Cooke was the latter group's president; Lawrence Fleischman, owner of Kennedy Galleries in New York, served as vice president. The Rome meeting followed a previous seminar, Influence of Spiritual Inspiration in American Art, held at the Smithsonian in July 1976, that had been attended by Pope Paul VI, founder of the Vatican Gallery of Modern Art and a strong supporter of contemporary forms of ecclesiastical art.

Maloof's mid-morning talk, Opinions and Goals of Artists, followed Paul J. Smith's presentation, Standards for Collecting Craft Art, and as he sat in the audience beforehand, he looked up at the great vaulted ceiling of Synod Hall, constructed in 1300, admiring the evident pride the anonymous masons had taken in their work. He later shared the ideas that had come to mind: "The reverence that the object maker has for the materials, for the shape, and for the miracle of his skill transcends to God, the Master Craftsman, the Creator of all things, who uses us, our hands, as His tools to make these beautiful things. Sitting there in the Vatican, surrounded by beautiful work, I was thankful and thought how fortunate I am to be able to work with my hands."[27]

Read from a great wooden lectern, his half-hour talk was a summation of his humanistic craftsman's credo. "As long as there are men who have not forgotten how to work with their hands," he began, "there will remain for the heritage of craftsmen a bright light of hope that began at the dawn of civilization." In the affluent and materialistic culture of present-day America, he continued, the spiritual awakening to be personally discovered in the process of handwork was all too often forgotten. Indeed, the forces of industrialization had significantly diminished the role and power of the individual: "we have been entrapped and swallowed up by the system," he declared. But, as hardy individualists, contemporary craftspeople were making a stand, choosing a way of living and working apart from the overwhelming influence of technology. "We marvel and exclaim about the machine," he stated, "and yet nothing has been designed or made, nor ever will be, as wondrous as the hands of man. What it produces has no element of surprise or feeling that an object made by hand may have. It leaves no room for change."

But he cautioned that, by imitating others' successful work, craftsmen could turn into conformists, or, alternately, become too innovative. His personal opinions about the latter course were firmly held: "Originality only to be different has no value. An object that is derived to make an impression only survives that first impact." He concluded his presentation with an affirmation—that the language of crafts was truly international, and no matter where one traveled, a common bond of understanding was to be discovered among all craftsmen. "The crafts make the world a universal family," he said. Without them, "we lose a meaningful part of our lives."[28]

After only two-and-a-half months at home, in September 1978, Maloof and Freda flew to Japan with 248 other American craftspeople and advocates to join their "universal family" at the eighth biennial general assembly and conference of the World Craft Council held in Kyoto. Maloof had been invited to participate on the wood panel organized by English studio furniture maker and teacher, John Makepeace. Fifteen hundred Japanese craftsmen were in attendance and in an issue of *Craft Horizons* devoted to Japan, Rose Slivka wrote that, since the local contingent had brought "real ideas into this meeting," it was likely to be "the most far-reaching conference in wcc history."[29] The theme was a familiar one to American conferees, if not to those from developing countries—The Role of Crafts in Industrialized Society.

Returning to California, the Maloofs extended their own hospitality to eighty-eight-year-old Aileen Webb, who stayed with them for several days of rest before returning to New York. (She died the following year, mourned by craftsmen.) But there was to be little rest for Maloof and Freda. In November, they were off to Manhattan for the acc Trustees' meeting, then on to Layton, New Jersey, for a two-day workshop at the Peters Valley Crafts Center, followed by a further two-day sojourn in Washington, D.C. In the nation's capital, they had tea with Joan Mondale in the vice president's official residence and discussed her plans for increasing the national visibility of crafts. Afterward, Maloof gave an evening talk at the Renwick Gallery, the second in its new artist-craftsmaker lecture series. The busy month concluded with yet another trip—to Denver for a symposium.

New Handmade Furniture

In April 1979, after a year's closure, the Museum of Contemporary Crafts reopened as the American Craft Museum in a renovated building at 44 West 53rd Street—virtually across the street from its former headquarters. (In the path of the city-approved westward expansion of MoMA, the original building had been slated for demolition.) The five-story structure included two floors of exhibit space and the inaugural show, organized by director Smith, was titled *New Handmade Furniture: American Furnituremakers Working in Hardwood.* (The lumber industry's Hardwood Institute was a major sponsor.) The exhibit clearly demonstrated not only a new enthusiasm for studio furniture, but also the broadening of the field. The thirty-seven individuals selected included not only long established practitioners such as Maloof and Joyce and Edgar Anderson (fellow exhibitors in the first studio furniture show in 1957), and Wendell Castle (many of whose followers in stack lamination were invited), but also a variety of younger newcomers. Among the latter were several who would become celebrated members of the so-called "second generation" of studio furniture makers—Garry Knox Bennett, Thomas Hucker, Michael Hurwitz, and Judy McKie.

While Smith had chosen fifty-three pieces that were furniture, not sculpture, the forms of a number of objects did not strictly follow their expected function. A case in point was Michael Speaker's fall-front *Rhinoceros Desk,* a 300-pound, horned behemoth whose plywood form had been covered with 15,000 small, Koa wood tiles. Other pieces were likewise humorous: a triumph of trompe l'oeil sculpture, Castle's wooden *Umbrella Stand* contained its own meticulously carved umbrella; and Stewart Paul's saucy, double-tongued jewelry box, *French Kiss,* mimicked its title. (A continuous slide show of sixty otherwise worthy pieces that for the sake of space could not be included introduced visitors to the broad range of current work that, like the exhibit itself, revealed no dominant stylistic directions.) Maloof contributed two works to the exhibit—a sleek five-foot-long walnut desk (fig. 164) and an all-wood, low-back settee. Plagued by both back orders and back problems (he would undergo surgery for a herniated disk in June), he completed them in a two-week burst of activity just before the deadline. Based on the original Evans settee, with its thirty-six-inch-long, unsupported back (a remarkable feat of engineering made possible by his new joint) and well-developed hard and soft lines, the two-seater had evolved into one of his most appealing sculptural forms (fig. 165).

But as sculpture, it was eclipsed by another settee in the show—a large, free-form love seat chain sawn from a giant poplar burl and smoothly polished by Howard Werner. By contrast, *Table Structure,* a work by Daniel Loomis

Fig. 164 Executive desk, walnut, 1979. Reproduction by permission of Jonathan Pollock.

Valenza, was elementally constructed, mimicking the minimalist sculpture of the period: an English brown oak board had been bolted directly onto a triangular stack of three red oak beams. However, more conventionally functional pieces by Osgood, Hucker, and Hurwitz demonstrated the era's new interest in technically sophisticated joinery.

The diverse show was reviewed by *Fine Woodworking* magazine, a four-year-old journal devoted to the technical interests of cabinetmaking and directed to the skilled, home-shop woodworker. The editor was pleased to note that "the pieces most closely derived from traditional furniture embody the best craftsmanship, whereas the wilder fancies sometimes aren't as well made." The magazine praised Maloof's visible joinery for its inventive and exacting qualities.[30] *New Handmade Furniture* was also pictorially featured, if not critically reviewed, in *American Craft*, a new, glossy magazine filled with advertising and color photographs. Making its first appearance in June 1979, it was the official replacement for the less commercially oriented *Craft Horizons*. The visible change in the ACC's bimonthly journal was more than cosmetic: it mirrored a metamorphosis in the craft movement itself.

A New Orientation

By the late 1970s, the market for crafts had boomed, and ACC members now insisted on the organization's practical help in promoting sales, not philosophically asserting their place in an industrialized society as artists. The trustees firmly supported this position, and faced with "ideological differences in approach to the crafts experience," Rose Slivka resigned her position as editor-in-chief of *Craft Horizons*, which she had held for twenty-four years. To a large extent, her fear that commerce would overtake aesthetics as the driving force of the movement had been realized. In the first issue of *American Craft*, she published a farewell statement, "Affirmation." The new magazine was decreed "another voice for a new time," for the "needs and pressures of the marketplace," she noted with some bitterness, now "precede and eclipse the meditative, philosophic stance that was my way of perception and my inclination."[31]

Reviewing the situation since Asilomar—when "we were all young in the crafts . . . a small, intimate, talky group"—Slivka noted how the craftsman movement had grown from "a unified assemblage of friends" into a "diversified population" going in many different directions and with multiple needs. The decade-long development of independent guilds and specific, media-based groups (often with their own publication) had fragmented the once-cohesive movement. Rather than spiritual rewards, members now looked to their work for financial ones. No longer "the ethical way of doing and seeing . . . creating responsive and responsible lives," the embattled philosopher-editor charged the craft movement with abandoning the age of ideas for an era of philistinism:

This is a new time. The marketplace has become large and demanding. Only the acceleration of consumerized media can justify its appetite for more visibility, more promotion, more public relations, more dollar volume, more products, more selling, more and more. . . . But if life-style replace lifecraft, if commodity replaces conviction, if volume replaces value, we may have success, but we will no longer have craft.[32]

American Craft indeed mirrored the new time. Given the recent collecting boom, craft galleries had proliferated and received new journalistic attention. So, too, did individual collectors, now given the celebrity status of fine arts collectors.[33] Sales figures for ACE's blossoming crafts fairs likewise were a subject of new editorial interest. In 1978, for example, the summertime Northeast Craft Fair at Rhinebeck, New York, was reported to have generated $2,531,068 for the 497 participating craftspeople. Total sales for the 1979 winter fair, staged in Baltimore after a blizzard, were projected to be a record-setting $1,174,000, while those for San Francisco's subsequent, fog-bound Pacific States Craft Fair were estimated at $800,000.[34] The snowstorm stopped Joan Mondale from attending the Baltimore fair, but her arts assistant, Elena Canavier, was able to attend. She noted how "businesslike" craftsmen at the fairs had become: many now accepted credit cards from wholesale buyers and retail customers and proffered printed sales brochures.

In May 1979, Joan Mondale was the commencement speaker at Pomona College and asked her Claremont hosts if she could visit Maloof and Freda beforehand. A breakfast meeting was arranged, and the grove was duly ringed by Secret Service agents and local sheriff's deputies, to whom Freda served home-baked Danish rolls with coffee. Mondale was delighted by the house, the furniture, and the collection of crafts; she stayed so long she almost missed her official lunch at the college. In November, after attending the ACC meeting, the Maloofs in turn were invited to a reception at the vice president's residence where Mrs. Mondale had assembled a small loan exhibition, *Handcrafted Furniture.* The pieces, which included Maloof's rocker from the Boston Museum of Fine Arts, a Wharton Esherick library ladder, and Wendell Castle's *Umbrella Stand,* were located throughout the ground floor rooms that she used as an informal, but effective crafts showcase.[35] To ensure that a Maloof rocker would remain in the official residence, "Joan of Art" bought one for the permanent collection—the first to be acquired by a White House incumbent.

Fine Woodworking

On the eve of the presidential election in November 1980, won by the Republican governor of Maloof's home state, Ronald Reagan, *Fine Woodworking* magazine published an in-depth article, "Sam Maloof: How a Home Craftsman Became One of the Best There Is."[36] A photograph of the furniture maker kneeling on his workshop floor while vigorously planing a chair arm was reproduced on the cover (fig. 166). In many respects, it marked a transition point in Maloof's career, signaling a shift in the critical context in which his work henceforth would be judged. As models of skillful and sophisticated joinery, his exquisitely crafted, traditional functional furniture now found greater appreciation among fine woodworkers than readers of *American Craft,* who were generally more interested in the latest style trends.

Fig. 165 Low-back settee, 1979. Reproduction by permission of Jonathan Pollock.

Author Rick Mastelli explained that Maloof typically used less expensive, No. 2 grade common walnut because of the liveliness of its grain patterns and the pale, contrasting sapwood that often appeared. Readers also learned that Maloof was primarily a chairmaker, and that he believed their forms to be the most demanding in a cabinetmaker's repertoire. He had developed some twenty different designs to date, he stated, each with variations, and added two or three new ones annually. Overall, his work had evolved from an early concentration on lathe-turned parts meeting at right angles to a present dependence upon compound bandsawn and hand-shaped curves. Adding visible and tactile interest to the latest chairs, the author noted, was an increasingly sophisticated use of a hard line, "which on some pieces can be traced through every part." Moreover, well-worked joints had now become "integrated with the overall shape of the piece." Readers also learned about Maloof's extraordinary skill with a band saw. He could cut out a pair of compound-curve arms freehand in five minutes, Mastelli wrote, and fifteen minutes further work with rasps, Surform, files, and scraper produced a pair of arms that, even though he relied solely on his thumb and forefinger as calipers, were symmetrical "to within a hundreth of an inch."[37]

For the article, Maloof himself contributed a technical account of his joinery, stating that he wanted to spare others the difficulties he himself had encountered over the years in "figuring it out." Since they removed too much wood, thus weakening the joint, he rejected mortise-and-tenons on table legs. Instead, he substituted simple, 3/4-inch dowels hammered in and laterally secured by a short row of 1/4-inch wood pins. But for chair legs, he substituted sheet metal screws that removed even less wood and assured greater strength. (The holes were then plugged with disks of darker wood, often ebony, drawing attention to the joints and creating pleasing visual accents.) Maloof described his inventive, dado-rabbet chair-leg joint, illustrating it further through exploded drawings. It was a generous gift to readers, but, as he argued, there were "no secrets" in woodworking and "a person who doesn't share is losing something."[38] However, sharing had its downside: it generated a host of imitators and copyists.

Mastelli had called Maloof the conservative progenitor of the often "flamboyant" West Coast style of studio furniture making. This regional movement, marked to date by an organic style of flowing lines that generally emanated from the work of Arthur Espenet Carpenter, was the subject of a twenty-person exhibition, *California Woodworking*, organized by the Oakland Museum in December 1980.[39] The show attracted large numbers of enthusiastic visitors who enjoyed not only the works, but the innovative installation design. (A number of chairs had been placed on high pedestals for closer scrutiny; a few, like Maloof's updated Evans model, were even elevated to eye level.) In his catalogue essay, curator Harvey L. Jones noted the current tendency to link custom-designed, handcrafted furniture with contemporary fine arts instead of traditional cabinetmaking. But the works he had selected all demonstrated sophisticated woodworking techniques, as well as an unexpected new trend in California—the exploration of historical styles.

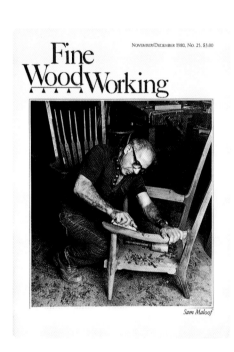

Fig. 166 Cover of *Fine Woodworking* magazine, November/December 1980. Courtesy *Fine Woodworking*.

A dining table by Philip O'Leno, for example, was a near reproduction of a 1906 design by Pasadena architect-designers, Greene and Greene, while the sinuous lines of Martha Rising's bent-laminated rocker, and another curvilinear one by John Cederquist, suggested art nouveau or Thonet bentwood examples. Even though Garry Knox Bennett's zebrawood and mahogany desk employed incongruous flat legs of brushed aluminum, it, too, reflected precedent—the silhouette was clearly derived from mid-eighteenth-century French furniture. Even the early modernist, De Stijl movement provided inspiration: Arthur Espenet Carpenter's dovetailed walnut *Mondrian Chest* had two plastic drawer fronts—one blue, another red—while Bob Wilhite's living room set suggested the pure geometry of Gerrit Rietveld's chairs—except instead of meeting at right angles, the precarious members intersected diagonally. But the "California Round-over" style of the 1960s and 1970s was also evident in several router-edged, dovetailed cases and desks. Sam and Slimen Maloof both exhibited work (the father a side chair, settee, and rocker; the son a coffee table and a round pedestal table) that Jones characterized as "artful combinations of tradition and modernity" reminiscent of Scandinavian design.

An additional catalogue essay by John Kelsey, editor of *Fine Woodworking* magazine, revealed studio furniture's new emphasis on technical skill. Since contemporary furniture was inevitably judged against the legacy of "old master" cabinetmakers, he argued, it should not pretend to be high art. It was "craft," and proudly so. Admittedly, a piece of furniture was like a work of sculpture—a composition in space of line, plane, texture, and form—but to be truly successful, not only did the maker have to balance aesthetic criteria with functional requirements, but demonstrate high standards of workmanship. But what truly characterized a fine furniture craftsman (as opposed to a furniture-as-sculpture artist), he stated, was his "unabashed passion" for the harmonious interaction between tools, techniques, and materials. As an example of the mastery of technical means for aesthetic, as well as functional ends, he cited the construction of Maloof's ingenious, interlocking, dado-rabbet joint developed five years before (fig. 167):

[Maloof] discovered that the curve cut by a half-inch rounding-over router bit will exactly fit into the curve left by a quarter-inch straight bit with ball-bearing pilot, when the latter has been run around an inside corner. The toolmaker never intended this correlation. But Maloof relies on its repetitive accuracy to make chair legs and seats interlock precisely.... Once the machines have done what they do best, he can turn to his hand tools to fair the intersection of line and plane into a pleasing combination of curves. The machine frees him from the need for mechanistic precision in joinery, and leaves him free to concentrate skill and attention on the form of the chair.[40]

The following year, Maloof's English friend and colleague, John Makepeace, published *The Art of Making Furniture,* a how-to book for amateur furniture makers filled with designs for pieces that could be built in a basement workshop. He had invited "some of the best known makers—of different ages, philosophies, and from various parts of the world"—to contribute plans, including Maloof and Wendell Castle. Sam drew up a simple dining room set—table, chairs, and buffet—while Castle produced drawings for a partially stack-laminated bedroom set. Both were quoted at length about their approach to woodworking. Maloof reiterated his long-held belief about the inseparability of design and craftsmanship: "I design as the pieces are made." He also stated that in formulating a design, one of the greatest difficulties was "to make a piece so simple that its very simplicity makes it a beautiful, functional object."[41] *Fine Woodworking* reviewed the book, criticizing many of the plans as too personally expressive to be translated easily into sets of drawings with sequential instructions, but declaring Maloof's drawings "excellent" with a strong appeal for the home craftsman.[42] In retrospect, they were just the sort Chilton Publishing had in mind when in 1961 it rejected his manuscript, "Contemporary Furniture as a Craft."

Fig. 167 Workshop photograph, 1980. Maloof demonstrating his slotted dado-rabbet joint. Reproduction by permission of Jonathan Pollock.

A Presidential Rocker

When asked to donate a work to the American Craft Museum's twenty-fifth anniversary auction held on October 1, 1981, Maloof decided to fabricate a new walnut rocker like the one he had just exhibited in *California Woodworking.* The evening gala in Manhattan proved a highly successful fundraiser and society page event, revealing the new celebrity status of crafts. Guests in formal dress first previewed the survey exhibition, *Beyond Tradition,* before following a three-block-long trail of silver footprints from the museum to the Time-Life Building. As dinner was served in the grand Tower Suite, they were greeted by Henry Geldzahler, the city's cultural affairs commissioner, and Mabel Brandon, White House social secretary. Brandon conveyed a reassuring message from President Reagan: despite recent cuts in the Federal budget, the Republican administration intended to continue the Democrats' tradition of financial support for the arts. She also saluted the eight new fellows honored that evening, among them woodworker Tage Frid and Maloof's California colleagues, Eudora Moore and Bernard Kester. ACC president Jack Lenor Larsen then, for the first time, presented the organization's highest award for artistic achievement, the Gold Medal, to Bauhaus-trained weaver Anni Albers.

The high point of the evening, however, was the spirited auction of fifteen donated pieces. Author George Plimpton wielded the gavel and virtually every piece was sold for more than its expected price. Castle's illusionistic wooden sculpture, *Table with Cloth,* received the highest bid, $15,000, while Maloof's rocker, its retail price $2,500, was knocked down for a rousing $8,000. The buyers were Philadelphians Robert and Nancy McNeil, already owners of a Maloof rocking chair. A co-chairman of the benefit, as well as ACC Trustee and member of the board of Friends of American Art in Religion, Nancy McNeil had attended the Vatican seminar and heard Maloof's talk in Synod Hall. Staunch Republicans, and buoyed by Mabel Brandon's message, the McNeils decided to donate their new acquisition to President Reagan.

Brandon quickly arranged a White House ceremony and, at 10:25 AM on November 11, 1981, the Maloofs, the McNeils, Brandon, and White House curator Clement Conger duly gathered in the Diplomatic Reception Room to await the president's arrival. (On the way in, Maloof and Freda had been briefly halted at the foot of a flight of stairs as the entire cabinet descended after their morning meeting.) The president appeared on schedule, shook hands, sat in the deep-seated rocker, expressed his pleasure, and was photographed smiling up at his fellow Californian, a lifelong liberal Democrat (fig. 168). As a personal gift, the chair was destined for the Reagans' private quarters, not the public areas of the White House, but nonetheless, it was the first piece of contemporary, handcrafted furniture to enter the antiques-filled precinct. Asked about the personal honor, Maloof modestly demurred, stating simply: "it opens a door for the American craft movement" and was "a sign that craft in general is beginning to get recognition."[43]

At the time, rocking chairs were Maloof's single most popular designs (fig. 169). In 1982, twenty-five were shipped to customers—a remarkable fact, since in June he suffered two successive heart attacks after giving a workshop

Fig. 168 President Ronald Reagan accepting the gift of a Maloof rocking chair, November 11, 1981. The first piece of studio furniture to enter the White House, it was used in the First Family's private quarters.

in Edmonton, Alberta. One chair was acquired by Barbaralee Diamondstein, host of the American Broadcasting Company's popular television series, *Handmade in America*. Maloof had been one of fourteen craftspeople she interviewed and his segment, filmed in Alta Loma, aired several times in early December that year. In the film, Diamondstein introduced Maloof to millions of primetime viewers as "probably America's number-one craftsman in wood . . . [who] has not had a day's formal training as a woodworker in his entire life."[44]

A lengthy and insightful on-camera interview, it was later published in a book that took its title from the popular television series. After recapping his history from childhood on, and recognizing Freda's essential role in his working life—"I don't think I would have stayed at it hadn't it been for my wife, really"— he discussed his evolutionary approach to perfecting designs, noting that, because of the amount of joinery required, chairs were the most difficult to make. In answer to Diamondstein's query about how his rockers moved so gracefully, Maloof replied, "every rocker I make rocks differently because the wood in the seat or the back may be denser than the previous ones. I use the same rocker [unit] on all of them . . . and by moving [it] back and forth [under the unattached legs] and then just tapping, I see if it rocks perpetually. Then it's fine."[45] Each chair, he continued, had its own set of characteristics, even its own personality. There were some twenty-five to thirty steps in making one, he said, and while he could cut out, assemble, and rough-shape an example in two days, with all the time required for his present shop assistants—Jerry Marcotte and newcomer Mike Johnson, a young man from Ontario hired in 1980—to shape, sand, and oil a piece, it took two to three weeks to completely finish it (fig. 170).

In the fall of 1983 (a year in which he made seventy-one pieces, eighteen of them rocking chairs), Maloof published a technical article in *Fine Woodworking*, entitled "How I Make A Rocker," detailing all the fabrication steps.[46] Of the twelve basic designs in his repertoire, he stated, the version with the solid, sculpted wood seat and seven flat spindles was the most popular—and the most imitated. "I don't believe in copying," he wrote, "but if knowing the way I work will help other serious woodworkers to develop their *own* ideas, I'm happy to share my methods." Since each differed slightly in terms of dimensions and material density of its parts, as he noted in the Diamondstein interview, a unique point of balance had to be discovered by trial and error during the actual assembly process. "I aim for a rocker that doesn't throw you back or tip you out," he stated, "and somehow I'm usually right on."[47] Since their appearance in the late 1960s, the laminated rocker units had been refashioned from short, simple curves into long, compound curves incorporating hard lines and strips of contrasting color (fig. 171). Rather than the stiff early examples, the later versions were composed of such curvaceous, sweeping lines that the chairs appeared, in the words of one reporter, "as graceful as a wide-winged bird floating on a sea breeze."[48]

The same issue of *Fine Woodworking* included an article on Wendell Castle's most recent work. No longer laminated or carved, many of his latest pieces reflected the new trend toward historicism and technical virtuosity. In fact, modeled on the mannered designs of Jacques-Emile Ruhlmann, the leading French art deco cabinetmaker, some works, employing exotic hardwoods (both solids and veneers) and incorporating delicate inlays of silver and ivory, were deliberately intended to push craftsmanship to its "outer limits," and, by emphasizing a philosophy of "more is more," in the words of his dealer, to present "workmanship as art."[49] Combining columns and other classical motifs, other fashionable designs by Castle mirrored the new post-modernist taste in architecture and interior decoration. Priced at unprecedented levels by his dealer to attract investors (a lady's desk and two matching chairs sold for $75,000), Castle's luxury furniture of the early 1980s—along with that of many of the younger studio furniture makers who found favor with new collectors—could not have been further removed from Maloof's straightforward, ergonomic designs with their sculpted joints. Maloof was troubled by the new, virtuoso style of cabinetmaking with its emphasis on mixed materials and conceptual designs. "There's a lot of work being done today that doesn't have any soul in it," he lamented in late 1983,

Fig. 169 Two Maloof rocking chairs, 1982. In the 1980s, there were a dozen variations on Maloof's classic rocker design. Clients could order them with spindles and wood seats, or fully upholstered. Different arm and headrests could be selected, along with backposts that were straight, or curved, either backward or forward. Reproduction by permission of Jonathan Pollock.

"The technique may be the utmost perfection, yet it is lifeless. It doesn't have a soul. I hope my furniture has a soul to it."[50]

Sam Maloof: Woodworker

That Maloof's work was indeed imbued with an intangible spirit or "soul" was evident to readers of a new book, *Sam Maloof: Woodworker*. This lavishly illustrated, 224-page autobiography was published in late 1983 by award-winning Japanese art and craft book publisher, Kodansha International, Inc. (Two years before, Kodansha had brought out George Nakashima's intensely personal record, *The Soul of a Tree: A Woodworker's Reflections*.)[51] Dedicated to Freda, Maloof's book was the realization of a persistent dream. Since the rejection of his manuscript in 1961, he had tried several times to interest other firms in a book on his life and work. Most recently, he had approached Scribner's in 1975. Although he wanted a monographic treatment, Scribner's had sought a more practical guide to cabinetmaking. Nonetheless, he persevered, making notes for an intended text and between late 1976 and early 1983, employing a

Fig. 170 Upholstered and spindle-back rockers in the sanding room, 1980. At night, Maloof would go over his assistants' day's work, testing the hard lines and sculpted curves as they were developing, marking some for greater emphasis. Reproduction by permission of Jonathan Pollock.

Fig. 171 Rocking chair, 1982. Walnut and ebony; 46 x 27 x 46½ inches; inscribed "No. 68 1982/Sam Maloof f.A.C.C./made for/Alfreda L.Maloof/Christmas '82/ P.S. and all/my love." and "j m."; Sam and Alfreda Maloof Foundation. The initials, "j.m.," refer to the assistant who worked on the chair, Jerry Marcotte.

Following pages:

Fig. 172 Primary workshop, 1981. Maloof used the machinery in this twenty-by-forty-foot room to cut out, assemble, and rough shape the more than 4,500 pieces he made between 1953 and 1999. Reproduction by permission of Jonathan Pollock.

young friend, Jonathan Pollock, to photograph recently completed pieces, examples in his own collection, workshop activities, as well as interior views of the house and its surroundings. In total, there were two hundred twenty-one black-and-white, and eighty-one color images in the book. Of particular interest is a series of photographs documenting the fabrication of a Maloof rocking chair. In large measure, the final text was based on a series of taped interviews conducted in the fall of 1982 with Jonathan Fairbanks during a trip to Anderson Ranch. But it also incorporated numerous statements about his ideals and beliefs that he had been carefully refining since the mid-1950s.

Fairbanks wrote an insightful introduction to his work, while Maloof supplied details of his personal history, anecdotes about clients, technical insights, and woodworking philosophy for five chapters—"Starting Out," "Sharing" (clients, exhibitions, craft organizations, apprentices, and teaching), "What I Do" (an overview of the process from initial idea to finished piece), "'Take a Picture with Your Eyes'" (concerning design), and "At Home" (a commentary on the evolving character of his residence, its collections, and the craftsman lifestyle). An epilogue, chronology, and bibliography rounded out the contents. Like the man himself, the writing was honest, revealing, and, his success and celebrity not withstanding, utterly unpretentious.

Reviewing the book in *Craft Horizons*, Glenn Loney noted that "there is such a generosity, even prodigality, of spirit in sharing ideas, methods, experiences, and observations in this book that . . . it is testimony to a unique way of working, thinking, and believing."[52] *Fine Woodworking* also evaluated the publication, praising the photography (especially the pictorial essays showing the "whiz of the bandsaw" at work; figs. 172–178), the typographical layout, Maloof's authorial "ingenuousness," as well as the simple, explanatory sketches and drawings he supplied. "A model for our era's self-taught craftspeople," the reviewer noted, "if Maloof is one of your inspirations, know this book is out."[53] Sales were brisk and demand remained strong for years. In 2001, *Sam Maloof: Woodworker* still prompts an outpouring of praise on the internet from young cabinetmakers.

Living Treasure

On January 19, 1984, the Creative Arts League of California opened its fourteenth biennial exhibition of contemporary crafts at the Crocker Art Museum in Sacramento. Unlike previous displays, this one, *Living Treasures of California*, was a retrospective view. Instead of celebrating the new, the organizers had decided to "look back and recognize those who . . . have contributed the most, and who most exemplify the quality and attitudes of the California Crafts since the late fifties."[54] To qualify as "treasures," each had to be a resident of the Golden State with a twenty-five-year history of craftwork, and to have significantly influenced developments in their respective fields.[55] After months of research and discussion, the selection committee winnowed a list of a hundred names down to nineteen individuals, all but Eudora Moore (honored for her longtime devotion to the *California Design* shows) were practicing craftspeople. Once selected, the State Assembly officially pronounced the nineteen "living treasures" of California.

Figs. 173–178 Workshop photographs, 1977–78. Maloof shaping the arms of partially assembled rocking chairs. Initially shaped freehand on the band saw, after the armrests were attached to the chair frame Maloof rapidly and intuitively sculpted them with a variety of simple hand tools—rasps, files, shavers, and chisels. Reproduction by permission of Jonathan Pollock.

Moore's contribution to the show, "The New Crafts Movement," was an essay published in the exhibition catalogue. "For the past thirty-five years," she wrote, "an activity whose genesis differs from mainstream art has been surging forward in the U.S." "Until fairly recently unrecognized, disavowed, or scorned by most facets of the organized art world," nonetheless, for over a decade, the crafts had actually influenced the fine arts. As evidence, she cited the fact that in the late 1960s, a sudden shift in direction could be seen in contemporary art magazines. "Cool Cubist shapes" and "Bauhaus pure forms" were replaced by a new interest in natural materials, organic lines, and the "palpable touch of humanity"—all characteristics of craft art. The "new movement," however, was split between a majority concerned with "the exuberant exploration of the material for its expressive purposes" and a lesser number seeking a "quiet beauty" in functional pieces. Compounding this schism was a recent and, from her point of view, unwelcome change:

In the past five years there seems, both in California and nationally, to be somewhat less of the philosophical commitment to the craftsman's way and more of a 'make it in the art world' attitude among young craftspeople . . . as one looks at work across the country one sees somewhat less vigor, yet considerably more refinement, more honing and perfecting of ideas. . . . The gut laughter that was sometimes boisterous, scatological, or erotic seems to have given way to more

refined and cynical snickers. There is a good bit of work which seems to be a contemplative statement about crafts—a vessel form which seeks to speak to the essence of the vessel through time immemorial, or a seating form which encompasses ruminations of the chair as function.[56]

Woodworkers Sam Maloof, Arthur Espenet Carpenter, and Bob Stocksdale had been selected to receive "living treasure" status. According to a reviewer in *Artweek,* their wooden works were a pleasure to behold: "Each creates objects of extraordinary craftsmanship; each enhances the quality of the wood grain and wood patterning with a sensitive attention to shape and detail; each produces objects so uniquely his own they are immediately identifiable." The simple honesty of Stocksdale's turned bowls were decreed Shaker-like, while Maloof's furniture "somehow combines Swedish-modern and early-American sensibilities with added elegance and beauty." Although Carpenter was described as "a serious joker," all three made the definition of craft "the simple and honorable thing it should be."[57]

Maloof had eleven furniture pieces on display in the exhibition, seven of them dated 1984 (one made especially for the show; fig. 179), the others ranging from the mid-1950s through 1979. Carpenter contributed ten works, including his colorful *Mondrian Chest* of 1974 and a signature-style, organically shaped bandsaw box with sculpted drawer pulls from 1983. Like Maloof's pieces, none were "ruminations" on function. Rather, in his artist's statement published in the catalogue, he declared: "My object is to design and make objects of everyday utility which are comfortable to live with, enjoyable to touch and to handle, will last aesthetically and functionally and will, it is hoped, communicate a level of care beyond the bare bones of utility."[58] By contrast, Sam's statement included a heart-felt declaration of his faith:

there is one thing that I remember very vividly as I look back over the years: my wife once said to me, 'Sam, God has been very good to us.' I hope somehow, in some way, that I have been able to give some of this blessing to others, perhaps in my writing, or in my lectures and workshops. I have tried to do this in the furniture that I have made for so many who have become my friends. So much of me goes into each piece that I make, how good it is, that in making each new piece, a renewal takes place. So it continues: a renewal in my commitment to my work and what I believe.[59]

For Maloof, the concentrated, sometimes obsessive, routine of daily work was such a potent force for rejuvenation that, for the next seventeen years, it not only sustained him physically and spiritually, but propelled him to new creative heights. Existing designs continued to evolve and be refined, and in his mid-eighties, he introduced new, ecclesiastical ones—altars, crosses, chairs, and lecterns—whose formal power surpassed anything he had previously achieved. His legacy was ultimately to be founded on this unquenchable thirst for work, the honors it continued to bring him, and the influence he continued to exert on younger generations of woodworkers.

Fig. 179 Occasional chair, 1984. Maple and ebony; 40 ¼ x 25 ½ x 23 ½ inches; inscribed "No. 1 1984/Made for/California Crafts XIV/Sam Maloof f.A.C.C."; Sam and Alfreda Maloof Foundation. On occasional chairs, in the 1980s Maloof favored tall backposts that bent forward at the top. With the short legs canted out below, they create a strong compound curve.

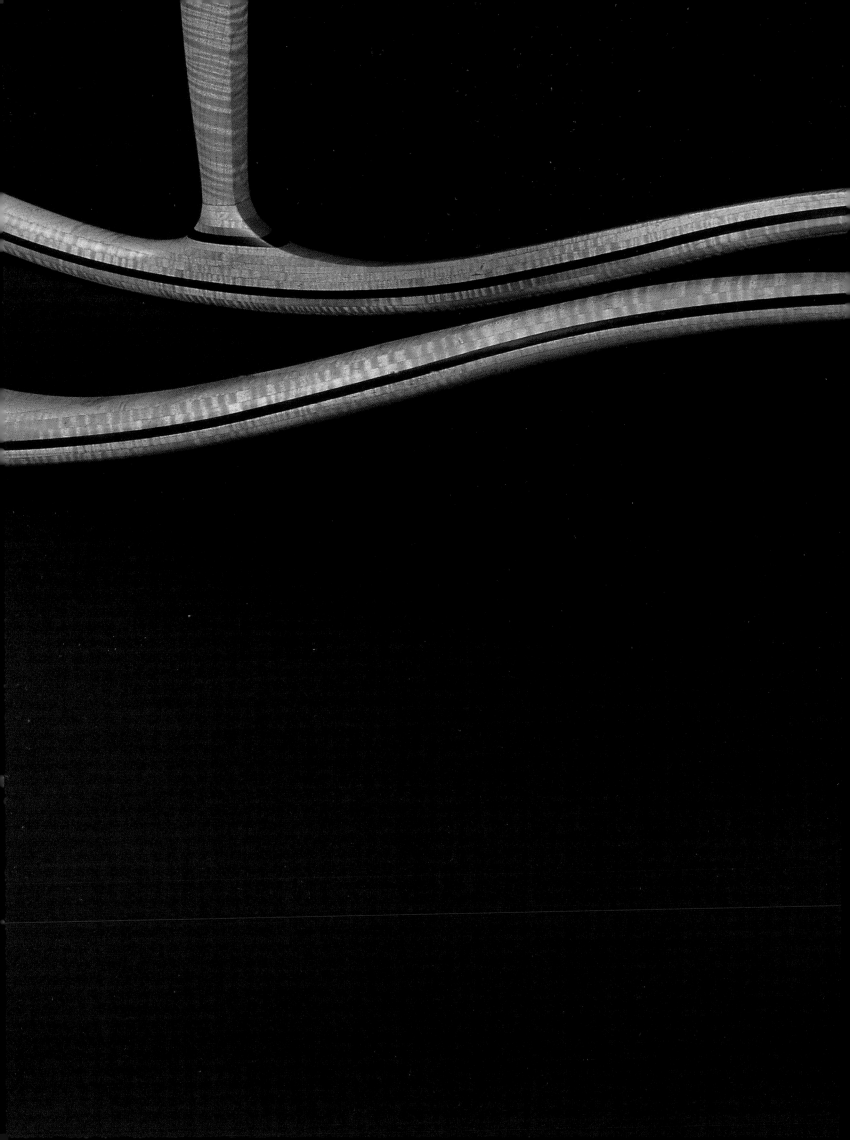

Chapter Six

LEGACY

In early June 1985, twenty-eight years after the first, ground-breaking ACC conference at Asilomar, Maloof and Freda traveled north to San Francisco to attend the organization's ninth national assembly. Convened under the title, Art/Culture/Future, the meeting drew more than 850 craftsmen, educators, collectors, dealers, and museum personnel, half from Northern California. It proved to be a cerebral get-together, "a feast of words" that, according to one writer in *American Craft*, put "a heavy tax on the left side of the brain."[1] By choosing most of the keynote speakers from academia, conference organizers deliberately avoided craft's booming commercialism, advancing instead the identity of the craftsperson as an innovative artist, not a successful entrepreneur. Indeed, the increasingly prevalent "business attitude" among craftsmen was viewed by many conferees as an impediment to aesthetic progress. Ceramic sculptor Stephen DeStaebler urged artists in his audience to assert their inner vision in the face of external demands to produce for the marketplace. "The pressure out there to be productive is great, but what's the point of producing if it's hollow?" he asked rhetorically.

The never-ending debate, "is craft art?" embroiled many of the attendees. For his part, museum director Graham Beale criticized the use of the term "craft artist," seeing in it "the desire for inclusion," as well as a "plea for special treatment." Indeed, a reporter for *American Craft* noted that the "voices in defense of craft [as art] had the ring of a minority denying its uniqueness in order to claim equality," and in conclusion wrote: "Craft has come a long way in 30 years. The question now is, How far will it get as art?"[2] At one of the concurrent exhibitions on display in the Bay Area, the Maloofs had an opportunity to judge the issue for themselves.

Furniture in the Aluminum Vein was held at Oakland's Kaiser Center, the corporate headquarters of the Kaiser Aluminum Company, for whose executive suite Maloof had fabricated furniture in 1961. All Californians, the young studio furniture makers in the show—many had crossed over from craft to art—were provided materials from the company's research division with which to experiment. Employing a variety of aluminum products, along with different woods

Rocking chair (detail), 1999. Fiddleback maple and ebony; private collection and other materials, they created a diverse range of furniture-like sculpture, all with at least a tangential reference to function. Norman Peterson, the show's organizer, discerned a distinctive, West Coast approach in the display. "What separates me, [Garry Knox] Bennett, and others like us from the people on the East Coast," he stated, "is that we often start with an *object* which might develop into furniture. A more traditional furniture maker would most likely start with a chair or a table in mind."[3] Maloof was impressed by the experimental nature of the pieces and the technical mastery they displayed, but they belonged to that class of postmodern objects that Arthur Espenet Carpenter had described as "artiture"—artifacts that "have the traditional form of furniture, but are not of any practical use"[4]—and that Maloof himself regularly criticized as egocentric creations.

MacArthur Fellowship

On the morning of June 18, 1985, functional furniture and traditional wood-working skills received a tremendous boost. Just before lunchtime, the telephone rang at the Maloof home and as was often the case, Maloof and Freda both picked up the receiver at the same time—he in the workshop, she in the office. On the other end of the line was an official of the John D. and Katherine T. MacArthur Foundation in Chicago. He announced that the craftsman had been awarded a MacArthur Fellowship. "Fellowship? What's this all about?" Maloof asked. The caller then explained that Maloof had been granted one of the coveted "genius" awards, since 1981 annually conferred on "exceptionally talented and promising individuals who have shown evidence of originality, dedication to creative pursuits, and capacity for self-direction."[5] He also learned he would receive a total of $375,000, a tax-free sum to be dispensed over the five-year period of the fellowship, no strings attached. Maloof was stunned, "knocked for a loop." The unexpected windfall would provide the financial security he had never actively sought, but, for his family's sake, had often worried about. "For the first time in forty years," he told a reporter from *Fine Woodworking,* "I won't have to worry about cash flow."[6] At the time, if he made $40,000 a year after shop expenses, he thought of himself as "doing well."[7]

The *Los Angeles Times* later recalled the couple's reaction to the unexpected news: "Woodworker Sam Maloof's wife . . . listened in on the short conversation and came into his workshop with tears in her eyes. 'I said to her: "I just can't believe it, Freda. Why me?" And she said: "Because you deserve it," which I thought was very nice.'"[8] Among twenty-five recipients that year, Maloof was the first to receive an award in the "crafts and design" category. It was a ground-breaking decision. As one journalist later put it, "In bringing Mr. Maloof out of the woodwork, as it were, MacArthur sent a signal that its affections were not confined to geneticists, epigraphers, or literary critics."[9] Doubtless, the publication of *Sam Maloof: Woodworker* had helped promote his accomplishments far beyond the crafts and woodworking worlds, prompting a nomination.

In September, the new fellows and their spouses were invited to Chicago to be honored at a MacArthur conference, and Maloof was one of a handful asked to give informal talks on their work. He agreed and before he left Alta Loma—

after repeated drafts—he prepared a speech to read while he showed slides of his home and furniture. But when he reached the auditorium door, he unexpectedly had an anxiety attack. How could his non-academic presentation stand comparison with those by learned professors, poets, and research scientists? Freda listened briefly to his fears, but then seized the typewritten pages, tore them up, and sternly declared: "I bet none of those people can make a chair. Just get up and talk about what you do."[10] He did. The spontaneous talk was such a great success that he was asked to repeat it the next day to a larger group.

Maloof's award caught the attention of *People* magazine. A reporter and photographer visited Alta Loma and prepared a short feature on the new MacArthur Fellow. Published in January 1986, the headline decreed Maloof "King of the Rockers," while the text called the vigorous seventy-year-old "one of the world's leading artisans—a Hemingway in hardwood whose work has been graced by the bottoms of some of the top people in the country." (The latter were identified as Presidents Reagan and Carter, as well as Hollywood film stars Anthony Quinn and Gene Kelly.)[11] The article was accompanied by an engaging photograph of Maloof outdoors, flanked by two of his quintessential chairs. It was a dramatic image. Seen against the sky, he is dressed in jeans and cowboy boots, his hands on his hips, and his head thrown back, laughing joyfully. ACC president Bruce Sharpe was quoted: Maloof was "the dean of American woodworkers" and his designs were "treasured" as "some of the finest produced in the 20th century."[12] Read by millions of Americans, the story generated more orders for Maloof furniture than any previous publicity.

One academic writer, investigating the working methods of forty MacArthur Fellows, so as to establish common links in their "uncommon genius," interviewed Maloof at length for a book on creative thinking. Like Maloof, each of the winners had taken risks in their careers that required great courage. Maloof's act was to strike out on his own in 1949 and then to follow the same slow, evolutionary design philosophy, never changing for the sake of fashion. From his standpoint, it represented a moral commitment. "I've always believed in . . . aiming myself—oh, how shall I put it?—aiming myself *true*," he stated, "If your mind is right, I think that all things fall into place." Integrity, he told the interviewer, was the single most important aspect of his work—and of his creativity: "I always try to adhere to what I think is right, and that, to me, is the most important part of creative work. Fashion comes and goes, but my pieces have to have the integrity of my vision."[13]

Craft Today: Poetry of the Physical

During 1986, the "Hemingway of hardwood" shipped twenty-six rockers to new clients—his highest annual output of the popular design to date. One was fabricated out of a material that was unusual for Maloof, if not for other studio furniture makers—fiddleback maple. Numbered "28/1986," it was among the earliest of an increasing number of his sculptural seating forms employing hard rock maple, a wood that he had not used regularly since the early 1950s.[14] Indeed, he had been prompted to return to it after refinishing one of his early maple desks and admiring the light-toned wood's active grain.

Maple added a new, high-keyed color to Maloof's palette, dominated as it
was by the darker tonality of black walnut. The outer sapwood of the tree is a
bright, creamy white with a slight reddish tinge, while the inner heartwood
varies from light to deeper reddish brown. Although generally straight-grained
and uniform in texture, milled maple can also be obtained with variegated,
caramel-colored graining—line, fleck, and dot patterns known as "fiddleback"
(also called "curly" or "tiger-striped"), "bird's eye," and "quilted." (Maloof's
favorite, fiddleback, is typically used for the backs of stringed instruments.)
Since the grain on a polished, figured maple surface appears to move when
viewed under changing light conditions, he termed it "jazzy" and delighted in
its active visual effects (fig. 180).[15]

Maloof first exhibited a rocker made from fiddleback in *Craft Today: Poetry
of the Physical,* the biggest survey show to be mounted since *Objects: USA.*
Opened on October 26, 1986, the encyclopedic blockbuster (embracing more
than 300 works by 286 craftspeople) had been organized by Paul J. Smith to
inaugurate the new American Craft Museum (now thirty years old), a three-
story, four-level space in the recently completed E. F. Hutton Tower located
opposite MoMA at 40 West 53rd Street.[16] The sculptural chair proved a popular
icon both inside and outside the museum. During the show, a large, backlit
color transparency of the bright-toned, tiger-striped chair photographed against
a black background graced the Manhattan IND subway station at 53rd Street
and 5th Avenue (fig. 181). One of seventy-one reproductions of artworks in the
city's Arts for Transit program, it was enjoyed by hundreds of thousands of
mid-town commuters and tourists. The same dramatic image also served as the
opening, two-page illustration for one of four sections in the lavish exhibition
catalogue.[17] In the museum itself, the maple rocker was given pride of place at
the foot of the grand, spiraling staircase (an engineering marvel in its own
right) that visually and spatially tied the separate floors together.

One critic admitted that, initially, she dismissed the chair as banal. But upon
reconsideration, she found it "amazing," for every part was subtly exaggerated:

*It's a little oversized, the rockers a little elongated, the rippled shapings of the
seat are almost wavelets, the ebony lines along the rockers together with the
ebony dowels and slight swellings at the joints underline the logic and poetry of
the construction. The natural striations of its yellow hard rock maple were selected
to echo the forms, widening slightly at the swell of a support and clinging to the
curve of the back rest. This chair is not just a technical tour de force, its exagger-
ations lift it to a kind of Platonic idea of a chair.[18]*

In both the show and its glossy, accompanying book, the disparate craft works
were divided into four simple categories, revealing broad divisions within the
field itself in the mid-1980s: "the object as statement" (the largest of the sections, revealing close connections with the current art scene), "the object made
for use" (the rubric covering Maloof's rocker and other utilitarian forms), "the
object as vessel" (explorations of a popular crafts format), and "the object for
personal adornment" (clothing and jewelry). These sections were not intended

to create hierarchical distinctions, nor to pigeonhole individual pieces, but, given the stylistic diversity of the objects on view, to assist exhibition goers by helping to clarify makers' goals. From the curator's vantage point, however, *Craft Today* underscored his essential point that "the object is the message," one in which visitors would discover for themselves the "poetry of the physical."

The new showcase and its inaugural display prompted an outpouring of favorable press reports, many commenting on the new marketability of contemporary crafts. *The Economist* of London wondered aloud whether New York's "voracious art market" had not created "a new set of collectible objects, complete with their own temple," while *The Wall Street Journal,* noting the existence of a "crafts-hungry marketplace," imagined the field as a "growth stock" that was now "consolidating its gains." For its part, in a guide to gift-buying in Manhattan, *New Yorker* magazine suggested, tongue-in-cheek, that as a result of the inaugural show's success "there's a chance that in this city the craft outlets will soon outnumber the Italian shoe stores."[19]

In his catalogue essay, Smith, too, observed that craftspeople in the 1980s expected financial as well as spiritual rewards from their work. Since the market for crafts had increased substantially, many individuals, formerly dependent upon university teaching or other employment, had transformed themselves into successful small business owners. Operating limited production studios, they retailed their creations either directly, through an expanding gallery system, or in the popular craft shows organized by American Craft Enterprises.

The trade in one-of-a-kind or limited edition crafts was booming. In 1986, for example, the combined receipts from wholesale buyers at the ACE shows held in Baltimore, West Springfield, and San Francisco totaled $11,197,234, while retail sales added an additional $4.3 million to that sum. The following year, Minneapolis/St. Paul debuted as an annual ACE venue, the number of wholesale booths at Baltimore and West Springfield increased from 450 to 800, and an upscale, retail crafts exhibit was staged at the Seventh Regiment Armory on Manhattan's Park Avenue, the prestigious locale for lucrative antiques and fine arts shows.[20] Clearly, the "craftsman lifestyle" had metamorphosed from an anti-establishment crusade into a profitable profession catering to the establishment.

Fig. 181 First rocking chair in fiddleback maple, about 1983. For decorative purposes, he inserted strips of ebony in the rocker units, their long, black lines emphasizing linearity. Reproduction by permission of Jonathan Pollock.

In terms of craft aesthetics, Smith characterized the decade as a period of technical "refinement," rather than one of "experimentation for its own sake." With issues of technique now resolved, he recognized a widespread desire to make objects "as beautifully and as well as possible"[21]—something conservative-minded collectors of the 1980s clearly welcomed. He also identified another obvious attribute of recent craftmaking: a renewed interest in design traditions, both recent and historical. In the 1980s, the decorative, or applied arts of the art nouveau, art deco, Arts and Crafts, and Modernist eras had become popular collectibles, actively acquired through specialized or fine arts galleries, and at major auction houses. This new design consciousness not only broadened a respect for contemporary craft objects, but, at the same time, helped stimulate the historicism of younger studio furniture makers following Wendell Castle's recent lead.[22]

Craft Today also reflected another recent phenomenon—a resurgence of interest in functional forms. Indeed, a new enthusiasm among collectors for useful decorative objects (as opposed to more purely sculptural forms) was a major reason for the increase in small-scale production studios, as well as for the exhibit section, "the object made for use." In his essay, Smith noted that this renewed interest was particularly noticeable in recent handmade furniture.[23] For the show, he had selected pieces by fourteen woodworkers, including many well-established members of the second generation. In their works (often less than fully functional), the younger studio furniture makers explored artistic and technical directions anathema to Maloof—expressive content, ornament, virtuoso workmanship, new synthetic materials, and color.

While the exhibition was on view in Manhattan, *Contemporary American Woodworkers,* a richly illustrated book was published that chronologically reviewed the field beginning with the work of Wharton Esherick.[24] Maloof was one of ten individuals featured in depth. For many urbanites whose knowledge of new furniture was restricted to jazzy, mass-produced pieces by the idiosyncratic Italian design firm, Memphis, and American postmodern architects Michael Graves and Robert Venturi, the volume was a portal to the still under-appreciated world of handcrafted furniture. But even for craft-world insiders, as an historical tool the book provided a firm basis for scholarship in the field. Except for Wendell Castle, Jere Osgood, and Garry Knox Bennett, author Michael Stone focused on the "elders" of the movement, those who had set up shop in the decade after 1945. Through an analysis of their woodworking philosophies, careers, and workshop practices, Stone firmly established their collective legacy for the new generation.

In his chapter on Maloof, Stone emphasized that the Alta Loma craftsman concentrated on refining and improving existing models, not inventing new forms. Maloof was quoted on the subject: "People ask me why I don't go off on a tangent and work in different directions. My answer is that I have not really perfected what I am doing now. . . . I do not think you have to change just for the sake of change. If the piece is good, it's good. Ten different chairs can evolve from one design."[25] However, the author noted, many younger members of the university-trained generation of studio furniture makers criticized Maloof's design philosophy as stagnant, some even dismissing his work altogether as an outmoded emulation of Scandinavian Modern. But, as Maloof himself pointed out in the text, that similarity was merely coincidental. Indeed, as one book reviewer noted, the postwar desire for simple, functional wood furniture with sculpted shapes and exposed joinery was widespread, not a proprietary Scandinavian response. Moreover, ideas flowed both ways—from America to Europe, as well as vice versa.[26]

According to Stone, unlike George Nakashima and Northern Californian James Krenov (both of whom often set aside slabs of wood for years as they considered their most perfect use), Maloof revealed a wholly pragmatic approach to his materials: "Some woodworkers talk about the necessity of contemplating a piece of wood and letting it tell them how it wants to be used. . . . I have no time for leisurely conversations with a single piece. My communications with wood, therefore, are very efficiently condensed. . . . The pieces that will become furniture are chosen with a mixture of common sense and love, and there is no reason for this process to be long and arduous."[27] Furthermore, while others liked to work in a wide variety of woods, he restricted his palette: his renewed interest in maple notwithstanding, fully ninety-five percent of his pieces were made from black walnut. Nor did he mix different woods, use metal hardware or other manmade materials. The only surface embellishments he countenanced were natural ones, either integral to the material itself (knotholes, complex graining patterns, and contrasts between light-colored sapwood and darker heartwood), or ebony plugs to highlight joinery.

Workshops

In 1986 Maloof's freehand skill with a bandsaw received popular, nationwide attention. In February he gave a workshop in Atlanta at Highland Hardware, an unusual store that not only retailed tools, but offered first-class instruction in woodworking. One of those attending Maloof's workshop was Jack Warner, a local journalist who wrote a weekly column, "Working with Wood," for the *Atlanta Journal-Constitution.* Based on his seminar experience, Warner developed a series of four engaging articles (some of the best writing on Maloof's work) that, syndicated by United Press International, spread Maloof's fame among woodshop amateurs from coast to coast.[28] "The simple, catchy way to identify Sam Maloof," Warner decreed at the outset, "is to call him the best known, the most successful woodworker in the world—every basement craftsman's dream come true . . . but he's about as far removed from basement woodworkers like me as Rubens was from the local house painter."

By the end of the two-day workshop, to the delight of his audience sitting on bleacher seats, Maloof had assembled and rough-shaped a high-backed occasional chair and, as he left the demonstration room, he invited everyone to sit in it. "Moments like this can be very embarrassing," Warner later wrote:

Everyone stands around smirking at the current sitter, who often feels bound to offer some astute judgement on the matter. I was just about the last to sit in it; it took a little courage. The seats of Maloof's chairs are long and generous; a high center crest discourages perching, urging you to slide down the slightly canted seat to the deep hollows at the back. Once there, you have the feeling of being cradled. Relax and the stiles support your lower back and the crest cups your head. The long arms hold your elbows firmly and your fingers curl over the subtle shape of the ends. I suspect each of the three dozen men and women at this seminar felt Maloof had made the chair with him or her in mind. The chair was still rough and feathery from the rasp and band saw; no part of it had been sanded smooth. But it was still the most comfortable upright chair I have ever experienced—wooden or upholstered.[29]

Maloof's workshops were more inspirational than educational. While others, like Tage Frid—"the dean of American woodworking teachers"—provided detailed instruction, Maloof simply demonstrated his own methods, impressing his audiences more by his remarkably skillful handling of materials and tools, and his infectious enthusiasm, than by his technical insights.

The well-reported Atlanta demonstration was not the only one he conducted that year. In July, the Maloofs drove east to Snowmass, Colorado, for another of Maloof's fully subscribed, annual workshops at the Anderson Ranch Arts Center. This time (and in his honor) it was to be held in a new facility—the Sam Maloof Woodbarn. The following year, using revenues from his MacArthur Fellowship, he established the Sam and Alfreda Maloof Scholarship Fund to support two annual, summertime scholarships for tuition and housing at Anderson Ranch in separate categories: "excellence of design, craftsmanship, and creativity in form" and "excellence in presentation of a design through drawings." The MacArthur prize money was also the source that year for an unrestricted donation of $75,000 to the ACC.

The Eloquent Object and Craft's "Artification"

In 1987 Maloof was invited to exhibit recent work in a total of ten exhibitions. Two were local ventures: *Maloof, McIntosh, Soldner: Work in Wood and Clay*, staged at Scripps College and a survey, *Claremont Centennial: 1887–1987*, organized by Chaffey College and celebrating the legacy of the university town's artists' colony. His longtime friend, Richard Petterson, reviewed the Scripps display, writing admiringly: "Maloof's furniture is truly sculptural. He shapes wood so beautifully it's almost as if it has grown naturally into the form of a chair or table."[30] Among the other exhibitions in which he participated that year, ranging geographically from Worcester, Massachusetts, to Portland, Oregon, was a landmark show that opened in Tulsa, Oklahoma, and subsequently traveled nationally and internationally—*The Eloquent Object: The Evolution of American Art in Craft Media Since 1945.* Comprised of some two hundred works by 139 artists, in terms of intellectual significance and aesthetic challenge it was the most ambitious crafts display mounted in the 1980s, far more substantial than *Craft Today*.

Six years in the making, *The Eloquent Object* was organized by potters Marcia and Tom Manhart of Tulsa. She was director of the Philbrook Museum of Art, while he served as chair of the University of Tulsa's art department. Assisting them was a team of curatorial advisers that included, among others, Rose Slivka, Bernard Kester, and Jonathan Fairbanks. While the organizers' stated intent was to survey work since the end of World War II, their real objective was to prove that, since artists and craftsmen now often shared similar materials, intentions, and contexts, the boundaries separating them had collapsed and a new, more inclusive category had been born—"art in craft media."

To prove that point, among the craft objects selected they interspersed works by established fine artists who, for conceptual purposes, used craft-based materials, techniques, and/or formats. These included, for example, a ceramic sculpture of cast and glazed restaurant ware by Pop artist Roy Lichtenstein, a flat, wall-mounted sculpture woven from steel strips by Duayne Hatchett, and a free-standing, ten-page wood and paper *Book* by Lucas Samaras. In some instances, juxtapositions indeed revealed common bonds between artists and craftsmen, substantiating the show's thesis. For example, with its smooth, polished surfaces and Shaker-like simplicity of form, Martin Puryear's circular, wall-mounted wood sculpture was certainly similar in sensibility to the sculptural form of Sam Maloof's adjacent low-back, maple settee.[31] But other intended comparisons, such as Samaras's abstract *Book* and a figurative bas-relief with an elaborate textual surround by ceramicist Jack Earl, both formally and philosophically challenged the proposal that fine art and craft objects belonged together.

To demonstrate that contemporary fine artists and craftspeople shared other concerns, including cross-cultural influences that further revised and extended the canonical boundaries of art, the Manharts also included works by minority artists. As catalogue essayist Lucy Lippard noted: "Respect for other cultures brings interdisciplinary respect. Exhibitions that mix these sectors expose the false dichotomies between art and crafts and the 'folk art' of diverse cultures."[32] Unlike *Craft Today,* however, only a limited number of pieces in the Tulsa show—such as Maloof's settee—were fully functional forms. In fact, works of traditional utility had been all but barred. In Marcia Manhart's words, the objects selected were "not made to cut bread, hold water, or to clothe, adorn, or support the human body." Instead, "they were made for the reasons art is made: to question, assert, celebrate, and record."[33] (In her historical essay in the catalogue, she cited Maloof's rocking chairs of the 1960s as early examples of traditional furniture that "stretched the functional ideal toward a sculptural dignity and scale.")[34]

The Eloquent Object marked the triumph of Rose Slivka's long campaign to present non-functional craft objects as autonomous works of art. To reconceptualize crafts in terms of sculpture, the show was organized into six thematic categories, replete with explanatory wall texts: *Idea Rules Material, Idea Supercedes Function, Illusion is Rediscovered, Social and Political Statement Emerges, Ritual is Recreated,* and *The Arts Fuse All Cultures.*[35] These and other "boundary obliterating" ideas were further explored in eleven essays by artists, curators, historians, and critics published in the handsome, award-winning exhibition publication. The abundant texts were themselves divided into four sections, envisioning the craft movement from different standpoints: the direct experience of the artist, the view of curators and critics, cultural pluralism, and ritual and the sacred.[36] But, in the absence of a solid base of crafts-specific scholarship and criticism, the authors ventured into what one termed "uncharted areas of visual production" inappropriately applying fine-art criticism to craft objects.[37]

Rose Slivka's essay, "The Art/Craft Connection," described as a personal, critical, and historical odyssey, reviewed the history and significance of the new American craftsman's movement within an increasingly industrialized society. Repeating many of the humanistic ideas and themes she had published during her tenure as editor of *Craft Horizons* (uncharitably termed "gnomic utterances" by a reviewer in *American Craft*),[38] she supported the essential "apotheosis argument" of the exhibition: only when craft objects relinquish function can they rise to the level of the fine arts and realize their "actual value" as "containers of ideas."[39]

In their respective essays, historians Jonathan Fairbanks and Penelope Hunter-Stiebel both contended that the philosophical distinction between art and craft was fundamentally false, a historical phenomenon that had no contemporary validity. As Fairbanks put it: "No special boundaries separate art from craft, nor is one sort of creative work more important than another. Artists and craftspersons may use different materials and have diverse technical objectives, but they share the goal of transforming raw material into expressive, spiritually moving work."[40] To prove visually that "art" and "craft" were interchangeable, a color reproduction of one of Maloof's new fiddleback maple settees illustrated Fairbanks's essay (fig. 182). According to its caption, the sculptural design was "among the most eloquent of contemporary American furniture," its composition artfully balancing solids and voids, while the interplay of hard and soft lines and curving members rhythmically echoed the wind-eroded shapes of sand dunes or snow drifts.[41]

Art critic John Perrault (soon to become senior curator at the American Craft Museum) contributed a witty, dissenting essay, "Crafts is Art." It was not a coherent argument, but rather a series of discontinuous topics in which the author grappled with ideological, crafts-related issues. Unlike the Manharts or Slivka, he did not assert that the categories of crafts and fine art had either blurred, overlapped, or merged—nor had they exchanged places. Instead, he proposed that "art in craft media" was in the process of actually replacing "fine art in art media" in the artistic hierarchy. In his opinion, craftspersons, not contemporary painters and sculptors, were creating objects that he defined as art—works that addressed, expressed, or added to the sum of human experience.

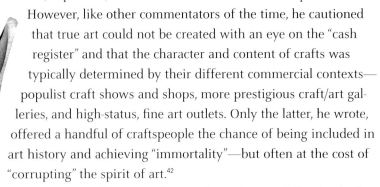

Fig. 182 Low-back settee in fiddleback maple, about 1985.

However, like other commentators of the time, he cautioned that true art could not be created with an eye on the "cash register" and that the character and content of crafts was typically determined by their different commercial contexts—populist craft shows and shops, more prestigious craft/art galleries, and high-status, fine art outlets. Only the latter, he wrote, offered a handful of craftspeople the chance of being included in art history and achieving "immortality"—but often at the cost of "corrupting" the spirit of art.[42]

From Perrault's point of view, the widespread dismissal of function was a direct result of craft's "artification." But putting crafts on a "pedestal," he argued, was risky, for usefulness determined essentials of form and meaning. The deliberate absence of utility transformed "art in craft media" objects into symbolic images of more conventional forms, denying them the "full force of the chief aesthetic virtue of crafts objects: their perceptual and conceptual complexity." Unlike fine art, he declared, craft had a unique "doubleness of being," one in which sight and touch were fused. Add function to the aesthetic experience, Perrault argued, and it was raised to transcendent levels: "If we can simultaneously manage seeing and touching *and* using," he wrote, "we have accomplished something quite miraculous."[43]

The Critique of Uselessness

In the late 1980s many argued that the immediacy and intimacy of touch was essential to emotional health, even to long term human survival. In the words of one critic reviewing *The Eloquent Object,* the fact that the craft world was so keen to shed function—"its last remnant of authenticity"—was pitiable. "For crafts to shift away from the tactility engendered by function and towards an entirely visual and conceptual notion of value," he wrote, was "the equivalent of suicide."[44] Another observer noted in *American Craft* that, as part of their physical and spiritual "completion," craft objects had to be handled. The daily use of artistically designed pottery, textiles, and furniture reinforced one's essential human identity and connected not only the user, but also the objects, to a shared, archaic past. "For this reason," she wrote:

it is tragic that so many of the most talented workers in clay, wood, and textiles have decided that making functional objects is a lower calling, one unworthy of the creative imagination. . . . To make unusable vessels that represent 'ideas about making vessels,' unsittable chairs that challenge the mind, furniture that looks good only in reproduction is to reinforce the striking rejection of the physical characteristic of today's debased visual arts. What these artists are doing is heeding the call of the philosophical idealists and voluntarily giving up a profoundly valuable heritage at a time when it is most needed.[45]

In the view of ceramics historian and dealer Garth Clark, utility (and its concomitant, tactility) could be preserved, even celebrated, if the debilitating art-versus-craft argument was resolved by positing another, more appropriate and supportive refuge for the crafts—the field of applied or decorative arts. In an article in *American Craft,* he noted an odd circumstance: many contemporary object makers "deny the crafts as their parent, claiming instead that they belong to the fine arts." But the fine arts, he noted, firmly denied this "paternity," ensuring that avant-garde objectmakers remained "cultural orphans." What these individuals really sought in an art-craft marriage, he concluded, was not greater aesthetic freedom, but rather the wealth and power of fine artists. "If a craft object were to fetch more money than a painting," he asserted, "there would be no debate (except that all the painters would hold conferences calling for their redefinition as craftsmen)."[46]

Although the vast majority of contemporary craft objects acquired by museums were placed in their decorative arts collections, there nonetheless remained a detachment between crafts and decorative arts, one that Clark decreed dated back to an ideological snobbishness adopted by makers of one-of-a-kind works during the Arts and Crafts era. This continuing isolation was strengthened by the fact that artist-craftsmen feared that a rapprochement with decorative arts would block their chances to join the fine arts. However, given the renewed interest in the applied arts on the part of museums, art dealers, and celebrity artists and architects, he cautioned that the decorative arts field might itself be co-opted, thus locking craftspeople out of their "ancestral home." A resolution to the on-going problem of identity and nomenclature, he argued, was simply to drop the term "crafts" altogether and merge with the applied arts, a field with a lengthy history, sound scholarship, and international outlook, and thereby relinquish contemporary craft's inherent isolationism, anti-intellectualism, and parochialism. Such a realignment would also result in "the achievement of an honest context and a re-connection with the umbilical cords of our past."[47]

As the title of a 1990 exhibition of useful crafts suggests, at least on a rhetorical level, Clark's proposed merger almost took place: *Art That Works: Decorative Arts of the Eighties, Crafted in America,* a show to which Maloof contributed a rare double rocker.[48] Moreover, since 1986, the annual Chicago International New Art Forms Exposition (CINAFE) featured craft objects retailed by upscale dealers under the rubric, *20th Century Decorative and Applied Arts.* (In 1987 one of Maloof's low-back maple settees was on sale in the booth of The Hand and The Spirit Gallery.) The latter's successor, the annual Sculpture Objects and Functional Art (SOFA) shows held in Chicago and New York, displayed crafts as "contemporary decorative art." But, the surrounding contentiousness notwithstanding, the term "crafts" proved inescapable.

In the late 1980s, a variety of voices joined in criticizing the "artiness" of crafts. In *American Craft* woodworker-writer, Glenn Gordon, censured contemporary "art furniture" for its rejection of honest serviceability. "What disturbs me most about the repackaging of the craft of furniture making as art," he wrote, "is that a lot of contemporary work is set forth as free of craft's original obligations." As a result, young woodworkers believed that completely useless forms were acceptable as works of "craft." To the despair of tradition-minded cabinetmakers, the creators of such "artiture" were amply rewarded with government grants and juried prizes, thereby reducing the craft of furniture making, in Gordon's words, "to a competition to see who can come up with the weirdest *objets de vertu.*"

By eliminating conceptual differences between art and craft, and construing furniture to be a form of sculpture, he asserted that studio woodworkers created pieces "unconvincing as art and pretentious as furniture." At best, such an object might be breathtaking in its virtuoso workmanship, at worst it "hyperventilat[ed] with the most desperate novelty." In Gordon's view, true works of furniture art had been produced—Shaker designs, for example—but they achieved that status through artlessness.[49] Generally, however, the less self-conscious, functionalist approach espoused by Maloof was rejected by younger studio furniture makers. To a public still largely unaware of its existence, the American Society of Furniture Artists, founded in 1985, vigorously promoted unique furniture forms as art objects.

New American Furniture

The 1989 exhibition, *New American Furniture: The Second Generation of Studio Furnituremakers,* however, rejected the idea of one-of-a-kind furniture as a subspecies of fine art, positing it instead as "an interactive medium combining art, design, and craft."[50] Organized by Edward S. Cooke, Jr., then a curator of decorative arts at Boston's Museum of Fine Arts, the show was inspired by the current revival of interest among younger woodworkers in historic furniture and design. As an important museum project, the display helped legitimize art-oriented studio furniture as a scholarly field.

In 1987, with the support of Jonathan Fairbanks, Cooke had invited twenty-six leading studio furniture makers to a lively, two-day symposium in the Department of American Decorative Arts and Sculpture. All were committed to craftsmanly processes and—in varying degrees—to function. They toured the furniture storage areas and examined masterpieces on display (including Maloof's contributions to the *Please Be Seated* program), learning about traditional design concepts, joinery, and production methods, and the practical and social uses—as well as symbolic values—of Colonial and Federal-era furniture.

Each of the participants was then invited to select a piece in the permanent collection on which to imaginatively base the design and fabrication of a new artwork that would be included in the proposed exhibition. Garry Knox Bennett chose a kneehole bureau-table in mahogany and poplar made in New York around 1760 as the basis for his remarkable revision that combined an aluminum carcase with Honduran rosewood, synthetic ColorCore, Fountainhead (a *faux* granite countertop material), set atop a base of interlocking fire brick (fig. 183).[51] Fellow Californian John Cederquist had been intrigued by a Newport, Rhode Island, high chest with a missing finial he encountered in storage. He created an illusionistic furniture sculpture (with parallelogram drawers) seemingly composed of stacked crates containing "deconstructed" sections of the historical piece. One of the leaders of furniture's "artification" in the mid-1960s, the iconoclastic Tommy Simpson contributed a whimsical, asymmetrical piece: a playful takeoff on a Windsor chair that combined a variety of carved and painted forms and imagery, as well as different woods. However, others, like Maloof's former Penland student, Thomas Hucker, and Kristina Madsen, combined high-quality workmanship with sophisticated design concepts to create functional forms that mirrored the aristocratic elegance of the originals they had selected.

In his exhibition catalogue essay, Cooke explored the background for 1980s studio furniture making, first reviewing the era of the 1950s when designer-woodworkers such as Esherick, Nakashima, and Maloof were on the "cutting edge." Then, he noted, the upscale furniture marketplace included three dominant modes: American Industrial (exemplified by Charles Eames and George Nelson), imported Scandinavian Modern (Hans Wegner and others), and custom designs by leading production designers (Edward Wormley and T. H. Robsjohn-Gibbings). Off-setting these contemporary expressions, however, was a more popular interest in colonial, or early American designs (an historicism anathema to modernist tastes in postwar Southern California). Although members of the nascent, nationwide crafts movement, Sam Maloof and other "first generation" designer-woodworkers, he accurately observed, labored in relative isolation, mostly serving a local clientele.[52]

The decade of the 1960s, however, saw crafts firmly established in university settings. Woodworkers employed as teachers were released from a dependence upon commercial sales and, as a result of cross-fertilization with other disciplines, new creative possibilities for furniture to evolve sculpturally were opened up. In that volatile decade, the ideals of form-follows-function and a reverence for "wood for wood's sake" (both central to Maloof's creative credo) were viewed as stifling, and Wendell Castle and Tommy Simpson helped reorient studio furniture toward more expressive and artistic ends. The cultural climate of the following decade, however, was more conservative and in the 1970s Swedish-trained cabinetmaker James Krenov strongly influenced younger woodworkers. Through his books and articles, he criticized the irreverent use of wood and the inelegance of carved lamination. Instead of freedom of expression, Krenov called for greater craftsmanly discipline and a restoration of the balance between formal design and high-quality workmanship. Like Krenov and Maloof, in the mid-1970s Nakashima also excoriated the domination of concept over material and execution. As he stated in *Fine Woodworking:* "Fast modern contemporary furniture, I want no part of it. People wanting to express themselves, it's just simply crap. That's what's causing all the ills of our society, individualism with nothing to express."[53]

On the East Coast, conservative-minded teachers of the "second generation" included Dan Jackson and Jere Osgood, two of Tage Frid's former students at RIT. Both recipients of additional training in Danish workshops, they became respected woodworking teachers in Philadelphia and Boston, helping to inculcate in their students high professional standards as well as fostering an interest in functional form, technical skill, and graceful design. During the expansive decade of the seventies, Cooke noted, academic courses in cabinetmaking multiplied (by 1985, some twenty degree-granting programs existed), the number of trained studio furniture makers proliferated, and the market for new one-of-a-kind pieces increased—all of which prompted museums to organize exhibitions such as *New Handmade Furniture* (1979) and high-end galleries such as Pritam and Eames (founded in 1980) to retail recent one-of-a-kind hybrids of art, furniture, and sculpture.

The 1980s, as Cooke noted, were marked by an increase in the exploration of synthetic materials—demonstrated in the Renwick Gallery show, *Material Evidence: New Color Techniques in Handmade Furniture* (1985), in which craftsmen employed the integrally colored laminate, ColorCore—and the mixing of a variety of woods with steel, aluminum, bronze, glass, plastic, and stone to create complex, visually pleasing assemblages. The dialogue with history also continued unabated, adding layers of symbolic meaning to the work and broadening public acceptability. In a summary, Cooke declared that the second-generation furniture makers of the eighties occupied a "firm middle ground between antique reproduction and first-generation reverence for natural wood and overtly functional works in safe styles," and the "radical new art furniture" of fine artists. Their work, he declared, fulfilled a need for a "participatory visual art" that, through combinations of extra-aesthetic meaning, fine craftsmanship, daring combinations of materials, and practical uses, evoked a variety of emotional responses.[54]

By restricting the furniture artists in the Boston show to useful forms reflecting the stimulus of historical models, one reviewer noted that Cooke had implicitly undermined modernism's stress on originality and its disassociation of art from mundane reality, and reaffirmed the importance of skilled work in

Fig. 183 Garry Knox Bennett, Kneehole Desk, 1989. The so-called "second generation" of studio furniture makers rejected Maloof's reverence for solid hardwoods. This postmodern desk by Bennett is composed of numerous manmade materials. Smithsonian Institution, Renwick Gallery. Gift of Anne and Ronald Abramson, the James Renwick Alliance and museum purchase through the Smithsonian Instiution Collections Acquisition Program. 1990.104.

the creation of art. As a result, *New American Furniture* brought a unique, "craftlike" viewpoint to a fine arts museum show. "The spectacle of craft aspiring to art is nothing new," she concluded, but asked provocatively, "could it be that the fine arts are moving closer to the perspective of craft?"[55]

New Honors

The idea of craft as skilled work was visually reinforced in October 1989, by the release of a 60-minute video tape, *Sam Maloof: Woodworking Profile,* by Taunton Press, publishers of *Fine Woodworking.* Carefully edited with voice-over technical explanations—and with a Schubert piano concerto playing softly in the background—watching the action on tape was even better than attending a workshop. Viewers not only witnessed Maloof's bandsaw virtuosity and his special joining and shaping skills, but enjoyed an in-depth tour of his celebrated residence. The director and cameraman had spent a week at the Maloof home, interviewing Maloof on camera about his philosophy of design and craftsmanship, and filming him as he selected the wood, and cut out, assembled, and rough-shaped a walnut rocking chair.

The videotaped chair was one of twenty-nine rockers Maloof fabricated in 1989, chairs that earned him $274,000—out of a total of $412,300 from sales of forty-four finished pieces.[56] That year, walnut rockers were priced at $8,000; models in fiddleback maple (the dense wood more difficult and time-consuming to shape and sand) cost $12,000, while those in more expensive Brazilian rosewood (another dense material) retailed for $15,000. However, when Maloof completed a back order (sometimes several years old), he was forced to charge the original, outdated price, so three customers who received rocking chairs made in 1989 were charged only four, five, and six thousand dollars.

Atlanta reporter Jack Warner reviewed the new videotape in a woodworking column that was syndicated nationwide by the Cox News Service. It was written just after Maloof had given a workshop at Highland Hardware. The journalist asserted that much of Maloof's work revealed a creative power that was "unearthly" and he concluded his report with an outright declaration: "there is no one who can reasonably be compared to Maloof. . . . He is simply one of a kind . . . the rarest of creatures, a true genius."[57] In California, noted Carmel Valley woodworker Alan Marks also reviewed the film, asserting the "talented, gregarious, prolific, generous" Maloof to be "a woodworking institution," the nation's "most acclaimed" worker in wood. While some cynical craftsmen found the open-hearted Maloof "ingenuous," Marks accepted him at face value: "I honestly believe he stands in awe of all the positive things that have happened to him during his life. Since he can't quite believe his good fortune, he makes it seem more real by sharing it with everyone."[58]

Maloof's "good fortune" had included winning in 1988 the ACC's highest honor, the Gold Medal for "consummate craftsmanship." Traditionally, winners were drawn from the college of fellows and were honored for their "exceptional contribution to the field as an artist, but additionally, by [their] influence as a teacher or mentor, and by the humanistic and philosophical values exemplified in their career."[59] (Instituted in 1981, the award previously had been given to such leading craftsmakers as Anni Albers, Harvey Littleton, Lenore Tawney, and Peter Voulkos.) The ceremony took place at an awards dinner held in San Diego and Maloof received his medal from city mayor and arts supporter, Maureen O'Connor (later a fellow ACC board member). He was not the only honoree that evening. For bringing a "humanistic approach and a poet's sensitivity" to her writing on crafts, Rose Slivka was presented with an Award of Distinction. As chairman of the Council's committee on fellows, Sam also witnessed the investiture of seventeen new fellows, among them woodworker Arthur Espenet Carpenter and his longtime Padua Hills friend, potter Harrison McIntosh. For their part in advancing the crafts, Paul J. Smith, director emeritus of the American Craft Museum, and Lloyd Herman, founding director of the Renwick Gallery, were made honorary fellows.[60]

In 1991, a year in which he made forty-four recorded pieces (twenty-three of them rockers) that earned him $386,700 (naturally, not all of it paid that year), the seventy-five-year-old woodworker received several more significant accolades. On February 8 a thirty-piece retrospective of his furniture opened at the Sweeney Art Gallery at the University of California, Riverside, the largest display of his work since his solo exhibition in Long Beach in 1970.[61] Dating from the early 1950s to 1990, many of the pieces came from his own collection. On May 10 Maloof received an even greater honor when Boston's august Society of Arts and Crafts (SAC), America's first crafts organization founded in 1897, conferred on him its prestigious Medal for Excellence in Crafts. (Inaugurated in 1913, the annual award had been discontinued in 1950 and only re-introduced in 1990.) Maloof was the first furniture maker to receive it. The Maloofs had flown to Boston for the event, staying with Jonathan Fairbanks and his family in their historic house in the suburbs. At the time, Maloof's health was not the strongest: he was recuperating from a mild heart attack—his third—suffered in February. (Freda, too, had been slowed down by heart problems. Three years earlier, she had undergone cardiac arrest and had only slowly regained her strength.) For the evening gala held at the SAC's Arch Street gallery, the woodworker uncharacteristically wore a suit and tie and was photographed beaming with pleasure as he was presented with the newly recast medal by President Ellen Grossman.[62]

The ceremony also heralded the opening of two adjacent exhibitions in the gallery that underscored the Californian's remarkable achievement over forty years: *Sam Maloof Retrospective* and *The Legacy of Sam Maloof: Woodworking as a Way of Life.* The solo display included twelve pieces, among them a new, single music stand, a fiddleback maple settee, and three rockers, including an example in greenish-gray, Mexican Zircote wood. The "legacy" show was comprised of work by seven furniture makers and fifteen wood turners, among the latter pioneer Bob Stocksdale. Following in Maloof's footsteps, all had pursued full-time careers in woodworking. A trustee of the SAC, Fairbanks had helped put together the one-man exhibit, while Edward S. Cooke, Jr., a member of the group's advisory board, had assisted in organizing the display of contemporary pieces, selecting examples of six of the furniture makers that had appeared in *New American Furniture.*

Fig. 184 Alfreda and Sam Maloof, 1982.
As a working couple, the Maloofs provided
a role model that in the 1970s and 1980s
many younger studio furniture makers
sought to emulate. Reproduction by permission of Jonathan Pollock.

In a short essay written for the occasion, Cooke noted one of the most intangible but influential results of Maloof's lengthy career was "his legacy as the
woodworker who validated furnituremaking as a career choice." More than anyone else active since the 1950s, Maloof had "set the example that someone can
earn a living by producing chairs, tables, and case furniture with high standards
of workmanship and finish." Moreover, "his clarity of expression, work ethic, and
generosity to aspiring woodworkers have contributed to this leadership role."[63]
Linking Maloof's functional pieces, with their strong, sculptural presence and
distinctive appearance, with the more conceptually oriented, eclectic, and mixed
media work of the second generation was somewhat contentious, especially
given the fact that Maloof regularly criticized such creations as emotionally cold
and egocentric. Somewhat defensively, Cooke addressed the issue of genera-
tional divergence: "While Maloof often laments the lack of recognizable aesthetic
'signatures' among members of the second generation, their furniture is consistent with current philosophy. Like many of his contemporaries, Maloof sought

to develop pure abstracted forms that highlighted the grain and warmth of solid wood. As a result, his style has been consistent and recognizable. The emphasis of work in the past decade has been less on the material itself, and more on the diversity of style that gives weight to idea, form, and choice of material and technique. . . . Many are using wood and traditional techniques in a different context." One of the participants, woodworker Tom Loeser, had begun using corrugated cardboard, challenging conventional preconceptions of beauty and craftsmanship. Cooke had included several of his recent painted pieces in the *Legacy* exhibit. While such an exploration in non-traditional materials veered far from Maloof's own philosophy of woodworking, Loeser's work was nonetheless decreed "a by-product of the master's leadership."[64]

As part of the celebrations, three furniture makers were invited to comment in writing on Maloof's impact. Tage Frid stated that he had first encountered Maloof at Asilomar in 1957. A "great artist and craftsman," and a man very serious about his work, he declared Sam's designs always "well thought through and executed" and his influence on postwar American furniture design "great." Alphonse Mattia, one of Frid's former students and a faculty member of the Rhode Island School of Design's (RISD) graduate furniture program—an artist known for humorous content and use of color—summed up the feelings of many in the second generation:

For students starting out in the mid-60s there was only a handful of studio furniture makers to look to for inspiration. Sam was one of the more visible. Through the integrity of his work, the size and setting of his studio, and the amount of work he could produce he set a mark of excellence. I don't think the contemporary furniture scene would be as rich or as far along as it is today without Sam Maloof's influence as a leader and dedicated craftsman. Sam and Freda Maloof have contributed much to the American Craft tradition. Through their commitment and generosity they have encouraged many of us in the way we work and the way we live.[65]

Another RISD teacher, Roseanne Somerson, whose own functional pieces combined different materials and featured applied ornament, contributed a statement underscoring the personal impact of Maloof's—as well as Freda's— influence: "People who meet Sam are always marked by his warmth, strength, and energy. As a young furniture maker just setting up shop I visited the Maloofs. Sam didn't know me at all then, yet he generously and openly took time to show me his work, studio, and home. Freda's hospitality matched his and I felt very lucky for the experience. Over the years, on his own, Sam watched my work evolve and always showed me support, support I never solicited. This meant an awful lot. As my commitment to furniture making grew, my respect for Sam's years of hard work grew as well. Sam and Freda are deeply caring people, the sort that make big differences in people's lives" (fig. 184).[66]

For his part, Jonathan Fairbanks wrote a lengthy and personal paean to his longtime friend, "Sam Maloof: Celebrating Forty-Four Years in the Fine Art of Furniture Making," reprinted in *Antiques & Fine Art*.[67] While affirming that function was fundamental to his philosophy, Fairbanks noted there were qualities of enduring beauty in Maloof's pieces that pointed beyond simply satisfying practical needs. What made Maloof furniture unique and compelling, he asserted, was the craftsman's concern for imparting the visual dynamics of sculpture to his designs—proportion, spatial division, articulation of parts, linear motion, textures, visual accents, and contrasts. From a distance, Maloof's dramatic seating forms (especially rockers) appeared visually as tall, gestural sweeps offset by shorter, more firm lines (fig. 185). Fluidity of movement was further conveyed by differently sculptured shapes—thick and thin, rounded or blade-like. When taking a closer look, the viewer could enjoy the quieter details of sculptural joinery, woodgrain patterns, and the perfect satiny smoothness of all surfaces. A reporter for the *Boston Herald* interviewed Maloof on the occasion of his small retrospective. "I never reach the perfection I want," he told her, "and I hope I never do. You're always searching for perfection. One can always climb the mountain. If you reach the top, you have to come down."[68]

Fig. 185 Rocking chair, 1999. Fiddleback maple and ebony; 46¼ × 27¾ × 45⅛ inches; inscribed "No. 2 1999/ Sam Maloof d.f.a r.i.s.d/ ©/ m.j. l.w. d.w"; collection of Bill and Rosanna Baldwin.

While the SAC shows were on view from May into August, another, more avant-garde furniture exhibition was on display at Manhattan's American Craft Museum, *Explorations II: The New Furniture.* Organized by curator John Perrault, it featured fifty-one objects by eleven artists and included pieces characterized as "original furniture, furniture-like forms, and furniture as sculpture."[69] None of the artists appeared in Cooke's concurrent *Legacy* show, and only three had been selected for his *New American Furniture* show—Garry Knox Bennett, Wendy Maruyama, and Ed Zucca. Along with woodworker David Ebner, they were the only ones among the participants working within the woodcraft tradition established in the 1950s by Esherick, Nakashima, and Maloof.

Indeed, it was Perrault's intent to move beyond the confines of even second-generation woodworkers to explore furniture as a "theme" in the hands of contemporary artists. He thus included a variety of individuals outside the furniture matrix—metalsmith Gary Griffin, production designer Dakota Jackson (formerly a dancer), and sculptors Allan Wexler (trained as an architect), Paul Ludick (a performance artist), and Elizabeth Egbert (a creator of outdoor seating as public art). Another exhibitor, Daniel Mack, had pursued a career as a radio and television journalist and teacher before almost single-handedly resurrecting the genre of rustic furniture as an art form, while Alex Locadia had previously embedded electronic devices or household appliances in housings of concrete or stone before creating interactive, sculpturesque seating with a post-apocalyptic, science-fiction look.[70]

In one way or another, all the participants employed furniture to make social commentary, relying on its symbolic use in social settings, or its obvious relationship (especially chairs) to the human body, as means of communicating ideas. But beyond the artistic strategy of transgressing categories, the reason why so many non-craft, avant-garde artists had turned to furniture, Perrault conjectured, was the fact that, since they were related to anatomy and at least implicitly signified functional use, chair-, desk-, and table-like forms naturally stimulated "the aesthetics of the physical"—a visceral response that nonfunctional sculpture resisted.[71] Like craftsmen in the late 1950s, the furniture object

Fig. 186 Inscription on rocking chair, 1999. After his honorary doctorate from the Rhode Island School of Design Sam dropped the initials "f.A.C.C." and substituted "d.f.a. r.i.s.d."

makers in *Explorations II* ignored the realities of their own technological era, he stated, seeking instead to reassert through their eclectic work the power of emotion and symbolism. But the forms and materials through which they sought to express such extra-aesthetic vitality bore little relationship to those of Maloof and the other pioneers of the studio furniture movement.

In May 1991, architect and author Witold Rybczynski wrote an article for the Sunday *New York Times,* "If a chair is a work of art, can you sit on it?" He noted that current studio furniture arose from the postwar achievements of Esherick, Nakashima, and Maloof who, rejecting industrial materials, techniques, and production methods, had revived the cabinetmaking skills, if not the styles, of the past. With its spare lines, lack of ornament, and ahistorical designs, Maloof's work was described as a "curious amalgam" of modernist aesthetics and pre-industrial methods. To Rybczynski, it displayed one of the chief attributes—and appeals –of traditional crafts: a rejection of novelty and passing fads, and a sense of permanence resulting from a slow, evolutionary rate of design change. However, in dynamic societies the stable values intrinsic to traditional crafts were threatened. "Either the crafts must embrace a hermetic and artificial existence," the writer stated, "holding fast to orthodoxies and reiterating old ways, rather than inventing new ones, or it must accept change." Clearly, studio furniture had accepted change and had moved swiftly in the direction of fine art. But, on the question "if it is a work of art, is it still a chair?" the movement was still divided, he commented, between those influenced by Wendell Castle who wished to be identified publicly as artists who invented new forms and those like Maloof who sought to address timeless issues of craftsmanship and function in classic designs.[72]

More Honors

Although far from art furniture's "cutting edge," during the 1990s Maloof was highy praised.[73] In terms of public recognition, decades of hard work committed to his singular vision continued to pay off. In 1992, Cypress College in nearby Orange County, California, organized a celebratory, twenty-seven-work survey of his furniture, while, more significantly, on the opposite coast, the trustees of the Rhode Island School of Design conferred on him an honorary doctorate of fine arts. It was a proud moment for the Depression-era graduate of Chino High School and he immediately dropped the inscription he had used since 1975, "f.A.C.C.," signing his work instead "d.f.a. r.i.s.d." (fig. 186).

That same year, Maloof International, the organization serving the interests of the worldwide Maloof clan, gave him its Lifetime Achievement Award for Outstanding Representation of the Family Name. His parents would have been overjoyed with this honor bestowed on their son. Scattered around the globe were tens of thousands of successful Maloofs, all descendants of original emigrants from the Levant. Proud of his Middle Eastern heritage, in the 1990s Maloof was embraced by the Arab American world. In 1991 the Kahlil Gibran Centennial Foundation of Washington, D.C., recognized him for his outstanding achievement in creative arts, while at Rice University in Houston the following year, the Arab American Education Foundation presented him its

Achievement of Excellence Award. In 1995 *Aramco World,* an English-language magazine aimed at readers in the Arab diaspora, celebrated Maloof's work in a lavishly illustrated article featuring his new maple pieces. To the delight of his Lebanese relatives and friends, the laudatory text was reprinted in the weekly *Beirut Times.*[74]

In 1993, a year in which he traveled with Freda and Slimen to Spain for three weeks in May, he contributed work to six exhibitions, including *The Fine Art of American Craft* at the Los Angeles County Fair,[75] the California Council of the American Institute of Architects (AIA) presented him with its Craftsmanship Award. The inscription read: "In recognition of your exceptional talent as a woodworker. The mastery you demonstrate with the fine art of woodcraft has influenced the world of art and architecture with original furniture designs. Your special and industrious commitment to your work is unique and inspiring to designers of all disciplines." The citation of industriousness was significant. Even in his late seventies, Sam Maloof was still the most prolific studio furniture maker in the nation. In 1992, for example, he fabricated some seventy-eight numbered pieces. This escalation in production (only forty-four were completed the previous year) was mostly due to his full recovery from his recent heart attack, but also to the fact that in March 1992, his first full-time employee, Larry White, rejoined the workshop staff. He and his wife Catherine moved into the adjacent guest house, no longer used as a showroom. Mike O'Neil had quit in late 1991, so with the masterful White signing on to work alongside the experienced Mike Johnson (the preeminent sander, bringing the subtleties of hard lines and sculptural transitions to the fore) and a young, talented newcomer,

Fig. 187 Workshop crew, 2000. In November 1999, the workshop was relocated to the Maloofs' new property. From left to right: Mike Johnson, Larry White, Slimen Maloof, David Wade, and Kern Briggs. Reproduction by permission of Jonathan Pollock.

David Wade (who joined in 1988), Sam's "boys," as he called them, irrespective of their ages, comprised the best team he had ever assembled (fig. 187).

Maloof, however, still cut out, assembled, and rough shaped every piece. Nothing left the shop that he had not designed, sawn, joined, or initially sculpted. Moreover, he closely supervised the detailing work of the others. Often in the evening, he went over work in progress in the sanding room (where seventy-five percent of the time that went into making a chair or table was spent), marking with a pencil hard lines that needed emphasizing, or sculptural transitions that required subtle shaping. Discovered in the morning, these penciled marks often dismayed Johnson and White, for they signaled additional hours of arm-numbing sanding. But it was the process by which the master subtly altered the tactile qualities of each piece in his ongoing search for perfection. In the office, Freda still put in a full day, managing the accounts, answering the busy telephone, confirming orders, and scheduling Maloof's myriad outside activities—as well as cooking meals and entertaining a constant stream of visitors and guests. She tried hard to keep her gregarious husband in check: when people stopped by unannounced, he spent generous amounts of time with them, often missing other appointments and tasks. But human contact was essential to his well-being and he made no real distinction between his business and social life. Maloof thoroughly enjoyed showing his work and home to visitors, whatever their motives.

Clients, Commissions, and New Directions

By the mid-1980s, requests for roomfuls or large suites of Maloof furniture had largely subsided. There was no dominant architectural style with which Maloof's distinctive designs coordinated, nor a regionally based clientele with collective needs and ideals to serve as there had been in the 1950s. Affluent homeowners now ordered single pieces or small sets to mix in with antiques or modern commercial lines in all manner of residences, from Manhattan high-rises to sprawling West Coast mansions. He even shipped pieces abroad, to customers in Europe and the Far East.

Generally, in the late 1980s and 1990s Maloof's American clients fell into two basic categories: repeat or new customers desiring well-designed, functional pieces for daily living, and newly established craft collectors seeking examples of Maloof's best known models to integrate into their collections. Photographs in *Sam Maloof: Woodworker* prompted many orders; customers used it like a catalogue, over the phone or in letters ordering such pieces as "the chair on page 131" or "the rocker on the cover."

Exemplifying the first client group, in 1985 the Harrises of Chicago ordered a set of twelve tall-back dining chairs with sculpted wood seats, flat spindles, and curved arms, then a popular chair type (figs. 188 and 189) to go with a custom-designed Maloof dining table. (Dining room furniture remained perennially popular.) Two years later, local friends Earle and Patty Kruggel took possession of another dining set that included ten chairs and a rectangular trestle table that extended to ten feet. The same year, Mr. and Mrs. Clinton Marr acquired a large oval, drop-leaf dining table that also opened up the same length.

While most of the twenty-four dining tables ordered by homeowners in the late 1980s and 1990s were made from walnut (in 1991 an example in rare curly walnut was made for Dr. and Mrs. Ralph Norman, strong supporters of Maloof's work), examples in lighter-toned, burled English brown oak were also constructed. In 1998 St. Louis investment manager, Alfred Goldman, who already owned a one-of-a-kind rocker, acquired a unique dining table with a top made from a solid slab of brown oak joined to a sculptured base in black walnut—along with a set of eight, low-back, Evans-style walnut dining chairs. Two other tables in the same wood were also completed that year, retailing for $25,000 apiece. Dining tables came in rectangular, oval, "square-round," or circular formats, either fixed, drop-leaf, or extendable. If round, like a forty-eight-inch-diameter example dating from 1988 (fig. 190), the top was firmly supported by a single pedestal with four branching legs. Long, rectangular tables, on the other hand, typically employed flat, sculptured pedestal supports at the ends joined by horizontal trestles.

Small pedestal side tables (usually with twenty-inch-diameter tops) were particularly popular. Easy to make, Maloof often gave them as gifts. In 1985 he donated one to his old client, actor Gene Kelly, as a seventy-fifth birthday gift, while others served as wedding gifts for the children of client-friends or as

Figs. 188–189 Dining chairs with flat spindles and curved arms, 1979. Walnut and ebony; 42 ½ x 21 x 24 inches deep; inscribed: "No. 41 1978" and "No. 44/Sam Maloof f.A.C.C."; private collection.

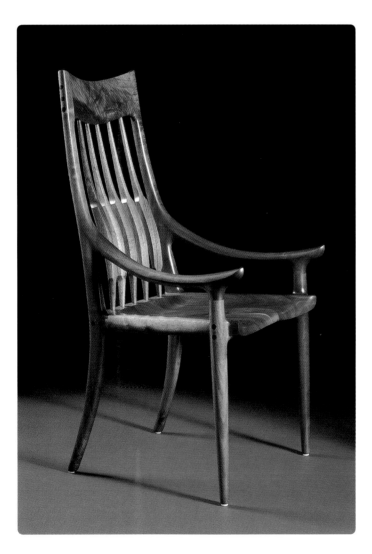

charitable donations. In 1988 he contributed one to an auction at Anderson Ranch, the proceeds of which went into the Sam and Alfreda Maloof Scholarship Fund. (The following year, he donated a rocker to the annual auction for the same purpose.) Designed at various heights, and made from different woods, small round tables were bread-and-butter sales items. Maloof often had several made up at one time which he quickly sold to visitors in search of ready-made pieces. When he discovered wood with spectacular graining, he sometimes fabricated them for his own private use. An example in walnut with dramatic, flame-like sapwood patterns (fig. 191) graced the master bedroom. Like all works made after 1992, it was inscribed with the chronological number and year of production, along with his now-standard, burned-in signature, "Sam Maloof d.f.a. r.i.s.d."—and the initials of his workers: "m.j." (Mike Johnson), "l.w." (Larry White), and "d.w." (David Wade).

Several new clients were celebrities. In 1988 puppeteer Jim Henson, creator of the Muppets, purchased an unusual rocking chair. Made of dark Gabon ebony, for decorative purposes it employed two strips of bright maple in the laminated rockers, as well as maple plugs inserted in the drill holes where the seat and crest rail were screwed to the legs. Henson also commissioned a low-back, Evans-style settee for his Manhattan apartment. The object-filled setting was featured in *Art For Everyday: The New Craft Movement* (1990), a book that promoted contemporary crafts as not only fashionable, but practical furnishings. Henson enjoyed the commissioning process. "What I like best," he was quoted as saying, "are craft pieces that I can use, not the sort of thing I have to put on a shelf. When craft moves away from function in order to be 'high art,' I lose interest in it."[76] Maloof was shocked to learn of the puppeteer's untimely death in 1990, writing in a letter to the editor of the *Los Angeles Times:* "Jim Henson was the kindest and most gentle person I have ever known—a giant who gave all of us a feeling of laughter and love. He shall not be forgotten."[77]

Another notable client who ordered a similar settee in fiddleback maple was Boston-based investment fund manager, Peter Lynch, a strong supporter of Jonathan Fairbanks's curatorial activities. For their home in coastal Marblehead, Massachusetts, already replete with outstanding examples of eighteenth-century cabinetmaking, Lynch and his wife Carolyn acquired four additional pieces from Maloof: a walnut rocker, two large pedestal tables, and the solo music stand from the craftsman's 1991 retrospective at the SAC. Like so many clients, the Lynches became fast friends with the Maloofs, keeping in touch and inviting Maloof and Freda to stay with them in Marblehead. "Sam's not what you'd expect," the financial expert declared to one reporter, "He's so down to earth . . . so enthusiastic. My goodness, on a scale of 1 to 10, he's about a 303. Whenever you talk to him or Freda, you feel better."[78]

The same year Maloof made Henson's settee, he fabricated another low-back example in tiger-striped maple for the Metropolitan Museum of Art in New York (fig. 192). With its daring structural engineering, strong sculptural presence, and formal vitality, it proved a fine addition to the museum's small, but select collection of twentieth-century decorative arts and design. The handful of postwar furniture makers already represented included Finn Juhl, Wharton

Fig. 190 Pedestal side table, 1997. Walnut; 28½ x 32 inch diameter; inscribed: "Sam Maloof No. 50 1997/ d.f.a. r.i.s.d./m.j. l.w. d.w.": Sam and Alfreda Maloof Foundation. Maloof often saved wood with dramatic graining for his private use. This table was used in his master bedroom.

Fig. 191 Pedestal dining table, 1988. Walnut; 28½ x 42 inch diameter; unmarked; private collection. Circular dining tables required strong sculptural pedestal supports.

Esherick (a music stand from 1962), Charles and Ray Eames, George Nakashima, and Wendell Castle (an organic, carved settee of 1977).

In a lavish book illustrating the Metropolitan's design collection, Maloof's settee was situated in a chapter focusing on work by ten craftspeople whose functional craft objects had "transcended" into "high art."[79] As curator R. Craig Miller noted in his text, the postwar craftworks did not reveal a shared style—as had been the case with earlier design movements—but rather a "common attitude" among artists who had spent their lives working within a single medium without bending to fashion trends. As a result, the sole criterion for judging their work, he rightly noted, was the singular context of their own unique development, not the wider culture of twentieth-century design.[80] In terms of Maloof's distinctive output over forty years, it was an apt conclusion. It made little sense to judge it against "artiture." The august Manhattan museum was not the only institution of its kind to acquire examples of Maloof's low-back settee design in fiddleback maple. In 1986 the Los Angeles County Museum of Art had ordered four of them as public seating. Three years later, the Philadelphia Museum of Art purchased a single example and in 1993, a year after Maloof was awarded his honorary doctorate, two were added as gallery seating in the new Daphne Farago Wing at the museum of the Rhode Island School of Design.

While major craft collectors typically sat on or dined off their Maloof acquisitions, they still considered them a discrete part of their collections. In 1988, Washington, D.C., art furniture collectors, Anne and Ronald Abramson—major supporters of second-generation studio furniture makers[81]—acquired their first Maloof piece, a high-backed occasional chair in maple with flat spindles and sculpted arms. It was a rarely ordered design; with its low, deeply shaped wood seat, and short legs it was like a rocking chair with the rockers removed. The Maloofs had one in their bedroom (*see* fig. 179). The Abramsons also purchased two other popular models that year—an updated Evans chair and the settee modeled on that design, likewise in maple, the most popular wood for collectors.

Another Washington-area couple, Samuel J. and Eleanor T. Rosenfeld, ordered a similar two-seater, later adding a rocker and a small pedestal table, also in fiddleback maple. In 1990 San Francisco collectors George and Dorothy Saxe acquired a maple Evans chair, later adding a recent hornback side chair (now called a "Texas" chair) in walnut and a rocker in Zircote. The maple chair toured nationally in the exhibition *Contemporary Crafts and the Saxe Collection,* further popularizing the sculptural, low-back design as a canonical "collectible." After Maloof was named a MacArthur Fellow in 1985, other nationally known collectors also added Maloof pieces. Sydney and Frances Lewis of Richmond, Virginia, whose assembly of modern decorative arts and design is among the highlights of the Virginia Museum of Fine Arts, acquired a fiddleback maple rocker made in 1986, while Providence, Rhode Island, prolific crafts collectors Peter and Daphne Farago purchased, in addition to ten other Maloof pieces in their collection, the landmark maple rocker exhibited in *Craft Today.*

In early 1987 Maloof introduced a new, forty-two-inch, double rocker design (fig. 193). With thirteen flat spindles fitted between the wide-spanning,

Fig. 192 Low-back settee, 1987. This example was acquired for the twentieth-century design collection of the Metropolitan Museum of Art. The Metropolitan Museum of Art, Gift of the artist, and Purchase, Anonymous Gift, 1988. (1988.90).

sculptured seat and back rest, it was the largest and most complex of his seating forms. It was also the showiest of his chairs. Nine of the eleven constructed by 1999 were made from bright, fiddleback maple decoratively and strikingly accented at the joins with black Gabon ebony plugs and with ebony strips laminated in the long, slender rocker units. Over the years, the prices of these new double rocking chairs escalated sharply from $9,500 to $30,000. One of the first was acquired in 1988 by Barbaralee Diamonstein (author of *Handmade in America*) and her husband, Carl Spielvogel. (Later the couple donated the walnut rocker they acquired in 1982 to the White House Collection of American Crafts.) The Faragos purchased the example that had toured in the 1990 exhibit, *Art That Works,* and in 1993 Maloof made another in maple especially for his friends, Jimmy and Rosalynn Carter (fig. 194). Maloof's San Diego patron, businessman John C. Moores (among his most prominent clients in the 1990s), first ordered a pair of double rockers in 1991, then another to complement two

Fig. 193 Double rocker, 1992. Maloof introduced double rockers in 1987. By 2000, he had made eleven examples. Smithsonian Institution, Renwick Gallery. Gift of the Hafif Family Foundation, the James Renwick Allince and museum purchase made possible by the Smithsonian Collections Acquisiton Progrm. 1992.115.

Fig. 194 President Jimmy Carter in the Maloof workshop. In December 1981, the former president, himself an amateur woodworker, had visited the Maloofs. The Carters subsequently acquired two Maloof rockers, one a double version.

single-seaters in walnut and Zircote. The next year, Maloof's Claremont friend and longtime client, Herb Hafif, donated a model to the Renwick Gallery, along with a small pedestal side table in similar maple. The last of the series, numbered 8/96, was purchased by Renwick supporters Deena and Jerry Kaplan of suburban Washington, D.C.

During the period from 1985 to 2000, Maloof acquired one important corporate client, the art-conscious Los Angeles utilities giant, Pacific Enterprises, whose orders for its new 3,000-square-foot executive offices in the Library Tower kept him busy during 1990 until his mild heart attack in the fall. The chief executive officer and his wife had visited the shop one day and casually asked whether he was interested in a commission for office furniture. It proved a large order. Eventually, Maloof ended up making some seventy pieces. For his own office suite, the CEO ordered two maple rockers and a small pedestal table, along with a ten-foot-long executive desk with a maple top and walnut base, as well as office chairs and a long credenza. For his private conference room, he requested a six-foot-diameter, oval table with four high-back, spindled chairs. For the executive reception area, Maloof made eight hornback chairs.

He was also asked to make an eighteen-foot, circular conference table for the board room along with twenty-seven matching, high-back executive swivel chairs—all upholstered in black leather and priced at $10,000 each. The table was much too large to fabricate in his Alta Loma workshop, so he initially proposed building a new shop. But the construction project was too much of an undertaking, so he arranged instead to make it in a large woodworking facility in Aspen, Colorado. The piece was the largest he had ever constructed. Made up of twelve pie-shaped sections in fiddleback maple, the massive top was supported by a complex metal base designed and constructed by an engineer friend. As a decorative surface feature, Maloof inserted a circular, five-foot diameter section of walnut burl into the center.[82]

In the 1990s, religious institutions also requested Maloof furnishings, and for two of them Maloof designed and constructed work unprecedented in his oeuvre. In 1994 he began several pieces for the chancel of the newly renovated Kresge Chapel at the nearby Claremont School of Theology, a United Methodist institution on whose board of trustees he served. One was a majestic, twenty-foot-high walnut cross. To suggest the body of Christ, he attached the crooked bark edges of sawn planks to the smooth face of the cross. It hung by two invisible wires high above the altar, canting slightly toward the congregants. Maloof never measured the vertical space; he simply "eyeballed" it and intuitively designed a cross with proportions that perfectly fit the void. At the junction of the axes he placed a ring of pink ivorywood. A spotlight at the back of the soaring, white-painted church interior—a beam arranged like a piercing shaft of sunlight—dramatically illuminated the circle.

Beneath the cross was a simple, almost primitive, altar whose top was fashioned from a massive three-inch-thick slab of walnut, the untrimmed edges smoothed, but left irregular. A narrower plank, its ragged bark edges left untrimmed, was turned on its side and served as a trestle. Utterly simple, it maintained a powerful presence on the raised dias (fig. 195). For the clergy's use, he also made two plain, throne-like chairs out of thick pieces of plain walnut (fig. 196), as well as a lectern. In late January 2000, the pieces were dedicated. One of the speakers was Carolyn Sheets, now an ordained minister. As a thirteen-year-old girl, with a crush on Maloof, she had cried her eyes out when she learned her father's handsome studio assistant—her first true love, she admitted unrepentantly—would marry Freda instead. "Theirs was an uncommon harmony," she told the audience. "Her spiritual beauty lives on in his art."[83]

During six months in 1999–2000, Maloof and his three-man team of workers constructed another set of liturgical furniture for the sanctuary of a striking, new Roman Catholic church, St. Maximilian Kolbe, in Oak Park, California. This time, the massive wooden cross (built around a heavy steel armature made to be fixed to the floor and withstand earthquakes) measured twenty-eight feet high by fourteen feet across. Other pieces included a tabernacle whose doors closed with a latch cut from a tree branch, a lectern, two chairs for officiating priests, and a highly unusual altar. Like the examples in the Claremont chapel, all were massive forms constructed from walnut slabs selected from his large stockpile of lumber. While Maloof had drawn detailed plans of the furniture for the approval of a church committee, to check the actual proportions and serviceability of the monumental lectern, he had Larry White make a full-scale model in plywood, before ordering the final, block-like walnut version cut out and put together. Five thick strips, the irregular bark edges face forward, were inserted vertically between the extended side planks, giving the front a powerful, rough-hewn look.

One evening, Maloof was in the sanding room considering the work in progress. Vaguely dissatisfied with the design, but unable to identify the reason for his growing doubts, he off-handedly picked up and placed another, natural-edged walnut plank atop the front edge, like a lintel. (The tops of the single-slab sides raked backwards.) Suddenly, with this new horizontal element balancing the vertical thrusts, the entire piece took on a whole new—and wholly satisfying—formal character. As a designer-craftsman, he had been altering designs during fabrication for four decades. When White and the others arrived the next morning, the added slab was cut to size and joined to the carcase, creating a far more effective and resolved composition.

The top for the altar was made from a slab sawn from the crotch of a large walnut tree; the naturally occurring split was an essential part of the design (fig. 197). Unlike the version made for the Claremont chapel, the solid sides of this elemental altar were dovetailed to the massive top, the whole made more secure with an irregular plank fixed to the underside of the top and joined to the sides. Like the rustic lectern, its bold, sculptural form was direct and impressive. The set also included two uncompromising, slab-sided chairs. The formal power of the suite of sanctuary furniture matching that of the towering brick interior with its skylight ringed with an angular redwood structure that appeared like a crown of thorns. In his enthusiasm for the project, Maloof had gone far over the church's allotted budget (he also provided a processional cross and a pew design to be manufactured commercially), but he was adamant that his vision be realized completely, so he was willing to take a financial loss. The commission would remain an important part of his design legacy. In retrospect, the use of walnut slabs for ecclesiastical furniture was partly an homage to his friend George Nakashima, whose 1990 obituary he had written for *American Craft*.[84] In 1986 the Japanese American woodworker had donated to the Cathedral of St. John the Divine an immense *Altar for Peace,* a masterwork comprised of two heroically scaled, irregular, book-matched sections sawn from a huge black walnut log and joined with massive dovetails.[85]

In the post-1985 period, seating forms were by far the most commonly ordered designs and, among them, rocking chairs predominated. Some 270 were fabricated. The vast majority had wood seats, flat spindles, and upright horns. Although craft collectors preferred maple, most were made from walnut. One visiting magazine writer, impressed with the exquisite balance of these chairs, undertook an experiment: He gave the back of one a firm push and timed how long it rocked. It finally stopped after four-and-a-half minutes.[86] Aside from walnut and maple, between 1985 and 2000 Maloof occasionally used other woods in his popular rockers: two of teak, two of Macassar ebony, three of purpleheart, five of rosewood, six of Zircote, and eight of cherry.

If chairs retained their perennial popularity, in the late period case pieces were rarely ordered. Indeed, for dressers and armoires, Maloof proved to be among his own best customers (fig. 198). As for other designs in his extensive repertoire, only occasionally was his earliest signature piece—the laced bench introduced in 1953—requested by clients. Once-popular bar or counter stools likewise were rarely commissioned. Free standing cradles, too, were infrequently ordered. In 1992 the DeYoung Museum in San Francisco acquired one in fiddleback maple—the first Maloof had made since 1977, when a walnut version was sold at the Philadelphia Craft Show. But in 1995, three examples with

Fig. 195 Kresge chapel altar, 1994. Claremont School of Theology. Reproduction by permission of Jonathan Pollock.

Fig. 196 Kresge chapel chair, 1999. Walnut; Claremont School of Theology. Reproduction by permission of Jonathan Pollock.

Fig. 197 St. Maximilian Kolbe altar, 2000. Oak Park, California. Reproduction by permission of Jonathan Pollock.

Fig. 198 Dresser, 1984. Walnut and ebony; 40½ x 66¾ x 21¾ inches; inscribed: "No. 16 1984/Sam Maloof f.A.C.C./j.m.": Sam and Alfreda Maloof Foundation.

Fig. 199 Dictionary stand, 1989. Macassar ebony; 38 ¾ x 38 ¼ x 25 ¼ inches deep; inscribed: "No. 60 1989/Sam Maloof f.A.C.C."; private collection. Although Maloof's work was usually executed in black walnut, he occasionally used exotic woods such as Macassar ebony.

wheels were fabricated, including two for the Moores in San Diego. As for print or dictionary stands, only one was fabricated after 1982—a spectacular example fabricated in Macassar ebony in 1989 for fellow Lebanese American friends, Dr. and Mrs. Joseph J. Jacobs of Pasadena (fig. 199).

Music racks fared better: some fifteen were ordered. But in the mid-1990s, the original 1964 design underwent revolutionary changes. Instead of solid, booklike holders fixed on horizontal bars with wooden screws, like Wendell Castle's landmark example, the new sheet music racks were composed of six gently curved ribs (the ends joined to a strip of ebony) that attached to a central spine. The wooden assembly slid up and down a vertical post supported by a pedestal base (fig. 200). The new stands also came in solo, duet, trio, and quartet versions. They were the showiest and most intricate of his designs—and when made in fiddleback maple, incorporated decorative details in ebony and other exotic woods. The music holders themselves were intricately sculpted and shaped (fig. 201). Their unusually fancy nature—in Maloof's words, "they opened up like flowers"[87]—was partly in response to the complicated forms and virtuoso workmanship of second generation art furniture makers.

In the 1990s innovations continued. In 1997 Maloof introduced a new, high-back chair design into his still-expanding repertoire, applying it to occasional, settee, and rocker models. Instead of a typical broad, flat head rest and wide sculpted arms, the new pattern incorporated narrower, sinuous lines. Like dining chairs from the mid-1950s, the ends of the rounded arms were attached directly to the turned tops of the front legs. But instead of straight lines and right angles, undulating, compound curves predominated. The narrow arms snaked laterally outwards before turning inward curvaceously to join the long, upward thrust of the back post (figs. 202 and 203). The sinuous quality of the movement continued across the headrest, now a thin, arched form. Binding the whole rhythmic composition together into a single tactile entity were prominent hard lines that ran almost completely around the chair. All the contours of the late chairs could be traced by running a finger along these interconnecting ridges.

In the 1990s, Maloof began to elaborate and exaggerate his signature hard lines, making them much more apparent to the eye. As a result, his sculptural designs became even more expressive, visually and tactilely. Not only did he accentuate the ridges, elevating them higher from the smooth surfaces, but sometimes, on the tall backposts of his rocking chairs, doubling them, so they ran parallel to each other creating runnels down the back of the rear legs. Sharpened front edges of his scalloped, saddle-shaped seats likewise contributed to a new assertiveness.

By the 1990s, the more aggressive nature of the hard lines had helped redefine the shape and character of pedestal supports. Instead of being gently rounded, the arched legs were now modeled in bold, almost angular planes (*see* fig. 191). The increased accent on sharp rims and edges also stimulated Sam to augment the soft, sculptural quality of some of his design components, especially the swelling back and headrests of his chairs. Their curved tops dipped lower and, from behind, assumed an almost biomorphic character.

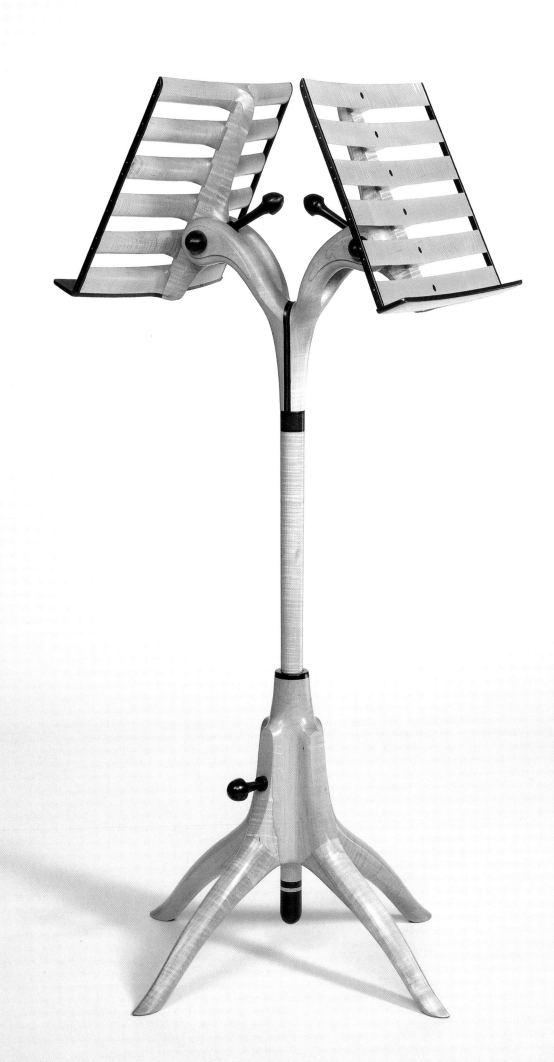

Fig. 200 Duet music stand, 1998. Maple, ebony, and purpleheart; 51½ x 26 inches; inscribed: "No. 52 Sam Maloof d.f.a. r.i.s.d./1998 m.j. l.w. d.w./Freda Maloof Collection"; Sam and Alfreda Maloof Foundation.

Fig. 201 Duet music stand (detail), 1998.

One reviewer likened the plump, swollen rear contours of a 1999 rocker's head-rest to a pregnant woman's belly[88]—a far cry from the gentle, understated crest rails of the 1960s. Once strictly maintained, the balance between form and function now tipped in favor of form and a new, sometimes disturbing assertive-ness resulted. In the 1990s, a new note of excitement runs through lines and contours—especially those of rockers and chairs (compare figs. 204 and 205).

In October 1999, a young *Los Angeles Times* art reporter, unfamiliar with Maloof's rich legacy of furniture design, was struck by a "breathtakingly beauti-ful" Maloof rocking chair on view at the Tobey Moss Gallery. To the uninitiated, Maloof's most popular creation always seemed fresh. Surprised by the sleekness of its design, the reviewer claimed that the woodworker had transformed a "grandfatherly" furniture form into a "sexy home accessory," that "if not quite futuristic" was at least "far ahead of its time." By comparison, it made a state-of-the-art stealth bomber appear "clunky and cheap." Such an aesthetic experience forced spectators not only to see their surroundings differently, he wrote, but to "live in a new and improved world."[89] But even those versed in Maloof's work re-mained deeply impressed by the long-tailed chairs. Another art correspondent—a former decorative arts curator—had encountered a recent rocker at the 1998 SOFA exposition in Chicago. For an international crafts readership he enthusiasti-cally wrote: "the shining star at SOFA Chicago this year in the field of wood . . . is a rocking chair by Sam Maloof. For those who are not familiar with Maloof's furniture, you will be astonished. For those who are, you will be amazed by this artist's ability to make a landmark object of such spiritual beauty."[90]

The Freeway and the Citrus Grove

Maloof's ability to keep producing "spiritually beautiful" work in the late 1990s was extraordinary, given the fact his shop and home were threatened with imminent destruction by forces far beyond his control. At the beginning of the decade, the California Department of Transportation (CalTrans) finally had been authorized to construct a long-rumored, twenty-eight mile extension of Los Angeles's Foothill Freeway east along Route 30 from La Verne (Freda's birthplace) to the junction of Interstate 215 in the City of San Bernardino. To the Maloofs' dismay, the eight-lane expressway was destined to slice straight through their unique oasis (fig. 206). By 2001, every tree, shrub, and structure within a central, 210-foot swath was to be leveled. As it inexorably advanced, month by month, the deadline forcing him off his property exerted great psychological pressure on Maloof, but more especially on Freda whose health was becoming increasingly frail. She loved where she lived and yearned to stay there peacefully for the remainder of her days.

The concept of a transportation corridor running east from the end of the Foothill Freeway had been approved in principle by area authorities not long after the Maloofs moved from Ontario to Alta Loma in 1953. As citrus ranches gave way to subdivisions of stuccoed tract houses, a right-of-way was maintained along much of the proposed route, abutting the Maloof's property on either side. But for decades, the highway had remained simply a rumored possibility, not an eventuality. In the 1950s and 1960s, when Maloof wished to add new rooms to his expanding house, he was told by local San Bernardino County building inspectors to seek permission first from the State highway engineer's office in Ontario. Twice the staff there told him to go ahead and build, since it was unlikely the roadway would ever be constructed. Later, the local inspectors explained the engineer's prior approval was no longer needed, so he naturally assumed that his compound was safe from the highway's depredations. But in the 1980s, local advocates kept promoting the idea of the new express road—the two major freeways already running east-west nearby (the San Bernardino and Pomona freeways) were becoming jammed with commuter traffic to and from Los Angeles, as was nearby Foothill Boulevard, historic Route 66.

In June 1990, the California legislature finally gave in to the mounting pressure, passing Measure 111 authorizing construction funds. Realizing that opposition to freeway building in California was fruitless, Maloof and his friends and supporters had already prepared a defensive strategy of their own. On August 27, their plan was publicly enacted: the California Office of Historic Preservation officially designated the Maloof residence and workshop as historic property. Since they satisfied two essential criteria—"property associated with a significant person," and "property possessing high artistic value"—the original linked structures (but not the guest house) were listed on the National

Fig. 202 Arm of rocking chair seen from the back, 1998.

Fig. 203 Rocking chair, 1998. Walnut and ebony; $44\frac{7}{8} \times 26\frac{1}{4} \times 44\frac{7}{8}$ inches long; inscribed "No. 23 1999/Sam Maloof d.f.a. r.i.s.d./ m.j. l.w. d.w. 1st prototype May 24, 1999."; private collection.

Fig. 204 Rocking chair, 1969. Oak and leather; 46½ × 29 × 45⅜ inches; signed with brand "designed. made/MALOOF/California"; embossed "74. 6. 69"; private collection.

Register of Historic Places. The highway builders were now forced to find a way to save the buildings. Various alternatives were explored: bend the freeway around the grove; tunnel beneath or bridge over it; or move the buildings—either fifty-five feet north to a point just beyond the highway's projected shoulder (and construct a sixteen-foot-high sound barrier), or off the property altogether. The most logical and cost effective solution was to relocate off-site.

On May 24, 1994, after nearly four years of stressful negotiations, the Maloofs entered into a binding agreement with CalTrans and the local municipal authority charged with condemning the land, San Bernardino Associated Governments (SANBAG). The 5.279 acre site was to be purchased for $2.4 million (money to be raised by temporarily hiking local sales taxes), a property of similar size and character nearby would be acquired, and, after careful recording by the Historic American Building Survey, the designated structures would be dismantled and rebuilt on the new site. At his own expense, Maloof would have to reconstruct the guest house, four auxiliary woodsheds, and his separate, two-car garage (fig. 207). The budget for the relocation project (which proved woefully inadequate) was put at $12 million.[91] As part of the deal, the Maloofs agreed in 1994 to set up the Sam and Alfreda Maloof Foundation (to be endowed both by them and by state agencies) to maintain and operate the

Fig. 205 Rocking chair, 2000. Walnut and ebony; 47 $\frac{1}{2}$ x 27 x 47 $\frac{1}{2}$ inches; inscribed: "No. 3 2000/Sam Maloof d.f.a. r.i.s.d./m.j. l.w. d.w."; collection of Dr. and Mrs. Robert W. Edgar.

relocated residence, shop, and landscaped grounds as a museum and non-profit cultural center.

In May 1996, a comparable site in Alta Loma was purchased some two and-a-half miles to the northeast—a vacant 5.5 acre plot at the north end of Carnelian Street at Hidden Farm Road. An elevated property, it backed up against the towering flanks of the San Gabriel mountains and had once been part of a larger citrus grove. A number of straggling lines of orange and lemon trees still remained. From its height, the plot overlooked the broad sweep of the Pomona Valley with the San Juan mountains in the distance. Now filled with housing developments and strip malls, during Maloof's childhood it had been covered with farms and citrus ranches. But even with these drastic environmental transformations, he was still emotionally and physically rooted in the valley in which he had grown up. As the crow flies, his new homesite was less than ten miles from the small bungalow on Sixth Street in Chino (now occupied by his sister Eva), where, some sixty years before, he had lived with his parents, siblings, nieces and nephews. The Padua Hills Theater was not far to the west along the same rocky hillsides. And his bank in nearby Claremont which he visited regularly was just two blocks away from Harold Graham's old shop (still looking the way it did in the late 1930s) and only four more from the

Vortox Company's office and factory. As he drove home, he often passed Seal Court at Scripps College, where in 1947 he had first met Freda. His continued sense of rootedness in the landscape gave him the strength to continue his operations at full pace.

The impending relocation focused renewed press attention on the meandering, U-shaped house embowered in foliage. Between 1981, when Henry Dreyfuss's son, John, architectural critic for the *Los Angeles Times,* had written an affectionate account of the Maloofs' "nourishing environment" for *American Craft* and 1991, when the next detailed description was published in *Fine Homebuilding,* a number of important architectural additions and improvements had taken place, adding to the organic sense of flow.[92] In fact, in the course of the 1980s, as his revenues rose, the interior space had increased from five to nearly seven thousand square feet and the number of separate rooms and semi-enclosed nooks had doubled to twenty-two. Moreover, the decor had changed: the once-spare interior was now richer and warmer toned—and much more lavishly ornamented with colorful objects and artworks.

When the freeway was approved in 1990, the two-story office and studio Maloof had built for Freda in 1975–76—the room for which he constructed his laminated and carved spiral staircase to reach the loft area—was a showroom/gallery filled with art and examples of his latest work (fig. 208). The business files and the walnut executive desk Freda used—the one exhibited in *California Design* in 1960—had been moved back into the original master bedroom, now reconverted into an office. Beyond the spiral staircase room, and connected to it by a glassed-in breezeway, was a recently built, square guest room with attached bath. The window on its southern wall was constructed as a glass display case for some of the couple's Indian pottery collection. Maloof was a master at adaptive reuse: in its former incarnation, this new tiled room had been an open carport-cum-woodshed, erected in 1978. Attached to the guest room was a towering new wood storage shed. Since the tree canopy dimmed much of the natural light, Maloof repeated the stratagem he had used in the master bedroom in 1968, adding a clerestory addition to the guest room. The guest house received the same treatment.

In the original nucleus of the labyrinthian residence, its floor composed of loosely arranged, raw bricks (they clinked as one walked across them), in 1976 Maloof had remodeled the existing kitchen, introducing skylights and enclosing a former service porch to create an indoor eating area. This new redwood-lined room was like a greenhouse: from its shed ceiling Freda had hung a dozen potted plants raised and lowered by cords on pulleys. In the 1980s the woodworker also constructed two new second story rooms that opened off the ends of the eastern side of the balcony built above the living room in 1978. One of the new rooms was a large display space with picture windows and filled with furniture, craft objects, and paintings. The second, at the top of the stairs was a smaller aerie with a colorful, leaded glass entry door and a built-in, book-lined sleeping nook (fig. 209). The trunk of a eucalyptus tree felled in a storm served as a beam running the length of the room, while a thick, curved branch functioned as the nook's lintel. With triangular clerestory windows, this new

Fig. 206 San Gabriel Mountains seen from the heart of the Maloof's citrus grove, 1979. Reproduction by permission of Jonathan Pollock.

"tree house room" had been erected on a rooftop deck Maloof previously had made so Freda could sunbathe in privacy. He napped in the hideaway during the late afternoon; at night, she used it as a retreat when he snored too loudly in the master bedroom.

Like the very first structure, all the piecemeal additions had been designed with similar clean, spare lines, their geometric volumes proportionate to the rest. Outside, they were sheathed with rough-sawn redwood boards, maintaining the rustic look of the original house (fig. 210). Inside, many of the windows were framed with smoothed and oiled redwood boards decoratively joined with outsized dovetails. Larger openings (such as between the kitchen and breakfast room) incorporated curved eucalyptus lintels fixed to milled supports or tree trunk posts with wedges and dowels. Flat ceilings were composed of black beams and white panels; clerestory additions employed black-painted rafters and bevelled pine boards colored with an off-white, pickled finish.

Throughout, the labyrinth of organically expanding rooms overflowed with books and artworks—objects of all shapes, colors, materials, sizes, and sorts.

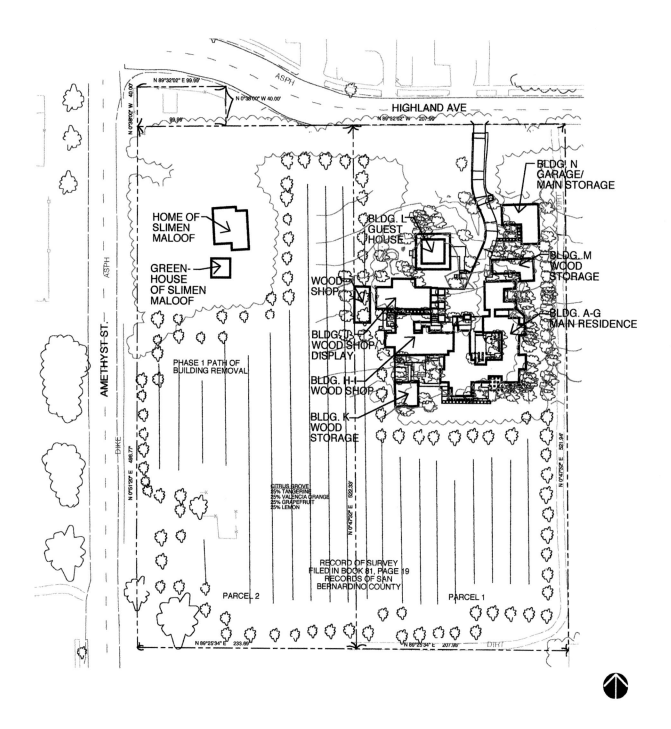

Fig. 207 Site plan of original Maloof compound, surveyed for relocation, 1999. Thirtieth Street Architects. Courtesy SANBAG.

Maloof simply couldn't slow his acquisitive habits. He enjoyed collecting immensely. It was one of the principal reasons he kept adding rooms. Initially, visitors were overwhelmed, but then delighted by the sheer number of pictures, pots, baskets, weavings, turned wood bowls, sculptures, found objects, dried and living plants, to say nothing of the more than one hundred pieces of Maloof furniture, that they encountered upstairs and downstairs, from one end of the house to the other. The dwelling was a mecca, a living monument to the creative impulse. In the 1990s, more than three thousand a year visited the idyllic site, leaving refreshed by what many termed an almost magical experience.[93]

For those who could only make the visit imaginatively, the fabled residence was featured in furniture maker Tommy Simpson's lavishly illustrated book celebrating the unique personality of craftsmen's homes, *Hand and Home* (1994), as well as in professional and shelter magazines, such as *Fine Homebuilding.*[94]

The Passing of Freda

In the spring of 1998 *This Old House* magazine published an article on Maloof's unique environment. "The question everyone wants answered is," the writer asserted: "would Sam Maloof's craftsman's genius have blossomed if he had not first created this world in which to live and work? In other words, did his genius create this place, or did this place create his genius?" Asked for his response, Maloof demurred: "Oh, I don't know. What do you think, Freda?"[95] As usual, her response was non-verbal. She simply smiled a gentle, ironic smile and looked quietly at her partner of fifty years, her blue eyes shining.

Although in the 1990s Maloof's vigor was barely diminished by his mounting years (since his heart attack in 1990, he had been attending a rehabilitation program twice weekly at a local hospital), Freda's health slowly ebbed. Nonetheless, she always accompanied her husband on his various travels, dressed casually, but always in great style, her silver hair tied at the back in a twist, often with a bright ribbon. After its reorganization and expansion in late 1991, Sam had retired from the ACC board, so the semi-annual trustees' meetings were no longer on their travel schedule, but she attended all his workshops, lectures, and exhibition openings. In April 1998, the couple were on hand at a reception for the opening of the Smithsonian Craft Show in Washington, D.C. But she was recuperating that spring from a bout with the flu, and Maloof was increasingly worried about her delicate condition and declining strength. During his daily visits, Slimen found his father distracted and unusually pensive, barely able to concentrate. In August, Freda seemed better and Maloof's spirits picked up. But, on September 23, 1998, after a short illness and brief hospitalization, she died in her sleep from a massive heart attack.

Although not entirely unexpected at age eighty-six, her sudden departure was a terrible blow, especially for Maloof. She was not only his constant companion (except for his solitary sojourn in Iran in 1959, they had hardly spent a day apart), but she was also his guardian angel, keeping him focused on the important things. In the compound itself, always imperiled by his passions, Freda was the peaceful epicenter. The gossamer web of emotional calm and moral order she gently imposed held everything in balance. But Maloof had no time to agonize over his loss. With sympathy cards, letters, and phone calls literally pouring in from around the nation and world, he threw himself into an unprecedented woodworking project: a casket for Freda. With Slimen and his own three-man team—all of them often in tears—he worked feverishly to produce a magnificent walnut, ebony, and Zircote coffin. No other Maloof design had been fabricated with such intense devotion.

The funeral was held on October 1 in the Kresge Chapel of the Claremont School of Theology. The chapel overflowed with friends and family. Freda's two sisters were present, as were her relatives from Sweden. For the ceremony,

Fig. 208 Spiral staircase room, 1997. In 1981–82, Maloof added a hand carved, spiral staircase to reach a guest bedroom. Courtesy *Fine Woodworking*.

which took place beneath his great suspended walnut cross, Maloof had designed a special cover to enclose the printed order of service. Beneath a reproduction of a recent photograph of Freda, he had penned a heartfelt farewell: "Freda my loved one/ Still waters run deep/ Thank you/ for ever and ever/ Godspeed my gentle one/ Sam." Six ministers, present and former pastors of their congregation at Trinity United Methodist Church in Ontario, participated, along with Dr. Robert W. Edgar, president of the theological school, and Monsignor O'Reilly of St. Maximilian Kolbe. Rabbi Leonard Beerman from the Leo Baeck Temple also gave a eulogy. While sad, it was nonetheless a joyful occasion, correctly styled "A Celebration in Thanksgiving for the Life of Alfreda Ward Maloof." There were songs, recitals, poems, and testamonials to a woman many called an angel. Certainly, she had touched the hearts and graced the spirits of everyone in the chapel.

Fine Woodworking published a short appreciation of Freda. While she ran the office of "an enormously successful business," she would be remembered, senior editor Jonathan Binzen wrote, for her remarkable personality: "Perceptive, unpretentious, and kind, she made new friends easily, and valued her many old ones. She was a beautiful woman with a natural sense of style and a discerning eye for fine craft and art. Her demeanor was placid, and her sense of humor was gentle and wry."[96] Alerting the woodworking community to her death, the article prompted such a flood of condolences (many readers had met her at chair-making demonstrations) that Maloof could only reply to them collectively in a letter to the editor. "Freda played such an important part in what I have done," he wrote:

She was my partner not only in our fifty years of marriage, but a partner in the work I have done. There were many times in the very early days when I talked about going back into graphics, and she would say, 'No, you can do it. I know you can.' I can honestly say that if it wasn't for her, I wouldn't have stuck to it. It was her strength and faith and belief in me that kept me going, and that's what keeps me going now. I know that her spirit is with me in everything that I do. Blessings and peace to all of you.[97]

New Residence

In design, the lid of Freda's coffin mirrored the gabled rooflines of the new home that Maloof had designed for the two of them at the Carnelian Street site. Since the old dwelling was to become a museum, SANBAG had agreed to construct another residence for the Maloofs, to be owned by their foundation and in which they would enjoy life occupancy rights. Afterwards, it would become the showcase-headquarters for the Maloof Foundation. After considering the problem of a hybrid structure, combining both private and public functions, in 1997 Maloof worked up rough plans and elevations for a distinctive, timber-frame building sheathed in redwood. It was the first time since the architectural drafting course he took during his senior year at Chino High in 1934 that he had conceived such a plan in its entirety.

Fig. 209 "Tree top" room, 1997. Maloof built this secluded aerie in the mid-1980s. Courtesy *Fine Woodworking.*

Maloof's sketches were given to an architect contracted by SANBAG for full elaboration. But the plans he reviewed were not to his liking; certain details, proportions, and relationships proved unsatisfying. But instead of making changes on the drawings, in early 1999 he had Larry White build a detailed, scale model that, like a prototype furniture design, he could "eyeball" critically from all angles (fig. 211). Furthermore, by peering through the small open doors and windows, and removing the roof sections, he could more accurately gauge the spatial effects of the interior. From his long-practiced, aesthetic vantage point, it was a better way of judging artistic quality than staring at abstract, two-dimensional representations of a three-dimensional structure. After several months of adjusting window placements and amending other structural and decorative details, he was satisfied with his new creation which the architect then used to redraw the plans.

In model form, the residence now included a new feature not initially envisioned by SANBAG planners—a burial plot for Freda and himself modeled on a Zen garden. White made an additional model based on sketches. It comprised a square, low-walled sanctuary entered by a tall, post-and-lintel gate. A water-filled moat (intended for koi) surrounded a central island on which lay an enormous, natural granite slab covering a crypt. The overall design reflected sacred Japanese environments he and Freda had seen in Kyoto during the wcc meetings in 1978. On the site plan, Sam located it just beyond the new master bedroom. When he awakened in the morning, he wanted to be able to look out and see it.

Completed in May 2000, Maloof's showcase residence, with its low-pitched, blue metal roofs and redwood siding, was axial (fig. 212). The west wing of the one-story axis included a garage and a large kitchen, while the east wing contained the master bedroom (in design much like the old one) and bath, and a small guest room and additional bath. Formal access to the house led along a path outside the kitchen to a magnificent front entryway and a narrow foyer that opened into an airy great room that comprised the entire secondary, cross axis. Like the Maloofs' former living room, this three-story-high, atrium-like space had a balcony/gallery at the second level, and was surmounted by an imposing clerestory. The interior was clearly a woodworker's creation: posts, beams, rafters, and massive roof trusses were dominant features; all joinery details were clearly visible. At either end of the upstairs balcony Maloof located sitting areas with tall windows that looked out over the landscape—to the south the panoramic valley, to the north the cluster of relocated old buildings with the mountains behind forming a dramatic backdrop. At the old house, the thick tree canopy had produced a sense of enclosure and privacy; the world beyond the compound remained invisible. At the new site, however, as the core of a cultural center, the buildings would remain, appropriately, on public display.

In June 2000, the relocated workshop reopened for business. The previous November, it had been emptied of forty-three years' worth of tools, machinery, wood, furniture templates, and other paraphernalia, and disconnected from its footings. Rigged with steel armatures inside, it was then lifted up by crane and

Fig. 210 Exterior view of guest room addition, 1997. The square guest room was connected to the spiral staircase room on the right by a short windowed passageway, while to the left, it was flanked by a tall wood storage shed. Courtesy *Fine Woodworking.*

removed from its concrete pad in one piece. All that remained was a clean, vacant space whose dimensions, for all the work produced within them—more than 3,500 pieces—seemed surprisingly small. Breaking Maloof's heart, and presaging future destruction, bulldozers had to flatten part of the grove to create access for the movers' equipment. But there was one bright note that otherwise bleak month.

In late November, the woodworker traveled to Beirut to receive Lebanon's Prize for Innovation awarded by the Makhzoumi Foundation, a philanthropic organization dedicated to local educational, cultural, and economic development. It was an uplifting moment. Ninety-four years after his parents had immigrated to Southern California in search of a better life, their Lebanese American son returned in triumph, honored at receptions and dinners by the country's president and prime minister. Many of his cousins attended the ceremonies. Supplied with an armed driver (who drove like a demon), he traveled north into the mountains to Douma to visit his relatives. This time, no one was saddened by the fact that the son of Slimen Nasif Nadir Maloof worked with his hands. In Beirut, he looked up his old friend, Akram, the owner of the furniture factory with whom he worked closely in 1959. But without Freda at his side, his delight in traveling abroad was greatly diminished.

In order to carry on with their work in late 1999 (already they were behind schedule with several projects), Maloof and the "boys" had moved the bandsaw and essential tools and materials into a smaller, adjacent workshop erected in the mid-1980s to serve as a furniture finishing and storage area. Larger woodworking machines had to be set up outdoors in a tent, and Mike Johnson moved his sanding operations into a nearby woodshed. Under these less-than-ideal, but still workable, conditions, the St. Maximilian Kolbe commission was completed on time, the great cross actually taking shape in Maloof's two-car garage. Even with chaos and uncertainty rising as the relocation process moved into ever higher gear, the commercial enterprise continued unabated.

Retirement was out of the question. At eighty-four, he had enough back orders to keep him busy, he said, until he reached a hundred.[98] Moreover, the thought of giving up the sights, smells, and sounds of working in wood was too painful to contemplate seriously. And what would he do with himself if he quit? Daily, he found spiritual renewal in work and his mind was brimming with ideas for novel pieces and subtle changes in existing designs. If and when he was forced out by failing health—or joined his beloved Freda—the business would carry on. The workshop was an entity separate from the foundation, and after Sam's demise, Slimen, Johnson, White, and Wade would become the new employee-owners, responsible for its continuing success. Like George Nakashima's workshop, directed by his daughter, Mira, Maloof's woodworking tradition was intended to endure into the foreseeable future, ensuring a supply of authentic, superbly crafted Maloof rockers and other designs. His legacy as a furniture designer, too, would survive, even expand.

As a museum, his extraordinary home—his greatest masterpiece—was saved for future generations to enjoy as a monument to the "craftsman lifestyle." As visitors walked through the furnished and decorated rooms, they would

Fig. 211 Model of new Maloof residence, 1999.

Fig. 212 New Maloof residence, 2000 His old dwelling, officially designated an historic structure, was dismantled and moved to the new site, where as a museum it forms a unique cultural center dedicated to the arts and crafts.

unconsciously absorb not only Maloof's artistic vitality, but Freda's quiet moral spirit and depart, like so many others during her lifetime, gently uplifted by the aesthetic and spiritual experience. The Sam and Alfreda Maloof Foundation would also ensure the survival of their legacy as a working couple, supporting not only the daily operations of the new cultural center, but educational programs related to arts and crafts in general. His legacy as a designer-craftsman and as an inspiration to woodworkers past, present, and future was assured.

Notes

Chapter One

[1] Stephen Dean Kirby, "Sam Maloof, Woodworker: His Life and Work" (master's thesis, California State University, Long Beach, 1974), 36.

[2] "American Craftspeople Oral History Project: The Reminiscences of Sam Maloof" (Columbia University, 1987, typescript), 7. Hereafter, "Reminiscences of Sam Maloof."

[3] Ibid., 14.

[4] For a history of the Padua Hills theater and its famous resident troupe, the Mexican Players, see Margaret Hall Simpson, "Padua Hills Mexican Theater: An Experiment in Intercultural Relations" (master's thesis, Claremont Graduate School, 1944); Pauline B. Deuel, *The Story of the Mexican Players and the Padua Hills Theatre* (Claremont: Padua Institute, 1961); and Matt Garcia, "'Just Put on that Padua Hills Smile': The Mexican Players and the Padua Hills Theater, 1931–74," California History 74 (1995): 244–61. See also, "We visited the Padua Hills Community," *Better Homes & Gardens* 33 (Oct. 1954): 24.

[5] "Contemporary American Crafts Forum" (Renwick Gallery, 26 Sept. 1992, panel discussion typescript; permanent collection files, Renwick Gallery).

[6] He had actually constructed his earliest functional piece for his parents as a ten year old: a wooden baker's paddle whose long handle was attached by a dado joint, riveted with a nail. Used for baking Lebanese flat bread at home, it lasted for decades.

[7] "Reminiscences of Sam Maloof," 11.

[8] Kirby, 52.

[9] "Reminiscences of Sam Maloof," 12.

[10] Ibid., 27–28.

[11] Ibid., 21.

[12] Ibid.; Sam Maloof, *Sam Maloof: Woodworker* (Tokyo: Kodansha International, 1983; hereafter, *Sam Maloof*), 27.

[13] Kirby, 59.

[14] For a short discussion of California furniture design in 1947, inevitably the context for Maloof's early work, see "Made in California: Hand- and Machine-Made Products," *Interiors* 107 (Sept. 1947): 100–104. In Los Angeles, aside from the Herman Miller showroom, the latest contemporary production furniture could be seen in Barker Brothers' block-long "Modern Shop," Van Keppel-Green, Inc., in Beverly Hills, and Glenn of California on West Gage Street.

[15] "Reminiscences of Sam Maloof," 25.

[16] See Barbara Goldstein, ed., *Arts & Architecture: The Entenza Years* (Cambridge, Mass., and London, 1998).

[17] As a consolation, Bird convinced Maloof that they should use their G.I. Bill educational benefits and study art abroad. In April 1947 they were both accepted by the celebrated Paris art school, l'Academie Julian. Only Bird departed for Europe. Sam had recently met his future wife and in the fall refused Bird's entreaties to go to Paris.

[18] *Arts & Architecture* 63 (Aug. 1946): 26.

[19] Unpublished interview with Blake Green of the *San Francisco Chronicle*, 20 Nov. 1982, typescript, 9. Maloof workshop papers.

[20] Janice Lavoos, "Millard Sheets: The Man and His Life," in *Millard Sheets: Six Decades of Painting* (Laguna Beach: Museum of Art, 1983), 20.

[21] For a full account of Sheets's career, see Janice Lovoos and Edmund F. Penney, *Millard Sheets: One-Man Renaissance* (Flagstaff, Arizona: Northland Press, 1984).

[22] "Reminiscences of Sam Maloof," 25.

[23] Kirby, 60.

Chapter Two

[1] See "Craftsman's World. The Workshop: Plywood or Solid Wood—pro and con," *Craft Horizons* 13 (Oct. 1953): 40.

[2] Sam Maloof, quoted in Kirby, 68.

[3] "String chairs" were then popular items among such contemporary Los Angeles furniture designers and manufacturers as Greta Magnusson and Dan Johnson, Functional Furniture, and Van Keppel-Green. See "A Portfolio of Contemporary Furniture," *Arts & Architecture* 67 (May 1950). Maloof's Plaza Serena furniture was more avant garde in design than most current modern manufactured designs. See William J. Hennessey, *Modern Furnishings for the Home* (1952; reprint, New York: Acanthus Press, 1997).

[4] Quoted in Rick Mastelli, "Sam Maloof: How a Home Craftsman Became One of the Best There Is," *Fine Woodworking* (Nov./Dec. 1980): 51.

[5] Ibid.

[6] In 1950, for example, Maloof was commissioned by the California State Historical Society to prepare a series of architectural renderings of Spanish Mission buildings and spent two weeks driving up and down the coast with Freda and his infant son, Sammy, sketching sites.

[7] John Webster, "Handsome Furniture You Can Build," *Better Homes and Gardens* (Mar. 1951): 258. In September, the *Los Angeles Times* Sunday Home magazine skirted copyright law and reprinted the drawings and photographs in a series of short articles by Donald Braun. Legal action ensued, but Maloof's plans reached a broad local audience. According to the craftsman, his early drawings could be seen for sale in amateur woodworking magazines as late as the 1980s.

[8] Jean Burden, "All This and Economy, Too," *Los Angeles Times*, 28 Oct. 1951, Home magazine, 24–25. The flat-roofed, open plan residence was

described as "modern." The Mauls' son was a Scripps College-trained architect.

[9] "How to Relate Furniture, Fabrics, and Ceramics," *Los Angeles Times,* 30 Mar. 1952, Home magazine, 11.

[10] *Sam Maloof,* 31.

[11] Ibid.

[12] P. K. Thomajan, "Henry Dreyfuss: Industrial Designer," *American Artist* 15 (Sept. 1951): 52.

[13] "Reminiscences of Sam Maloof," 29.

[14] Ibid., 32.

[15] Ibid.

[16] For a period study of Finn Juhl's furniture designs, see "Finn Juhl," *Interiors* 110 (Sept. 1950): 82ff. For views of Juhl's chair with a floating seat and contrasting dark "feet," see Baker Furniture advertisement, *Arts & Architecture* 69 (Oct. 1952): 17.

[17] See "Exhibitions. Modern Periodized," *Interiors* 110 (Sept. 1952): 10.

[18] "Reminiscences of Sam Maloof," 33.

[19] Henry Dreyfuss to T. H. Robsjohn-Gibbings, 3 Feb. 1953. Maloof workshop papers.

[20] "Reminiscences of Sam Maloof," 33.

[21] Sam Maloof, unpublished interview with Jonathan Fairbanks, 1 Sept. 1982, typescript, 5. Maloof workshop papers.

[22] Ibid.

Chapter Three

[1] For discussions of the terms "contemporary" and "modern" as related to the decorative arts, architecture, and cultural history of the post-war period, see Lesley Jackson, *Contemporary: Architecture and Interiors of the 1950s* (London: Phaidon Press, 1998) and George H. Marcus, *Design in the Fifties:*

When Everyone Went Modern (Munich and New York: Prestel, 1998). Jackson's book illustrates many Los Angeles area interiors, the sorts of architectural settings in which Maloof's furniture was often found.

[2] Sam Maloof, unpublished interview with David Gardner, 1 Sept. 1982, typescript. Maloof workshop papers.

[3] Ibid.

[4] *House Beautiful* (Feb. 1954): 84.

[5] *House Beautiful* (May 1954): 151. In its December issue, the magazine again featured Millard Sheets in an article entitled "How a Famous Artist 'Decorates' for Christmas." In a photograph, two Maloof occasional arm chairs flank the fireplace. *House Beautiful* (Dec. 1954): 117.

[6] Sherley Ashton, "Maloof: Designer, Craftsman of Furniture," *Craft Horizons* 14 (May/June 1954): 16.

[7] Sam Maloof, "Furniture as a Craft," about 1961, unpublished typescript, 4–12. Maloof workshop papers.

[8] Ashton, 18.

[9] Ibid., 17.

[10] Ibid.

[11] Vivian Bateman, "Alta Loma Furniture Designer Displays Talent of True Artist," *Upland Daily Report* [1954].

[12] Virginia Stewart, "The Work of Sam Maloof—Strength, Beauty, Utility," *Los Angeles Times,* 8 Aug. 1954, Home magazine, 13.

[13] Pomona *Progress-Bulletin,* 2 Oct. 1953, Sec. 2, 7.

[14] Foster Rhodes Jackson, "Fine Arts Exhibit at Fair Praised as Wedding of Arts, Architecture," Pomona *Progress-Bulletin* [Sept. 1954].

[15] James Toland, "A Fine Arts Exhibit for the County Fair," Pomona *Progress-Bulletin,* 12 Sept. 1954, 19. A clear precedent for the show was "For

Modern Living," an exhibition of furnished rooms organized in 1949 by the Detroit Institute of Arts. Designers selected to furnish rooms included Florence Knoll, Charles Eames, and George Nelson. The Los Angeles firm, Van Keppel-Green, supplied outdoor furniture for a patio-garden area.

[16] Ibid.

[17] "A County Fair Preview," *Los Angeles Times,* 9 Sept. 1955, Home magazine.

[18] Oppi Untracht, "Chairs from Hans Wegner's Shop," *Craft Horizons* 15 (Jan./Feb. 1955): 30–35.

[19] "The House of George Nakashima, Woodworker," *Arts & Architecture* 67 (Jan. 1950): 22–26. Wharton Esherick's handcrafted home and studio were featured in Mary Roche, "A New Feeling for Material," *House Beautiful* 93 (Mar. 1951): 116–19, 130–31. Maloof was familiar with both articles.

[20] "The Studio Craftsman Observed," *Craft Horizons* 24 (May/June 1964): 103.

[21] "First World Congress of Craftsmen," *Craft Horizons* 24 (Sept./Oct. 1964): 8.

[22] Sam Maloof, 42. *California Design II* was held in January 1956. The series was then presented annually until 1962, after which it was organized on a triennial basis. The series ended with the 1971 show.

[23] W. Joseph Fulton, introduction to *California Design* (Pasadena, 1954).

[24] See for example, Alfred Auerbach, "Good Design," *Arts & Architecture* 67 (Jan. 1950): 20–24, 49; Edgar Kaufmann, Jr., "Good Design '51," *Interiors* 110 (Mar. 1951): 100–105, 160–62; Ada Louise Huxtable, "How Good is Good Design?," *Craft Horizons* 15 (Mar./Apr. 1955): 35–37. The layouts were models of their kind; the early installations were designed by Charles Eames, Finn Juhl, Paul Rudolph, and Alexander Girard. Among jurors for 1951 was William Friedman, director of the Walker Art Center in Minneapolis. In 1947, Friedman had opened the pioneering "Everyday

Art Gallery," an ongoing, post-war museum exhibit of modern furnishings dedicated "to help build a better environment for daily living."

25 Ceramicist Susan Peterson in "How the West Was Won," *American Craft* 57 (Aug./Sept. 1997): 6.

26 *Arts in Western Living,* exhibition brochure (Los Angeles: Los Angeles County Fair Association, 1955).

27 "Booming California. Want to Move There?," *Changing Times* 11 (Feb. 1957): 28.

28 Wayne Whittaker, "A Salute to the California Influence," *Popular Mechanics* 110 (Oct. 1958): 128. In its own salute to the house building boom, the magazine published an annual "home section."

29 Edward P. Eichler of Eichler Homes, quoted in ibid., 129.

30 Carey McWilliams, *Southern California Country—An Island on the Land* (New York: Duell, Stone, and Pearce, 1946). Quoted in *Arts & Architecture* 63 (June 1946): 25.

31 For a study of this post-war architectural program, see *Blueprints for Modern Living: History and Legacy of the Case Study Houses* (Cambridge, Mass., and London: MIT Press, 1989).

32 Paul Darrow, "The Arts in Western Living," *Craft Horizons* 15 (Nov./Dec. 1955): 23.

33 C. B., "California," *Craft Horizons* 16 (Sept./Oct. 1956): 11.

34 "California Designed," *Arts & Architecture* 72 (July 1955): 26.

35 Eileen Ball, *Independent-Telegram* (Long Beach) [Dec. 1955], "Southland Magazine."

36 "California Designers Present," *Living for Young Homemakers* (Dec. 1955): 25. The show was also highlighted in *Craft Horizons* 16 (Sept./Oct. 1956): 45, and *Retailing Daily,* 1 Mar. 1956.

37 Richard Petterson, "A Climate For Craft Art," *Craft Horizons* 16 (Sept./Oct. 1956): 11.

38 "Leadership Came West," *Los Angeles Times,* 15 July 1956, Home magazine, 20–21.

39 *New York Herald Tribune,* 2 February 1957.

40 Thomas S. Tibbs, preface to *Furniture by Craftsmen* (New York: Museum of Contemporary Craft, 1957).

41 Faith Corrigan, "Museum Shows 78 Furnishings by Craftsmen," *New York Times,* 15 Feb. 1957.

42 Sam Maloof, unpublished interview with Jonathan Fairbanks, 10 March 1983, typescript. Maloof workshop papers.

43 John Kapel was a graduate of Cranbrook Academy of Art who, after reading Sherley Ashton's 1954 article on Maloof in *Craft Horizons,* had decided to devote himself to fine woodworking and moved to California. He discovered, however, it was economically more viable to design furniture for George Nelson.

44 Greta Daniels, "Furniture by Craftsmen," *Craft Horizons* 17 (Mar./Apr. 1957): 34–38.

45 Norbert Nelson, letter to Sam Maloof, 23 Mar. 1957. Maloof workshop papers.

46 Creighton Peet, "Quality," *American Forests* 63 (June 1957): 12–13.

47 For the distinction between "risk" and "certainty" in workmanship, see David Pye, *The Nature and Art of Workmanship* (Cambridge, England: University of Cambridge Press, 1968).

48 "Asilomar Conference: An On-the-Scene Report," *Craft Horizons* 17 (July/Aug. 1957): 17.

49 Ibid.

50 American Craftsmen's Council, *Asilomar: First Conference of American Craftsmen sponsored by the American Craftsmen's Council, June, 1957* (New York: ACC, 1957), 5.

51 "Asilomar: An On-the-scene Report," 20.

52 The quotations used are taken from both the American Craftsmen's Council report and the article that appeared in *Craft Horizons.*

53 Sam Maloof, "Wharton Esherick, 1887–1970," *Craft Horizons* 30 (Aug. 1970): 10.

54 Conversation with the author, 8 Feb. 2000.

55 American Craftsmen's Council, 22.

56 Ibid.

57 *Sam Maloof,* 46.

58 American Craftsmen's Council, 31.

59 While completing the drawings, Maloof suffered serious burns in a fire in his cottage which incapacitated him for months. The commercial cabinetmaker therefore made the bed frame, TV cabinet, dresser, and bedside tables from the plans, adding marble and brass as per the hotel's instructions.

60 Kirby, 132. Between 1955 and 1957, Guy Brink ordered some fifty-two pieces of furniture from Maloof for his private and corporate clients.

61 For decades, having no expertise in the matter, Maloof relied on the upholstery skills of Ballard's in Pomona. For chair backs, he generally fabricated wooden panels which, when upholstered, fitted so tightly into the open walnut frame that fasteners were unnecessary.

62 Sam Maloof, unpublished interview with Jonathan Fairbanks, 1 Sept. 1982, typescript, 5. Maloof workshop papers.

63 Richard Whitney, letter to Harry Lawenda, 26 July 1956. Maloof workshop papers.

64 Clifford Nelson, introduction to *California Design 4* (Pasadena, Calif.: Pasadena Art Museum, 1958), 3. See also the show's press release.

65 Arthur Millier, "Some of the Faces Behind 'California Design,'" *Los Angeles Times,* 2 Feb. 1958, "Midwinter" magazine, 18.

66 This group was an off-shoot of the state-wide California Designer-Craftsmen, formed to distinguish themselves from San Francisco Bay area craftspeople. During the 1950s, many individual States had "designer-craftsmen" or "artist-craftsmen" groups. Their annual exhibitions were reviewed in *Craft Horizons.* The ACC hoped to be the national umbrella organization for these separate and often isolated groups.

67 See "On Display, Skilled Work in Many Crafts," *Los Angeles Times,* 26 Jan. 1958, Home magazine, 18–19. Three photographs of Maloof working in his shop were reproduced, one caption noting "Sam Maloof, though embodying old traditions of craftsmanship, is still helping to develop a new tradition of design."

68 The annual Arts Fiesta is described in "Lively Arts Festival, Scripps College," *Los Angeles Times,* 10 Sept. 1961, Home magazine, 16–17. The festival's theme was vintage Millard Sheets: that art should be integral with daily life, not an awesome, untouchable museum object.

69 Aside from the MCC show, Maloof's work was displayed outside the Los Angeles area in 1957 at the University of Illinois, Chicago, *American Craftsmen,* and University of Washington's Henry Gallery, Seattle, *Twenty-Four American Craftsmen. California Design 3* traveled that year to San Antonio, Texas.

70 "Design Exhibit. Art Museum Shows New Furnishings," *Oakland Tribune,* 3 Mar. 1958, C5.

71 "Artist-Craftsman Stays Busy," Upland-Ontario *Daily Report,* 10 Oct. 1958, n.p.

72 The stereographic slides and other period photographs are among the Maloof workshop papers.

73 In the late 1950s, legendary Los Angeles artist-engineer, Jan de Swart, was an even more adept virtuoso sculptor with the bandsaw. Without preliminary drawings, and as fast as the saw would cut, he created complicated, intertwining forms from purely visualized designs. See "Jan de Swart," *Craft Horizons* 18 (Jan./Feb. 1958): 16–18. For a description of Maloof's arm-making process, see Sam Maloof, "Master Class. Shaping the Arm of a Chair," *Fine Woodworking* 137 (Aug. 1999): 102–6.

74 Wharton Esherick, letter to Sam Maloof, 26 Aug. 1958. Maloof workshop papers. Author's italics.

75 See editorial, "Crafts: A Bridge to Peace," *Craft Horizons* 18 (Jan./Feb. 1958): 8.

76 *Designer Craftsmen U.S.A.* (New York: Brooklyn Museum, 1953), 11.

77 Sam Maloof, 37.

78 "ICA," Craft Horizons 18 (July/Aug. 1958): 28–36.

79 "Local Artist Leaving Today for Lebanon Assistance Program," *Upland-Ontario Daily Report,* 9 Feb. 1959, B1. See also *Craft Horizons* 19 (Mar./Apr. 1959): 7.

80 Sam Maloof, Middle East diary, 1959, n.p. Maloof workshop papers.

81 Ibid.

82 *Sam Maloof*, 32.

83 See Catalog of Furniture Produced under the Furniture Design Project, Iran and Lebanon, February1959–December 1959 (Chicago: Dave Chapman, Inc., 1960).

84 Quoted in Kirby, 177–78.

85 *Sam Maloof*, 34.

86 Sam Maloof, unpublished interview with David Gardner, 8 Nov. 1982, typescript, 12. Maloof workshop papers.

87 The July 1959 issue of *House Beautiful* was devoted to the "worldwide influence" of Scandinavian design.

88 Sam Maloof, "'This is My Best.' Functional Beauty Shaped by Hand," *Los Angeles Times*, 14 July 1959, Home magazine, 22.

89 Robert C. Niece, *Art: An Approach* (Dubuque: W. C. Brown, 1959), 24.

90 *Art: USA: 59; a force, a language, a frontier* (New York: American Art Expositions, Inc., 1959), 8.

91 Rose Slivka, "The Art/Craft Connection: A Personal, Critical,and Historical Odyssey," in Marcia Manhart and Tom Manhart, eds., *The Eloquent Object: Evolution of American Art in Craft Media since 1945* (Tulsa, Okla.: The Philbrook Museum of Art, 1987), 67.

92 Rose Slivka, "U. S. Crafts," *Craft Horizons* 19 (Mar./Apr. 1959): 21.

93 Ibid., 10. The G.I. Bill of 1944 provided that "any person who served in the active military . . . shall be entitled to receive education and training." In 1947, nearly one half of 2.3 million students enrolled in college courses received veterans' benefits. A surprising high percentage of them enrolled in fine arts courses, many of them electing to work in craft media. See Calvin Tompkins, "The Art World: Erasing the Line," *The New Yorker* (July 28, 1980): 83.

94 Ibid., 20.

95 Sam Maloof, "Furniture as a Craft," typescript and photographs. Maloof workshop papers.

96 Conrad Brown, "The Trouble with Craft Books," *Craft Horizons* 19 (May/June 1959): 8.

97 Ibid., 9.

98 Available in flat, half round, and full round, the Surform was a cutting tool that replaced rasps, spoke shavers, and other traditional cutting tools. In "Furniture as a Craft," Maloof recommended the following machine tools: 12-inch planer, 8-inch jointer, bandsaw, drill press, table saw, shaper, boring machine, lathe, grinder, and pneumatic drum, belt, and disc sanders. The following power hand tools were indispensible: 3-inch belt sander, drill, router, hand electric saw, saber saw, and oscillating sander.

99 *Sam Maloof*, 57. 100 "Furniture as a Craft," 4–13.

101 Ibid.

102 See "Crafts/Interiors: The Southern California Designer-Craftsmen," *Creative Crafts* 1 (Oct./Nov. 1960): 14.

103 The tapering double-back chair was illustrated in the New York *Herald Tribune*'s review of the show, "Designed and Handcrafted for Use," 27 May 1960, 13.

104 David R. Campbell, "Designer-Craftsmen USA 1960," *Craft Horizons* 19 (July/Aug. 1960): 19.

105 Ibid., 17.

Chapter Four

1 "3 Southland Designers," *Los Angeles Times*, 12 Feb. 1961, Home magazine, 18.

2 "Maloof: The Craftsman," *Los Angeles Times*, 12 Feb. 1961, Home magazine, 18.

3 See *Los Angeles Times*, 25 Mar. 1962, Home magazine, 12, and *Los Angeles Herald-Examiner*, 25 Mar. 1962, *Pictorial Living*, 19.

4 Beverly E. Johnson, "California Design 8: Essential Link Between Artist and the World," *Los Angeles Times*, 25 Mar. 1962, Home magazine, 14.

5 "California Design 8," *Arts & Architecture* 79 (Apr. 1962): 22.

6 Paul Laporte, "Letter from Los Angeles," *Craft Horizons* 22 (May/June 1962): 61–62.

7 Revenues for 1961 were $22,357.05, and for 1962 $15,727.50. Maloof workshop papers.

8 Kirby, 88.

9 Sam Maloof, unpublished interview with Blake Green of the *San Francisco Chronicle*, 11 Nov. 1982, typescript, 8. Maloof workshop papers.

10 *Sam Maloof*, 35.

11 Sam Maloof, unpublished interview with Jonathan Fairbanks, 2 Sept. 1982, typescript, 4. Maloof workshop papers.

12 Ibid., 4.

13 The annual dates of operation were 4 Apr.–18 Oct. 1964 and 21 Apr.–10 Oct. 1965.

14 Newspaper clippings. Maloof workshop papers.

15 See "Pavilion of American Interiors," *Interiors* 123 (Mar. 1964): 102–5. The American Cyanamid Corporation's "Formica House" had been decorated with craft objects by some forty-two craftsmen.

16 "The Studio Craftsman Observed," *Craft Horizons* 24 (May/June 1964): 95.

17 *Sam Maloof*, 43.

18 For a photo of the model of the proposed exhibit design by Sam Richardson, see "Pavilion of American Interiors," *Interiors* 123 (Mar. 1964): 105.

19 Paul J. Smith, "An Introduction to the American Craftsman," in *The American Craftsman* (New York: American Craftsmen's Council, 1964).

20 "The Studio Craftsman Observed," *Craft Horizons* 24 (May/June 1964): 103.

21 "First World Congress of Crafts," *Craft Horizons* 24 (July/Aug. 1964): 8.

22 Ibid. In 1965, the wcc was accepted as a non-governmental member of UNESCO and the following year prepared a report on the global situation of crafts, *World Crafts: A Mid-Twentieth Century Report* (New York, 1966). wcc activities included biennial General Assemblies in different countries, an information service, a slide purchase program, traveling exhibitions, and a newsletter sent to some five thousand recipients worldwide. In each country, wcc members elected their own representatives to serve on the General Assembly who in turn elected a board of directors. Sam Maloof became a director of the American section of the wcc in the 1970s.

23 Ibid., 9.

24 Ibid., 55.

25 Ibid., 12–14.

26 "First World Congress of Craftsmen," *Craft Horizons* 24 (Sept./Oct. 1964): 17.

27 Quoted in Davira S. Taragin and Edward S. Cooke, Jr., *Furniture by Wendell Castle* (New York: Hudson Hills Press, 1990), 24.

28 Rose Slivka, "The American Craftsman/1964," *Craft Horizons* 24 (May/June 1964): 10ff. The author's analysis of the role and significance of the contemporary artist-craftsman within an international, industrialized society is further developed in "The Persistent Object," in *The Crafts of the Modern World* (New York: Bramhall House and wcc, 1968), 12–20.

29 Taragin and Cooke, Jr., 17.

30 "First World Congress of Craftsmen," 14.

31 "In the Western Tradition," *Los Angeles Times*, 24 Jan. 1965, Home magazine, 15.

32 "Craftsman. Wood Comes Alive in Fine Furniture by Sam Maloof," *Los Angeles Times*, 24 Jan. 1965, Home magazine, 21.

33 Upland-Ontario *Daily Report*, 4 Apr. 1965.

34 Eudora Moore, letter to Sam Maloof, 16 June 1964. Maloof workshop papers.

35 One half were craft objects; the others manufactured items or industrial prototypes. Of the handmade works, one-third were by invitation (including Maloof's pieces); the remainder juried in Los Angeles and San Francisco. See *Arts & Architecture* 82 (Mar. 28, 1965): 5–9.

36 With a white leather upholstered seat, it was subsequently sold that year to Dr. Michael Langan of Greenwich, Conn., the first of Maloof's clients to own a rocker.

37 *Wall Street Journal,* 30 Mar. 1961, 1.

38 Henry Dreyfuss, letter to Sam Maloof [1961]. Maloof workshop papers.

39 Maloof admired Parrott's brightly colored, textural weavings and, along with Jack Lenor Larsen's fabrics, regularly used them as upholstery material and for loose settee pillows. Freda enjoyed them too, and during summer visits to Santa Fe ordered long skirts and simple tops made from the distinctive fabrics. Aside from *Maloof/Parrott* and *California Design 9,* Sam participated in two other California shows in 1965—the ACC-organized *Craftsmen of the Southwest* in San Francisco and *Some Claremont Artists* at Scripps College. He also had a piece in *Designer-Craftsman Invitational* organized by Brigham Young University in Provo, Utah.

40 Glenn Loney, "Sam Maloof," *Craft Horizons* 31 (Aug. 1971): 19.

41 *Fantasy Furniture,* MCC, 21 Jan.–13 Mar. 1966. The other participants included American Thomas Simpson, Mexican Pedro Friedeberg, and the Italian duo, Fabio de Sanctis and Ugo Sterpini.

42 *Fantasy Furniture* (New York: Museum of Contemporary Crafts, 1966), n.p.

43 See Donald McKinley, "Craftsman-Designer-Artist," *Craft Horizons* 26 (June 1966): 83–84

44 Mary Roche, "A New Feeling for Material," *House Beautiful* 93 (Mar. 1951): 116–19, 130–31; Gertrude Benson, "Wharton Esherick," Craft Horizons 19 (Jan./Feb. 1959): 33–37.

45 See "The New American Craftsman: First Generation," *Craft Horizons* 26 (June 1966): 15–34.

46 Ibid., 18–19.

47 Ibid., 19.

48 See client file, Maloof workshop papers.

49 Kirby, 119.

50 ACC, *The Bed,* 23 Sept.–6 Nov. 1966. The twenty-seven pieces included historical and contemporary examples of beds, cradles, and hammocks, both custom made and industrially manufactured. The intention was to "encourage and inspire new ideas . . . and to arouse interest in bed design."

51 Loney, 19, 70. See also *Sam Maloof,* 188–89.

52 Lecture, 31 Aug. 1982, typescript. Maloof workshop papers.

53 See "Umbrella House," *House & Garden* 4 (Apr. 1968): 94–99.

54 Unidentified newspaper clipping. Maloof workshop papers.

55 "Sam Maloof. A Visit with a Noted Craftsman in His Home," *Los Angeles Times,* 29 Sept. 1968, 14.

56 In October 1968 Nordness relocated his Manhattan contemporary art gallery to East 75th Street, creating a separate, but adjacent space, Forms & Objects, in which works by artist-craftsmen were displayed. In his view, the best means of making the public aware of the quality of crafts was to associate it with the fine arts.

57 Lee Nordness, letter to Sam Maloof, 7 May 1968; Sam Maloof, letter to Lee Nordness, 16 May 1968. Maloof workshop papers.

58 Robert Hilton Simmons, "Objects: USA. The Johnson Collection of Contemporary Crafts," *Craft Horizons* 29 (Nov./Dec. 1969): 26, 66.

59 Ibid., 26.

60 "Commentary," *Craft Horizons* 26 (Sept./Oct. 1968): 28.

61 Lee Nordness, *Objects: USA* (New York: Viking Press, 1970), 269.

62 "Art News," *Los Angeles Times,* 15 Feb. 1970.

63 Nordness, 258.

64 Ibid., 7.

65 Ibid., 12.

66 Ibid., 15.

67 *Sam Maloof,* 72.

68 See Glenn Adamson, "California Dreaming," in John Kelsey and Rick Mastelli, eds., *Studio Furniture: Heart of the Functional Arts* (Free Union, Virginia: Furniture Society, 1999), 35–39.

69 Quoted in Kirby, 97.

70 *Sam Maloof,* 47–48.

71 Ibid., 48.

72 Gerry Williams, ed., *Apprenticeship in Craft* (Goffstown, N.H.: Daniel Clark Books, 1987), 146–47.

73 *Sam Maloof,* 49.

74 Ibid.

75 Williams, 146.

76 Quoted in Kirby, 92.

77 Ellen Krec, "Magnificent Maloof," *Long Beach Independent–Press Telegram,* 22 Mar. 1970, Southland Sunday magazine, 24–25.

78 Bernard Kester and Susan Peterson, "Letter from Los Angeles," *Craft Horizons* 30 (May/June 1970): 64.

79 See Christine Orr-Cahill, ed., *The Art of California. Selected Works from the Collection of The Oakland Museum* (San Francisco: Chronicle Books, 1984), 162.

80 Quoted in Kirby, 100.

81 Ibid., 168

82 Ibid., 166.

83 *Artweek* (Mar. 27, 1971).

84 Susan Peterson, "California Design XI," *Craft Horizons* 31 (June 1971): 52.

85 Ibid., 72.

86 Ibid.

87 *Honolulu Star-Bulletin and Advertiser,* 29 Nov. 1971.

88 The exhibition was on view in Washington from Jan. 28 through July 19, 1972, and in St. Paul from Oct. 22 to Dec. 31, 1972. In St. Paul a museum trustee asked to purchase a number of Maloof's works and Freda, to whom they had been promised, granted permission.

89 Anne Crutcher, *Washington Daily News,* 28 Jan. 1972, 27.

90 "In Smithsonian: Sam Maloof—The Big Time," Cucamonga, California *Times,* 17 Feb. 1972. Exhibition archives, Renwick Gallery.

91 Joan Pearson Watkins, "Pomp and Circumstance: The Renwick Gallery Opens for the Exhibition of Arts, Crafts, and Design in the Grand Manner," *Craft Horizons* 32 (Apr. 1972): 68. In the Feb. issue, the magazine noted an ecological angle to the show: "Behind the organization of the exhibition lies the contrast between our country's past dependence on wood as an abundant material suited to handcrafted furniture and our present realization that wood is rapidly becoming a rare natural material." *Craft Horizons* 32 (Feb. 1972): 3.

92 *Woodenworks: Furniture Objects by Five Contemporary Craftsmen* (Washington, D.C.: National Collection of Fine Arts and Minnesota Museum of Art, 1972), 6, 22, 30, 38. The use of the term "furniture objects" indicates the degree to which by 1972 all contemporary craftsmen, no matter how functional their work, were deemed to be "object makers."

93 Glenn Loney, "Sam Maloof," *Craft Horizons* 31 (Aug. 1971): 16–20.

94 See Maloof client system completed piece list, "Occasional Chairs," ship date 14 December 1970. Maloof workshop papers.

95 Sam Maloof, unpublished interview with Jonathan Fairbanks, 4 Sept. 1982, typescript, 2. Maloof workshop papers.

96 See photograph of desk chair submitted to *California Craftsman '76* exhibition at the Monterey Peninsula Museum of Art in Alan Marks, "California Woodworking: Intriguing Solutions to Traditional Problems," *Fine Woodworking* 1 (spring 1977): 34. Woodworker Marks criticized Maloof's use of a wood seat on this chair. He believed—falsely—that its annual shrinkage and expansion would stress and crack the joints where the back legs were doweled into the crest rail.

97 Sam Maloof, unpublished interview with Jonathan Fairbanks, 4 Sept. 1982, typescript, 2. Maloof workshop papers.

98 Sam Maloof, letter to Robert Turner, 10 Oct. 1972. Maloof workshop papers.

99 "Color for the House," *Los Angeles Times,* 16 Mar. 1964, Home magazine, 24. The rooms are

illustrated. In 1967, the magazine featured another new home for which Maloof created dining room furniture. The seating included two low-armed, two-seat benches with hornlike extensions upholstered with red-orange fabric. See "A House that Conquers Scale in a Grand Manner," *Los Angeles Times,* 14 May 1967, Home magazine, 18–19. The writer praised the furniture for suiting not only the human scale of the homeowners, but the grandeur of architectural space.

100 Sam Maloof, letter to Norman Bowler, Jr., 7 Mar. 1966. Millard Sheets papers, Archives of American Art.

101 Sam Maloof, unpublished interview with Blake Green of the *San Francisco Chronicle,* 20 Nov. 1982, typescript, 19. Maloof workshop papers.

102 "Upland News," Cucamonga *Times,* 26 July 1973.

103 Sam Maloof, "You Have to Seek It Out," *Perfect Home* (Apr. 1974).

104 Rose Slivka, "World's Crafts Council in Toronto: The First Decade," *Craft Horizons* 34 (Oct. 1974): 12, 61.

105 "In Praise of Hands," *Craft Horizons* 34 (June 1974): 48.

106 Ibid., 12.

107 James S. Plaut, "A World Family," in *In Praise of Hands: Contemporary Crafts of the World* (Greenwich, Conn.: New York Graphic Society and World Council of Crafts, 1974), 10–11.

108 Ibid., 12.

109 Octavio Paz, "Use and Contemplation," in *In Praise of Hands: Contemporary Crafts of the World* (Greenwich, Conn.: New York Graphic Society and World Council of Crafts, 1974), 22.

110 Ibid., 24.

111 Sam Maloof, letter to Robert Turner, 23 July 1974. Maloof workshop papers.

Chapter Five

1 See "American Crafts Council Creates an Academy of Fellows," *Craft Horizons* 35 (June 1975): 8.

2 *The Craftsman in America* (Washington, D.C.: National Geographic Society, 1975), 23.

3 "From Knives to Rugs . . . In a Mechanized America: A Comeback for Handicrafts," *U.S. News and World Report* (Nov. 1, 1976): 75.

4 Others included *Vignettes of American Art and Life, 1776–1976,* at the Honolulu Academy of Art; *California Craftsmen '76,* at the Monterey [California] Peninsula Museum of Art; and *Bicentennial Crafts Exhibition,* at San Diego State University.

5 Stephen Prokopoff, foreword to *American Crafts '76: An Aesthetic View* (Chicago: Museum of Contemporary Crafts, 1976), 3.

6 Bernard Kester, introduction to *American Crafts '76: An Aesthetic View* (Chicago: Museum of Contemporary Crafts, 1976), 8.

7 Ibid., 22–23.

8 See Eudora Moore, "The New Crafts Movement," in *California Crafts XIV* (Sacramento: Creative Arts League, 1985), 10.

9 See Bernard Kester, "California Deisgn '76," *Craft Horizons* 36 (Apr. 1976): 67–68.

10 Eudora Moore, introduction to *Craftsman Lifestyle: The Gentle Revolution,* by Olivia Emery (Pasadena, California: California Design Publications, 1978), [2].

11 Ibid., 53.

12 Julie Hall, *Tradition and Change: The New American Craftsman* (New York: E. P. Dutton, 1977), 10. Rose Slivka wrote the book's introduction, commenting that "the concerns with ideas, energy, irony, mystery, traditionally the realm of 'fine art,' are equally the concerns of modern craft."

13 Ibid., 18–20.

14 Ibid., 24, 27.

15 Rose Slivka, "The Decade: Change and Continuity," *Craft Horizons* 36 (June 1976): 14.

16 Ibid., 15.

17 For a discussion of the dilemma of the craft fair, see Leon Nigrosh, "The Craft Fair," *Craft Horizons* 32 (Oct. 1972): 51, 65–66.

18 *Masterpieces from the Boston Museum* (Boston: Museum of Fine Arts, 1981), 95. The chair was also featured the same year in Jonathan Fairbanks and Elizabeth Bidwell Banks, *American Furniture: 1620 to the Present* (New York: Richard Marek, 1981), 519. In the latter, Fairbanks called the double chair-back settee made for *Please Be Seated* as "among the half dozen most beautiful examples of seating made by a contemporary American craftsman." Ibid., 521.

19 "Art in Architecture," *Craft Horizons* 36 (June 1976): 6.

20 See Jonathan Fairbanks, "A Natural Devotion," *Antiques & Fine Art* 8 (May/June 1991): 66.

21 See Edward S. Cooke, Jr., *New American Furniture: The Second Generation Studio Furnituremakers* (Boston: Museum of Fine Arts, 1989). Hereafter *New American Furniture.*

22 Sam Maloof, unpublished interview with Jonathan Fairbanks, 4 Sept. 1982, typescript, 8. Maloof workshop papers.

23 Ibid., 9.

24 Elena Canavier, letter to Sam Maloof, 18 Mar. 1977. Maloof workshop papers.

25 Beth Fagan, "Maloof is a Sculptor of Furniture," *The Oregonian,* 4 Feb. 1977, n.p.; Suzanne Kuo, "Work Made to Be Handled," *Willamette Week,*

14 Feb. 1977, n.p. Maloof workshop papers. Kuo subsequently reviewed the solo show in *Craft Horizons* 37 (June 1977): 65.

26 "sw: Experience is the Spice of Craft," *Craft Horizons* 37 (June 1977): 46.

27 *Sam Maloof,* 53.

28 Sam Maloof, "Opinions and Goals of Artists," typescript. Maloof workshop papers. The text appears in part in *Craft, Art and Religion* (New York: Committee of Religion and Art of America, 1978), 34.

29 "wcc Kyoto Meet Draws Cream of the Craft World," *Craft Horizons* 38 (Aug. 1978): 49.

30 "Editor's Notebook. Art Furniture Show, Woodworking Conferences," *Fine Woodworking* 18 (Sept./Oct. 1979): 89.

31 Rose Slivka, "Affirmation," *American Craft* 39 (June/July 1979): 50, 88.

32 Ibid., 88.

33 See Marilyn Hoffman, "Collecting the Crafts," *American Craft* 47 (Feb./Mar. 1983): 15–19.

34 "Craft World," *American Craft* 39 (June/July 1979): 83; (Dec./Jan. 1979–80): 76.

35 "Crafts in the Vice-Presidential Collection," *American Craft* 39 (Dec./Jan. 1979–1980): 24–27.

36 Rick Mastelli, "Sam Maloof: How a Home Craftsman Became One of the Best There Is," *Fine Woodworking* 25 (Nov./Dec. 1980): 48–55.

37 Ibid., 49.

38 Ibid., 54.

39 Ibid., 49; "California Woodworking: An Exhibition of Handcrafted Furniture," Oakland Museum, 16 Dec. 1980–15 Feb. 1981.

40 John Kelsey, "Woodworking/Design/Technology," in *California Woodworking* (Oakland: The Oakland Museum, 1980), 5. For a further discussion of the engineering principles of the joint, see Zach Etheridge, "The Maloof Joint," Highland Hardware *Wood News* 20 (fall 1987): n.p.

41 John Makepeace, introduction to *The Art of Making Furniture* (New York: Sterling Publishing, 1981), 81.

42 "The Art of Making Furniture," *Fine Woodworking* 30 (Sept./Oct. 1981): 38.

43 Upland-Ontario *Daily Report,* 6 Dec. 1981, n.p. "Events," *Fine Woodworking* 32 (Jan./Feb. 1982): 48.

44 Barbaralee Diamonstein, *Handmade in America: Conversations with Fourteen Craftsmasters* (New York: Harry N. Abrams, 1983), 135.

45 Ibid., 141.

46 Sam Maloof, "How I Make a Rocker. A Master Craftsman Reveals the Details," *Fine Woodworking* 42 (Sept./Oct. 1983): 52–55.

47 Ibid., 52.

[48] Nancy Adams, "Artistry in Wood," *St. Louis Globe-Democrat*, 26–27 Feb. 1983, Magazine section, 10.

[49] Urbane Chapman, "Wendell Castle Tries Elegance," *Fine Woodworking* 42 (Sept./Oct. 1983): 69; *New American Furniture*, 27.

[50] Tom Jacobs, "Love of the Crafts Fuels Furniture Maker," *Palladium-Item* (Richmond, Indiana), 1 Jan. 1984, E6.

[51] The two men were the only contemporary studio furniture makers to be featured in Robert Bishop's landmark study, *The American Chair: Three Centuries of Style* (New York: E.P. Dutton, 1972; rpt ed., 1983).

[52] Glenn Loney, "Books," *Craft Horizons* 44 (Mar./Apr. 1984): 38.

[53] Rick Mastelli, "Books," *Fine Woodworking* 43 (Nov./Dec. 1983): 20.

[54] *California Crafts XIV: Living Treasures of California* (Sacramento: Creative Arts League, 1984), 12.

[55] The "living treasures" included metalsmiths Allan Adler, Arline Fisch, Svetozar Radakovich, Florence Resnikoff, and June Schwarcz; ceramicists Laura Andreson, Robert Arneson, Peter Voulkos, and Beatrice Wood; fiber artists Lillian Elliott, Ragnhild Langlet, and Ed Rossbach; and glass art makers Robert Fritz, Freda Koblick (cast acrylic), and Marvin Lipofsky; and woodworkers Arthur Espenet Carpenter, Sam Maloof, and Bob Stocksdale.

[56] Eudora Moore, "The New Crafts Movement," in *California Crafts XIV: Living Treasures of California* (Sacramento: Creative Arts League, 1984), 11.

[57] Joanne Burstein, "California's Senior Craftspeople," *Artweek* (Mar. 2, 1984): 1.

[58] Ibid., 66.

[59] Ibid., 73.

Chapter Six

[1] Patricia Malarcher, "Art/Culture/Future," *American Craft* 46 (Oct./Nov. 1986): 46.

[2] Ibid., 49.

[3] John Marlowe, "California Crossover: Multimedia Works Out West," *Fine Woodworking* 61 (Nov./Dec. 1986): 64.

[4] Arthur Espenet Carpenter, "The Rise of Artiture," *Fine Woodworking* 38 (Jan./Feb. 1983): 98.

[5] Website, MacArthur Foundation, "Fellows Program."

[6] "Maloof Named MacArthur Fellow," *Fine Woodworking* 54 (Sept./Oct. 1985): 126.

[7] Barbara Manning, "Master Craftsman Sam Maloof is King of the Rockers Because he Rocks by the Seat of His Pants," *People Magazine* (Jan. 6, 1986): 76.

[8] Dick Adler, "The 'Genius Award' Winners. Five Southern Californians Ponder What They Will Do with Their MacArthur Fellowships," *Los Angeles Times*, 27 Oct. 1985, magazine section.

[9] Richard Magat, "Waiting for a MacArthur: How I Missed Out on Becoming a Genius," *Chronicle of Philanthropy* (June 27, 1989): 27.

[10] Quoted in Bob Sipchen, "A Man of the Woods," *Los Angeles Times*, 24 July 1994, E2.

[11] In July, readers of *Life* magazine learned that "when Ronald Reagan goes upstairs after a hard day in the Oval Office, he may relax in the White House's $8,000 Sam Maloof rocking chair." The woodworker asserted his rockers were different than others' examples because "the seat is more sculptured, so when you sit down, the chair sits you down too." See "Made in America; From Coast to Coast Crafts Are Flourishing," *Life* (July 1986): 84–85.

[12] Manning, loc. cit.

[13] Denise Shekerjian, *Uncommon Genius: How Great Ideas Are Born* (New York: Penguin Books, 1991), 28–29.

[14] The earliest classic maple rocker with curved flat spindles and a saddle seat dates from 1985. See Paul J. Smith and Edward Lucie-Smith, *Craft Today: Poetry of the Physical* (New York: Weidenfeld and Nicolson, 1986), plate 109.

[15] Deborah Upshaw, "An Interview with Sam Maloof," *Woodwork* (summer 1989): 70. For a discussion of the wood from a cabinetmaking perspective, see Jon Arno, "Maple: A Versatile Timber," *Fine Woodworking* 85 (Nov./Dec. 1990): 73–74.

[16] See Lisa Hammel, "American Craft Museum: A New Era," *American Craft* 44 (Aug./Sept. 1984): 11–14; and Paul Goldberger, "A New Presence for Craft," *American Craft* 47 (Feb./Mar. 1987): 31–32. The former museum building at 44 West 53rd Street (the brownstone purchased by Aileen Webb in 1959 for America House and renovated as a display space in 1978) closed in February 1984, but its programming continued at American Craft Museum II in International Paper Plaza on West 45th Street. Across from MoMA, the new space was an autonomous condominium owned by the ACC in the northeast corner of the 30-story E. F. Hutton Tower. The exhibition space increased dramatically: from 2,500 square feet to more than 9,000 square feet.

[17] See Smith and Lucie-Smith, loc. cit. Smith contributed a short essay, "Poetry of the Physical," while English crafts historian Lucie-Smith produced a lengthy, historical review of American crafts, "Historical Roots and Contemporary Perspectives."

[18] Helen Giambruni, "ACC's New Museum: Functional Crafts to the Back of the Bus?," *Crafts International* (Apr.–June 1987): 21.

[19] Quoted in "Off Press," *American Craft* 47 (Feb./Mar. 1987): 12.

[20] "ACE Enters New Markets," ibid., 6.

[21] "Off Press," loc. cit.

[22] As an indication of this new interest, in 1985 the Whitney Museum of American Art presented the popular exhibition, *High Styles: Twentieth Century American Design*. In the catalogue, curator Lisa Phillips noted: "The revolution in design consciousness owes something to two recent phenomena: the resurgence of architect-designed objects for domestic use; and the increasing number of visual artists who have 'crossed over' into the design field, turning their attention to functional objects . . . during the seventies, the results of these activities were finally accepted as art." Lisa Phillips, "Total Style," in Phillips et al., *High Styles: Twentieth Century Design* (New York: Whitney Museum of Art, 1985), 192. Although there were a number of craftworks in the show—including a Maloof rocker—ideologically the crafts was still an orphan, isolated between the higher status fine art and design fields, and accepted by neither as an equal.

[23] "Off Press," loc. cit.

[24] Michael Stone, *Contemporary American Woodworkers* (Layton, Utah: Peregrine Smith Books/Gibbs M. Smith, 1986). The woodworkers selected were Esherick, George Nakashima, Maloof, Arthur Espenet Carpenter, Tage Frid, James Krenov, Wendell Castle, Jere Osgood, Garry Knox Bennett, and woodturner Bob Stocksdale.

[25] Ibid., 65.

[26] Edward S. Cooke, Jr., "Contemporary American Woodworkers," *American Crafts* 46 (Dec./Jan. 1986–1987): 16.

[27] Stone, 80.

[28] Jack Warner, "Maloof Gives Solace to Human Spirit," *Atlantic Journal-Constitution*, 16 Mar. 1986, 22L; ibid., "Watching Master Craftman Work," ibid., 23 Mar. 1986, 19L; ibid., "Teacher Puts His Soul into His Work," ibid., 30 Mar. 1986, 11L; ibid., "Maloof's Chairs Not Just Beautiful, They Feel Good," ibid., 6 Apr. 1986, 23L.

[29] "Maloof's Chairs Not Just Beautiful."

[30] Richard Petterson, "Three For the Show," *Claremont Courier*, 21 Mar. 1987.

[31] Susan Hamlet, "The Eloquent Object," *Metalsmith* 8 (spring 1988): 47.

[32] Lucy Lippard, "Give and Takeout: Toward a Cross-Cultural Consciousness," in Marcia Manhart and Tom Manhart, eds., *The Eloquent Object: The Evolution of American Art Since 1945* (Tulsa, Oklahoma: Philbrook Museum of Art, 1987), 225.

[33] Quoted in "The Eloquent Object," *Ceramics Monthly* 36 (Mar. 1988): 39.

[34] Marcia Manhart and Tom Manhart, "The Widening Arcs," in *The Eloquent Object*, 29.

[35] See *The Eloquent Object*, 42–64.

36 For reviews, see Michael Dunas, "The Eloquent Object," *Metalsmith* 8 (spring 1988): 55; "The Eloquent Object," *Ceramics Monthly* 35 (Dec. 1987): 77; and Tony Chastain-Chapman, "Aspiring to History," *American Craft* 48 (Apr./May 1988): 37, 91.

37 John Perrault, "Crafts is Art: Notes on Crafts, on Art, on Criticism," in *The Eloquent Object,* 197.

38 Chastain-Chapman, 37.

39 Ibid., 86.

40 Fairbanks, "Craft and American Art Museums," 157.

41 Ibid.

42 Ibid., 192, 197, 201.

43 Ibid., 201.

44 Derek Guthrie, "'The Eloquent Object' Gagged by Kitsch. Tradition Silenced in Traveling Crafts Exhibition," *The New Art Examiner* 16 (Sept. 1988): 29.

45 Jane Addams Allen, "Comment," *American Craft* 48 (Apr./May 1988): 64.

46 Garth Clark, "Comment," *American Craft* 46 (Dec./Jan. 1986–1987): 14.

47 Ibid., 14, 62.

48 See Lloyd Herman, *Art That Works: The Decorative Arts of the Eighties, Crafted in America* (Seattle and London: University of Washington Press, 1990). The show traveled nationally 1990–93.

49 Glenn Gordon, "Comment," *American Craft* 47 (Feb./Mar. 1987): 20.

50 Mary Frakes, "American Studio Furniture: Second Generation," *American Craft* 50 (Apr./May 1990): 38.

51 In 1984, Bennett had participated in the exhibition *Material Evidence: New Techniques in Handmade Furniture,* organized by the Workbench Gallery in New York and the Renwick Gallery. The show was intended to promote the integrally colored, synthetic material ColorCore.

52 *New American Furniture,* 11.

53 Quoted in John Kelsey, "George Nakashima," *Fine Woodworking* 14 (Jan./Feb. 1979): 46.

54 *New American Furniture,* 28.

55 Mary Frakes, "American Studio Furniture: Second Generation," *American Craft* 50 (Apr./May 1990): 38.

56 Workshop data indicate that fifty-eight numbered works were completed in 1989. However, revenues for only forty-four can be computed.

57 Jack Warner, "Woodworking: Video Profile of Maloof Shows a Singular Man," *Atlanata Journal-Constitution,* 11 Nov. 1989.

58 Alan Marks, "Videoscene," *Pacific Woodworker* [1989].

59 Memorandum, ACC, 3 May 1994. Maloof workshop papers.

60 See "American Craft Council Salutes 29 at Awards Dinner," *American Craft* 48 (Oct./Nov. 1988): 6–8.

61 "Sam Maloof: Woodworker," Feb. 2–Apr. 24, 1991, University of California, Riverside, California.

62 See "People and Places," *American Craft* 51 (Aug./Sept. 1991): 11. On November 6, 1991, at the opening of the 15th Philadelphia Craft Show, Maloof received another award: the Medal of Achievement from the Women's Committee of the Philadelphia Museum of Art.

63 Edward S. Cooke, Jr., "The Legacy of Sam Maloof in New England," Stuff Magazine [Boston], special edition (May 1991).

64 Ibid.

65 Ibid.

66 Ibid.

67 The original article appeared in *Stuff.* It was published as "A Natural Devotion: Studio Furniture Maker Sam Maloof," in *Antiques & Fine Art* 8 (May/June 1991): 65–69.

68 Joanne Silver, "'Retrospective' of Pioneering Woodworker," *Boston Herald,* 10 May 1991, S17.

69 John Perrault, "The New Furniture," in *Explorations II: The New Furniture* (New York: American Craft Museum, 1991), 7.

70 For an illustrated review of the show, see Joshua Markel, "Exploring the New Furniture," *American Craft* 51 (Aug./Sept. 1991): 56–62.

71 Ibid., 9.

72 Witold Rybczynski, "If a chair is a work of art, can you still sit on it?," New York Times, 5 May 1991, H38.

73 Several were given by Lebanese or Arab organizations: the Kahlil Gibran Centennial Foundation's 1991 award in "recognition of outstanding achievement in creative arts"; in 1992 Maloof International, "Lifetime Achievement Award for Outstanding Representation of the Family Name"; the Arab American Education Foundation's 1993 "Achievement of Excellence Award."

74 George Barakami Azar, "The Soul of the Hardwood," *Aramco World* (Mar./Apr. 1995): 10–11; *Beirut Times* (Apr. 6–13, 1995).

75 See Terry Estudillo, "The Art of Furniture," *Los Angeles Times,* 16 Oct. 1993.

76 Patricia Conway, *Art for Everyday: The New Craft Movement* (New York: Clarkson, Potter, 1990), 75.

77 Sam Maloof, letter to editor, *Los Angeles Times,* 26 May 1990, B7.

78 Quoted in Sipchen, "Man of the Woods," 3.

79 R. Craig Miller, *Modern Design in the Metropolitan Museum of Art, 1890–1900* (New York: Metropolitan Museum of Art and Harry N. Abrams, 1990), 236.

80 Ibid., 237.

81 See Conway, 94–108, for views and discussion of the Abramsons' apartment designed as a showcase for their art furniture collection. Maloof's more practical pieces graced their suburban home.

82 "Southland Profile: Sam Maloof," *The Southern California Woodworker* (May/June 1991): 24–25.

83 Pam Noles, "Chapel Dedication Celebrates Life of Spiritual Beauty," *Los Angeles Times,* 31 Jan. 2000, Inland Valley sec., 5.

84 Sam Maloof, "George Nakashima, 1905–90," *American Craft* 50 (Oct./Nov., 1990): 4.

85 See "Nakashima's Peace Altar," *Fine Woodworking* 64 (May/June 1987): 108–9.

86 Barakami Azar, 11.

87 Nancy Hathaway, "Woodworking—Class Hero," *Angeles Magazine* (Sept. 1990): 161.

88 John Perrault, "Crafts is Art: Notes on Crafts, on Art, on Criticism," in *The Eloquent Object,* 197.

89 Ibid.

90 Tran Turner, United States correspondent for *Craft Arts International,* as quoted on the 1999 SOFA website.

91 Pam Noles, "Dismantling Memories," *Los Angeles Times,* 9 Oct. 1999, Inland Valley sec., A4.

92 John Dreyfuss, "The California Home of Sam and Alfreda Maloof," *American Craft* 41 (Oct./Nov. 1981): 4–8; Charles Miller, "Sam Maloof's House," *Fine Homebuilding* 68 (June/July 1991): 36–41.

93 Fairbanks, "A Natural Devotion," 68.

94 Tommy Simpson, *Hand and Home: The Homes of American Craftsmen* (Boston: Bullfinch Press, 1994); Vincent Laurence, "The House That Sam Built: Endangered," *Fine Woodworking* 104 (Jan./Feb. 1994): 122–23; Jonathan Binzen, "Assessing an Icon: Sam Maloof. Home is Where His Furniture's Heart Is," *Home Furniture* 13 (Nov. 1997): 66–71.

95 Walt Harrington, "An American Craftsman," *This Old House* (Mar./Apr. 1998): 88

96 Jonathan Binzen, "Alfreda Maloof: An Appreciation," *Fine Woodworking* 134 (Feb. 199): 36.

97 Sam Maloof, "Thanks for Appreciation of Alfreda Maloof," *Fine Woodworking* 136 (May/June 1999): 8.

98 Mark Muckenfuss, "Blending Art, Love in His Life," *Press-Enterprise,* 1 Jan. 2000, 18.

Bibliography

(in chronological order)

"The House of George Nakashima, Woodworker." *Arts & Architecture* 67 (January 1950): 22–25.

Webster, John. "Handsome Furniture You Can Build." *Better Homes and Gardens* (March 1951): 258.

"Taste Portrait of One Man Who Played the Game." *House Beautiful* (May 1954): 151.

Ashton, Sherley. "Maloof: Designer, Craftsman of Furniture." *Craft Horizons* 14 (May–June 1954): 16.

Stewart, Virginia. "The Work of Sam Maloof—Strength, Beauty, Utility." *Los Angeles Times*, 8 August 1954, Home magazine: 13–15.

Niece, Robert C. *Art: An Approach*. Dubuque, Iowa: W. C. Brown Co., 1959.

Maloof, Sam. "'This is My Best.' Functional Beauty Shaped by Hand." *Los Angeles Times*, 14 July 1959, Home magazine.

"Maloof: The Craftsman. Completeness without Ornamentation." *Los Angeles Times*, 12 February 1961, Home magazine.

"Craftsman. Wood Comes Alive in Fine Furniture by Sam Maloof." *Los Angeles Times*, 24 January 1965, Home magazine.

McMasters, Daniel. "Sam Maloof. A Visit with a Noted Craftsman in His Home." *Los Angeles Times*, 29 September 1968, Home magazine.

Krec, Ellen. "Magnificent Maloof." *Long Beach Independent-Press Telegram*, 22 March 1970, Southland Sunday magazine.

Loney, Glenn. "Sam Maloof." *Craft Horizons* 31 (August 1971): 30.

Bishop, Robert. *The American Chair: Three Centuries of Style*. New York: E. P. Dutton, 1972. rpt ed., 1983.

Woodenworks: Furniture Objects by Five Contemporary Craftsmen. Washington, D.C.: National Collection of Fine Arts and Minnesota Museum of Art, 1972.

Kirby, Stephen Dean. "Sam Maloof, Woodworker: His Life and Work." Master's thesis, California State University, Long Beach, 1974.

Maloof, Sam. "You Have to Seek It Out." *Perfect Home* (April 1974).

Hall, Julie. *Tradition and Change: The New American Craftsman*. New York: E. P. Dutton, 1977.

Fagan, Beth. "Maloof is a Sculptor of Fine Furniture." *The Oregonian*, 4 February 1977, Weekend Leisure.

Kuo, Suzanne. "Portland." *Craft Horizons* 37 (June 1977): 65.

Moore, Eudora. *Introduction to Craftsman Lifestyle: The Gentle Revolution by Olivia Emery*. Pasadena, California: California Design Publications, 1978.

Maloof, Sam. "Opinions and Goals of Artists." *Craft Art and Religion*. New York: Committee of Religion and Art of America, 1978.

Mastelli, Rick. "Sam Maloof: How a Home Craftsman Became One of the Best There Is." *Fine Woodworking* (November–December 1980).

Diamonstein, Barbaralee. *Handmade in America: Conversations with Fourteen Craftsmasters*. New York: Harry N. Abrams, 1983.

Maloof, Sam. *Sam Maloof: Woodworker*. Tokyo and New York: Kodansha International, 1983.

Maloof, Sam. "How I Make a Rocker. A Master Craftsman Reveals the Details." *Fine Woodworking* 42 (September–October 1983): 52–55.

Stone, Michael. *Contemporary American Woodworkers*. Layton, Utah: Peregrine Smith Books/ Gibbs M. Smith, 1986.

"American Craftspeople Oral History Project: The Reminiscences of Sam Maloof." Columbia University, 1987.

Upshaw, Deborah. "An Interview with Sam Maloof." *Woodwork* (summer 1989): 70.

Fairbanks, Jonathan. "A Natural Devotion." *Antiques & Fine Art* 8 (May–June 1991): 65–69.

Sipchen, Bob. "A Man of the Woods." *Los Angeles Times*, 24 July 1994.

Maloof, Sam. "Master Class. Shaping the Arm of a Chair." *Fine Woodworking* 137 (August 1999): 102–6.

Index

Note: Page numbers in *italics* refer to selected figures in the text.

Photography credits

Jeremy Adamson: fig. 211; American Craft
Museum: figs. 132, 133; Harry H. Baskerville, Jr.:
figs. 17, 18, 19, 20, 21; Jonathan Binzen: fig. p.
xvii; Bob Carey: fig. p. ii; Cespedes Photos, Chino,
Calif.: fig. 1; Richard Di Liberto: fig. 123; John A.
Ferrari: fig. 109; Richard Fish: figs. 98, 99; Bill
Fitz-Patrick: fig. 168; Frasher's Fotos, Pomona,
Calif.: figs. 22, 23, 24, 25, 26, 29, 30, 31, 32, 35, 37,
41, 42, 43, 44, 45, 49, 52, 53, 54, 96; Burton
Frasher, Jr.: figs. 50, 51; Richard Gross: figs. 101,
111, 129, 130; Dale Healy Photography: fig. 67;
Hugh Laing: fig. 131; Alfreda Maloof: figs. 38, 40,
83, 84, 85, 86, 87, 90, 91, 93, 94, 100, 103, 108, 114,
194; Sam Maloof: figs. 16, 60, 61, 65, 66, 68, 69,
70, 71, 72, 75, 76, 79, 80, 88, 89, 92, 102, 104, 105,
106, 112, 116, 117, 118, 128, 135, 138, 139, 140,
141, 142, 155; Metropolitan Museum of Art: figs.
36, 192; Donald Lloyd McKinley: fig. 115; Bruce
Miller: figs. 183, 193; Charles Miller: figs. 208,
209, 210; Museum of Fine Arts, Boston: figs. 158,
159; Jonathan Pollock: front and back covers; figs.
pp. x, xi, xii, xiii, xv; frontispieces for chapters 2,
3, 4, 5, and 6; figs. 13, 28, 33, 34, 39, 46, 47, 48, 58,
62, 63, 64, 73, 74, 95, 97, 107, 113, 119, 120, 121,
122, 124, 125, 126, 127, 134, 136, 137, 143, 144,
145, 146, 147, 148, 149, 150, 151, 152, 153, 154,
156, 157, 160, 161, 162, 163, 164, 165, 166, 167,
169, 170, 171, 172, 173, 174, 175, 176, 177, 178,
179, 180, 181, 184, 185, 186, 187, 188, 189, 190,
191, 195, 196, 197, 198, 199, 200, 201, 202, 203,
204, 205, 206, 212; Gene Sasse: fig. 182; Julius
Shulman: fig. 56; Max Tatch Photos: fig. 27;
Valley Photo Center, Ontario, Calif.: figs. 57, 59,
77; Vortox Manufacturing Company: figs. 4, 11;
Wendell Castle Incorporated: fig. 110.